Ellen Meiksins Wood

The Retreat from Class

A New 'True' Socialism

VERSO

Verso is the Imprint of **New Left Books**

British Library Cataloguing in Publication Data

Wood, Ellen Meiksins
   The Retreat from Class:
   A new 'true' socialism.
   1. Title
   335   HX73

First published 1986
© Ellen Meiksins Wood 1986

Verso
15 Greek Street, London W1V 5LF

Typeset in Times by
Leaper & Gard Ltd., Bristol

Printed by The Thetford Press
Thetford, Norfolk

ISBN 0-86091-128-4
ISBN 0-86091-839-4 Pbk

Contents

To my father and Elsie

Acknowledgments

I am grateful to Peter Meiksins, Neal Wood, Neil Belton, Robin Blackburn, and especially to Gregory Meiksins and Perry Anderson, for their constructive criticisms and fruitful suggestions.

Parts of this book have appeared in print before: Chapter 2 is taken, with a few modifications, from 'Marxism Without Class Struggle?' *Socialist Register* 1983. Chapter 3 is based, with some changes, reorganization, and additions, on the discussion of Nicos Poulantzas in the same article. In Chapter 4, the few pages devoted to the earlier work of Ernesto Laclau are also taken, with minor modifications, from that article and from 'Liberal Democracy and Capitalist Hegemony: A Reply to Leo Panitch on the Task of Socialist Political Theory', *Socialist Register* 1981. Part of Chapter 10 is drawn, with small modifications, from 'Liberal Democracy and Capitalist Hegemony' and from 'C.B. Macpherson: Liberalism and the Task of Socialist Political Theory', *Socialist Register* 1978.

Ellen Meiksins Wood
Toronto, October 14, 1985

1

The New 'True' Socialism

In the 1840s, Marx and Engels directed some of their most elo-
quent polemics against an intellectual current described as 'true'
socialism. The 'true' socialists, they wrote in *The German
Ideology*, 'innocently take on trust the illusion ... that it is a question of the "most reasonable" social order and not the needs
of a particular class and a particular time.... They have
abandoned the real historical basis and returned to that of ideology.... True socialism, which is no longer concerned with real human
beings but with "Man", has lost all revolutionary enthusiasm and
proclaims instead the universal love of mankind.'[1] 'It is difficult
to see why these true socialists mention society at all if they believe
with the philosophers that all *real* cleavages are caused by *conceptual cleavages*. On the basis of the philosophical belief in the
power of concepts to make or destroy the world, they can likewise
imagine that some individual "abolished the cleavage of life" by
"abolishing" concepts in some way or other.'[2] In the *Communist
Manifesto*, 'true' socialism is summed up thus: since socialism had
'ceased to express the struggle of one class against another, ... [the
'true' socialist] felt conscious of ... representing, not true requirements, but the requirements of Truth; not the interests of the
proletariat, but the interests of Human Nature, of Man in general,
who belongs to no class, has no reality, who exists only in the misty
realm of philosophical fantasy.'

In the 1980s, we seem to be witnessing a revival of 'true' socialism. The new 'true' socialism (NTS), which prides itself on a
rejection of Marxist 'economism' and 'class-reductionism', has
virtually excised class and class struggle from the socialist project.

---

[1] *The German Ideology*, in *Collected Works*, New York 1976, vol. 5, pp. 455-7.
[2] Ibid., p. 467.

1

The most distinctive feature of this current is the autonomization of ideology and politics from any social basis, and more specifically, from any class foundation. Against the assumption, which it attributes to Marxism, that economic conditions automatically give rise to political forces and that the proletariat will inevitably be compelled by its class situation to undertake the struggle for socialism, the NTS proposes that, because there is no necessary correspondence between economics and politics, the working class can have no privileged position in the struggle for socialism. Instead, a socialist movement can be constructed by ideological and political means which are relatively (absolutely?) autonomous from economic class conditions, motivated not by the crude material interests of class but by the rational appeal of 'universal human goods' and the reasonableness of the socialist order. These theoretical devices effectively expel the working class from the centre of the socialist project and displace class antagonisms by cleavages of ideology or 'discourse'.

The NTS encompasses a variety of political stances and has found expression in various intellectual genres. Its exponents count among their number political and economic theorists, analysts of ideology and culture, and historians; they cover a broad range of interests and styles including, for example, Ernesto Laclau, Barry Hindess, Paul Hirst, and Gareth Stedman Jones. One of the major theoretical organs of the NTS in the English language is *Marxism Today*, the theoretical journal of British Eurocommunism, but, although the NTS has been closely tied, theoretically and politically, to the development of Eurocommunism on the Continent and in Britain, it has joined together a fairly broad array of socialists, from Communists to Labourites, and has found exponents on both sides of the Atlantic.

To a great extent, the NTS can be identified with what has been called the 'new revisionism'[3]; but distinctions need to be made, if only to mark out those 'new revisionists' who support their political views with elaborate *theoretical* formulations which, while purporting to be part of the Marxist tradition, represent fundamental departures from it and indeed a rejection of its essential premises. In general, the 'new revisionism' represents a 'spectrum of thought' with certain shared political principles. These include most notably the rejection of the primacy of class politics in favour of 'democratic struggles' especially as they are conducted by the 'new social movements'. For the NTS, these political principles demand a thorough reassessment of social reality or at least of the theoretical apparatus by which it is to be explained. It would also probably be true to say that those who have contributed most to this theoretical reconsideration tend to be situated at the far right of the new revisionist spectrum and have staked out positions which many of their comrades would find too extreme. Perhaps it might even be suggested that there seems to be a direct correlation between the extent of the rightward shift and the degree of theoretical elaboration and complexity, not to mention pretension and obscurity. In any case, the main object of the present study will be that part of the spectrum which is both devoted to theoretical reconstruction and located on the political right of the current.

Despite the diversity of this movement and the fact that not all its members are equally explicit about, or committed to, all the same principles, we can perhaps put together a kind of maximum construct, in the form of a few major propositions, to indicate the logic of the trend:

1) The working class has not, as Marx expected, produced a revolutionary movement. That is, its economic situation has not given rise to what was thought to be an appropriate corresponding political force.

---

[3] See especially Ralph Miliband, 'The New Revisionism in Britain', *New Left Review* 150, March-April 1985. See also Ben Fine et al., *Class Politics: An Answer to its Critics*, London 1985, where the 'new revisionism' is called the 'newer left'. The latter includes some prominent figures who have been excluded from this survey despite some important affinities with the NTS. Perhaps the most obvious omission is Stuart Hall, who by his own account has been substantially influenced by Ernesto Laclau and the politics of 'discourse'. Hall's theoretical statements are sufficiently ambiguous and his movements in an NTS direction are so often accompanied by qualifications and disclaimers that it is not always easy to know exactly where he stands. But it must be said that he does not explicitly deny the centrality of class politics, or even the organic connection of working class interests and capacities to socialist politics, so much as insist, more or less pragmatically, on the costs and inadequacies of a purely class-based politics. (He has, incidentally, recently dissociated himself from Laclau's latest work, 'Authoritarian Populism: A Reply', *New Left Review* 151, May-June 1985, p. 122). Eric Hobsbawm, who has gone at least as far as any other prominent Marxist in promoting a virtually unlimited cross-class alliance to defeat Thatcher, is a rather different case. He shows little interest in or sympathy for the 'new social movements', and his political approach is much more in the tradition of old Communist Popular Front strategies. Furthermore, there has been no sign of any explicit departure from Marxist theoretical orthodoxy as he has always understood it.

2) This reflects the fact that there is no necessary correspondence between economics and politics in general. Any relation between class and politics is contingent. In other words, ideology and politics are (relatively? absolutely?) autonomous from economic (class) relations; and there are no such things as 'economic' class interests that can be translated *a posteriori* into political terms.

3) More particularly, these propositions mean that there is no necessary or privileged relation between the working class and socialism, and indeed that the working class has no 'fundamental interest' in socialism.

4) Therefore, the formation of a socialist movement is in principle independent of class, and a socialist politics can be constructed that is more or less autonomous from economic (class) conditions. This means two things in particular:

5) A political force can be constituted and organized on the ideological and political planes, constructed out of various 'popular' elements which can be bound together and motivated by purely ideological and political means, irrespective of the class connections or oppositions among them.

6) The appropriate objectives of socialism are universal human goals which transcend class, rather than narrow material goals defined in terms of class interests. These objectives can be addressed, on the autonomous ideological and political planes, to various kinds of people, irrespective of their material class situations.

7) In particular, the struggle for socialism can be conceived as a plurality of 'democratic' struggles, bringing together a variety of resistances to many forms of inequality and oppression. In fact, it may even be possible to replace the concept of socialism with the notion of 'radical democracy'. Socialism is a more or less natural extension of liberal democracy; or at any rate 'democracy' as it exists, albeit in a limited form, in advanced capitalist societies is in principle 'indeterminate' and capable of extension to socialist democracy. (It is worth noting that in the United States, the NTS exists above all in the form of this proposition, which has received quite elaborate development at the hands of writers like Samuel Bowles and Herbert Gintis).

The declassing of the socialist project represents not only a redefinition of socialist goals, which can no longer be identified with the abolition of class, but also a rejection of the materialist analysis of social and historical processes. It should be evident that the logic of the whole argument requires a relegation of material production to at best a secondary role in the constitution of social life. As the socialist project is dissociated from any particular class, it is relocated in social collectivities — 'popular alliances' — whose identity, principles of cohesion, objectives, and capacity for collective action are not rooted in any specific social relations or interests but are constituted by politics and ideology themselves. Thus the NTS postulates historical forces which are not grounded in the specific conditions of material life, and collective agencies whose claim to strategic power and capacity for action have no basis in the social organization of material life. To put it more precisely, the possession of strategic power and a capacity for collective action are not treated as essential criteria in identifying the agents of social transformation.

The theoretical tendency to autonomize ideology and politics is, at its most extreme, associated with a drift toward the establishment of language or 'discourse' as the dominant principle of social life, and the convergence of certain 'post-Marxist' trends with post-structuralism, the ultimate dissociation of ideology and consciousness from any social and historical base. The flaws in this dissolution of social reality into language, the circularity and, finally, nihilism of this approach, have been forcefully exposed by Perry Anderson.[4] What is important from our point of view is how this approach has been harnessed to a political strategy which assumes that social and political forces are constituted by discourse itself, with little foundation in social relations.

The typical subject of the NTS project, then, appears to be a broadly conceived and loose collectivity, a popular alliance, with no discernible identity except that which it derives from an autonomous ideology, an ideology whose own origins are obscure. And yet, it may not be entirely true that the subject of the NTS has no determinate identity. The new 'true' socialists seem to share the view that the natural constituents of socialism are what might be called 'right-minded' people, whose common ground is not crass material interest but a susceptibility to reason and persuasion. More particularly, *intellectuals* tend to play a very prominent role. In some cases, the primacy of intellectuals is made quite explicit;

---

[4] Perry Anderson, *In the Tracks of Historical Materialism*, London 1983, pp. 40-55.

but it can be argued that even where it is not, the NTS project necessarily ascribes to intellectuals a predominant role in the socialist project, insofar as it relies on them to carry out no less a task than the construction of 'social agents' by means of ideology or discourse. In that case, the inchoate mass that constitutes the bulk of the 'people' still remains without a collective identity, except what it receives from its intellectual leaders, the bearers of discourse.

We can then add one final principle to our model:

8) Some types of people are more susceptible than others to the universalist and rational discourse of socialism, more capable of commitment to universal human goals as distinct from narrow material — or what Bentham used to call 'sinister' — interests; and these form the natural constituency of the socialist movement. (In this proposition, it is important to note the opposition, indeed antagonism, that is established between rational, humanitarian goals, on the one hand, and material interests, on the other.)

At the very least, the NTS all have one premise in common: the working class has no privileged position in the struggle for socialism, in that its class situation does not give rise to socialist politics any more naturally or readily than does any other. Some, however, would go further: the working class — or the 'traditional' working class — is actually less likely than other social groups to produce a socialist politics. Not only is there no necessity that the working class be revolutionary, its essential character is to be anti-revolutionary, 'reformist', 'economistic'.

Here, however, there may be a contradiction in the argument. While the essential principle is the autonomy of politics and ideology from class, it now appears that at least in the case of the working class, economic-class situation does determine ideology and politics — only not in the way Marx expected. The only thing that might rescue this argument from annihilating itself is the idea that economic conditions themselves determine the degree to which other phenomena are autonomous from them, or — to adapt a favourite Althusserian formula — the economic determines in the last instance, only in the sense that it determines which 'instance' will be determinant or dominant; and some economic conditions determine that the economy itself will be dominant, while others determine that politics or ideology will be 'relatively' autonomous and dominant. Put in more traditional terms, the argument is that certain class conditions determine that people will be bound to material necessity, while other conditions allow greater intellectual and moral freedom, a greater capacity, in other words, to be 'right-minded' and therefore a greater susceptibility to socialist discourse.

People are therefore more amenable to socialist politics, the greater the degree of their autonomy from material conditions and hence their capacity to respond to rational, universalistic goals. What makes the working class a less appropriate constituency for socialist politics, then, is not simply that its material class interests tend to produce an 'economistic' or 'reformist' politics, but rather the very fact that it is driven by material interests at all. And so, socialist theory has been reconstituted on the basis of a classic conservative principle whose lineage is traceable back throughout the long history of political thought to the anti-democratic philosophy of Plato. But more on this Platonic Marxism later.

This, then, is the new 'true' socialism. Needless to say, there is a great deal in it which is hardly new. To a large extent, it is just another repetition of banal and hoary right-wing social-democratic nostrums. The idea that capitalist democracy need only be 'extended' to produce socialism, or that socialism represents a higher ideal of life capable of appealing to all right-minded people irrespective of class, would, for example, be perfectly at home with, say, Ramsay MacDonald, or even, for that matter, John Stuart Mill. What is new about the NTS is that its exponents insist that they are working in the tradition either of Marxism, or of some sequel to it ('post-Marxism'). Even those — like Ernesto Laclau and Chantal Mouffe — who have departed most radically from the Marxist tradition and moved most emphatically to the rightward extreme of the NTS spectrum still claim Marxism as *one* of their principal constituent traditions, merely 'scaling down the pretensions and the area of validity of Marxist theory ...'.[5] These claims account for some of the most characteristic features of the current, in particular its complicated, pretentious, and — it must be said — evasive theoretical contortions, which are in sharp contrast to the rather more open and unadorned opportunism of traditional social democracy which sought no elaborate theoretical disguises.

The obvious questions to be answered are why this trend has

---

[5] Ernesto Laclau and Chantal Mouffe, *Hegemony and Socialist Strategy: Towards a Radical Democratic Politics*, London 1985, p. 4.

developed, why it is coming to fruition now, and why it has found such a particularly strong foothold in the English-speaking world. In very broad terms, of course, it is part of a larger trend which has affected the left in the past decade or so, undoubtedly conditioned by many defeats and failures of hope for socialists in various parts of the world. It must be stressed, however, as Ralph Miliband has remarked in his comments on the 'new revisionism', that this phenomenon 'has assumed much more virulent and destructive forms in other countries, most notably in France, where it has con-stituted not a "new revisionism", but a wholesale retreat into anti-communist hysteria and obscurantism, religious and secular.'[6] The NTS in Britain has certainly not plumbed these depths; and from this point of view, its refusal to cut itself off completely from the Marxist tradition, no matter how misleading that refusal may be, could be construed as a positive statement, which expresses an abiding commitment to some kind of socialist values. Nevertheless, there has been a significant abandonment of vital socialist positions which still needs to be explained.

The period during which the NTS current has developed is roughly 1976-85, though its immediate theoretical antecedents, its roots in Althusserianism, go further back to a theoretical-political formation for which 1968 was a pivotal moment. As we shall see when we explore the theoretical background, a typical trajectory has been from the transplanted Maoism of 1960s radicalism, which was informed by Althusserian theory, to Eurocommunism and points to the right of it. The line from Althusser to Poulantzas to Laclau more or less charts the theoretical and political course of the NTS, with the mid-1970s marking a critical breaking point. In Britain, a paradigmatic path has been followed by Hindess and Hirst, for whom 1975-6 represents an important turning point as, in the space of two short years, they travelled the distance from the last vestiges of Maoist-Althusserianism to the beginnings of a post-Althusserian right-wing Labourism. Others have taken similar journeys in somewhat different political surroundings, many of them, for example, remaining within the boundaries of British Communism. The current battles within the CPGB are testimony to this trend.

What was happening around the mid-1970s which might account for these developments? We need to explain not just a

---

[6] Miliband, p. 6.

general climate of despair or a failure of nerve on the left, but this particular retreat from socialism, in this particular form, and in these particular places: the English-speaking world and especially Britain. Enough has probably been said about the general reasons for 'rethinking' socialism, which Miliband has briefly summed up:

> The experience of 'actually existing socialism', Czechoslovakia and Afghanistan, the collapse of Maoist illusions, Cambodia and the sour aftermath of victory in Vietnam, the withering of Eurocommunist hopes, the emergence of 'new social move-ments' born of dissatisfaction with the limitations of traditional labour and socialist movements and parties, a growing disbelief in the capacity of the working class to be the agent of radical social change, and a consequent 'crisis of Marxism'. More specifically for Britain, there is also what has for many been the trauma of 'Thatcherism' and, even more traumatic, its ability to win elections.[7]

This last item points to a factor which may be the most imme-diately and specifically relevant one for explaining the NTS. The most obvious historical correlate of NTS development is the evo-lution of the 'New Right', especially in Britain and the United States. In very general terms, then, it might be correct to say that the NTS is a response to the growth of the New Right; but this in itself does not advance the issue very far. We would still need to know why this particular response. Since, for example, 'Thatcherism' is characterized by a perception of the world in terms of the class opposition between capital and labour, since the Thatcher government has had as its primary purpose to alter the balance of power between capital and labour which in their eyes has tilted too far in favour of labour, why should socialists respond by *denying* the centrality of class politics instead of confronting Thatcherism for what it is, theorizing it as such, and responding politically by taking the other side in the class war being waged by the Thatcherites? Why should socialists be more obsessed with the ideological trimmings of Thatcherism — its so-called 'authoritarian populism' — than with its real practice in prosecuting the class war against labour?

---

[7] Miliband, pp. 6-7.

Because the two trends are virtually contemporaneous, perhaps it would be better to regard the NTS not simply as a response to the New Right, but rather as a reaction to the same causes that produced the New Right. There can be little doubt that the immediate impulse for the development of the New Right in Britain came from the outbreaks of labour militancy in the 1970s, following the period of radicalism in Europe in 1968-69, particularly after the miners' strikes of 1972 and 1974, and the defeat of the Heath government. Thatcher emerged very clearly in the spirit of 'never again', and with a clear determination to fight and win the class war against organized labour. The 'winter of discontent' in 1978-79 added fuel to the fire. The evolution of the NTS has also coincided with these episodes of militancy, and has reached fruition during yet another dramatic moment in the history of working class struggle, the miners' strike of 1984-85. And each milestone of working class militancy has been followed by further developments of NTS theory.

It would not be unreasonable, then, to suggest that the growth of the NTS, bounded at both ends by dramatic episodes of working class militancy and spurred on by each successive outbreak in between, has had something to do with the recent history of working class struggles in the West, and in Britain in particular. In view of the historical coordinates, however, it would be difficult to maintain that the NTS and its rejection of the working class as the agent of socialist change represent a simple despair on the part of socialists at the quiescence of organized labour.

How, then, to explain the irony that the theoretical expulsion of the working class from the centre of the socialist project was being prepared at the very moment when workers in several European countries were exhibiting a new militancy, and that especially in Britain it has reached new heights whenever militant workers have dominated the political scene? One possible explanation for this apparent paradox is that a new pessimism about the revolutionary potential of the working class has been engendered by precisely such displays of militancy, because they have failed to issue in a decisive battle for socialism. It is as if the only struggle that counts is the last one. At the same time, the 'new social movements' have drawn attention to various issues inadequately addressed by organized labour. There are, however, other possible factors that cannot be discounted, such as the lure of intellectual fashion, as 'discourse' becomes the style of the eighties; or perhaps even a certain fastidious middle-class distaste for — not to say fear of —

the working class, and an indignant refusal of the discomforts occasioned by the withdrawal of service. The militancy eagerly awaited in theory becomes far less agreeable in practice.

At any rate, if the specific historical causes of the NTS must remain a question for speculation, its theoretical provenance is a matter of explicit record. We can proceed, then, to an exploration of its antecedents.

2

The Journey to the New 'True' Socialism: Displacing Class Struggle and the Working Class

I

Class struggle is the nucleus of Marxism. This is so in two inseparable senses: it is class struggle that for Marxism explains the dynamic of history, and it is the abolition of classes, the obverse or end-product of class struggle, that is the ultimate objective of the revolutionary process. The particular importance for Marxism of the working class in capitalist society is that this is the only class whose own class interests require, and whose own conditions make possible, the abolition of class itself. The inseparable unity of this view of history and this revolutionary objective is what above all distinguishes Marxism from other conceptions of social transformation, and without it there is no Marxism. These propositions may seem so obvious as to be trivial; yet it can be argued that the history of Marxism in the twentieth century has been marked by a gradual shift away from these principles. The perspectives of Marxism have increasingly come to be dominated by the *struggle for power*. Where the achievement of political power was originally conceived by Marxism as an aspect or instrument of the struggle to abolish class, class struggle has increasingly tended to appear as a means toward the achievement of political power — and sometimes not even as a primary or essential means.

Changes in the Marxist tradition have not been confined to movements whose clear objective has been the attainment of office, rather than power, by 'democratic' or electoral means. Important divergences have also occurred in revolutionary movements which have accepted insurrectionary action as a possible, even necessary, expedient in the struggle for power. The major revolutionary movements of the twentieth century — in Russia and

China — have in a sense been forced by historical circumstances to place the struggle for power above all else, and even to some extent, particularly in the Chinese case, to place the 'people' or 'masses' before class as the principal agents of struggle. In these cases, such developments have been determined by the immediate necessity of seizing power, of taking an opportunity that could not be refused, and doing so without a large and well-developed working class. The principles of 'popular struggle' and the primacy of the contest for power have, however, taken root in advanced capitalist countries in very different conditions and with very different consequences. Here, the struggle for power has increasingly meant electoral contests; and though the working class has been large and even preponderant, the 'people' or 'masses' has ceased to mean primarily an alliance of exploited classes, notably workers and peasants. Electoral strength has become the principal criterion of alliance, with little concern for whether the constituents of the 'popular' alliance can have as their objective the abolition of classes or even, more specifically, the abolition of capitalist exploitation, and whether they possess the strategic social power to achieve these objectives. The implications have been far from revolutionary and far more conducive to displacing class struggle and the working class altogether from the centre of Marxism.

These historical developments have had profound effects on Marxist theory. It might have been possible for theory to serve as a guiding thread through the complexities of historical change and the compromises of political struggle, a means of illuminating these processes in the constant light of class struggle and its ultimate goal, analysing changes in class structure and especially the development of new formations within the working class, laying a foundation for new modalities of struggle while keeping the revolutionary objective constantly in sight. Instead, Marxist theory, when it has concerned itself with matters of practice at all, has increasingly adapted itself to the immediate demands of the contest for political power, whether in the form of revolutionary action or electoral alliance.

In the more recent major developments in Western Marxism, theory has become in many respects a theorization of Eurocommunist strategy and especially its electoral strategy of 'popular alliances'. While the ultimate objective of Eurocommunism is still the construction of socialism, presumably a classless society without exploitation, this objective seems no longer to illuminate the whole process of revolutionary change. Instead, the process is coloured by the immediate needs of political strategy and the attainment of political office. So, for example, Marxist theory seems no longer designed to enhance working-class unity by dispelling the capitalist mystifications that stand in its way. Instead, as we shall see in what follows, these mystifications have in effect been incorporated into the post-Marxist theory of class, which is now largely devoted not to illuminating the process of class formation or the path of class struggle, but rather to establishing a ground for alliances within and between classes as they are here and now, for the purpose of attaining political power, or, more precisely, public office.

This reconceptualization of the revolutionary project has served to reinforce a tendency that has come from other directions as well: the displacement of the working class from the centre of Marxist theory and practice. Whether that displacement has been determined by the exigencies of the power struggle, by despair in the face of a non-revolutionary working class in the West, or simply by conservative and anti-democratic impulses, the search for revolutionary surrogates has been a hallmark of contemporary socialism. Whatever the reasons for this tendency and whether or not it is accompanied by an explicit reformulation of Marxism and its whole conception of the revolutionary process, to dislodge the working class is necessarily to redefine the socialist project, both its means and its ends.

Revolutionary socialism has traditionally placed the working class and its struggles at the heart of social transformation and the building of socialism, not simply as an act of faith but as a conclusion based upon a comprehensive analysis of social relations and power. In the first place, this conclusion is based on the historical/materialist principle which places the relations of production at the centre of social life and regards their exploitative character as the root of social and political oppression. The proposition that the working class is potentially *the* revolutionary class is not some metaphysical abstraction but an extension of these materialist principles, suggesting that, given the centrality of production and exploitation in human social life, and given the particular nature of production and exploitation in capitalist society, certain other propositions follow: 1) the working class is the social group with the most direct objective interest in bringing about the transition to socialism; 2) the working class, as the direct object of the most fundamental and determinative — though certainly not the only — form of oppression, and the one class whose interests do not rest on the oppression of other classes, can create the conditions for liberating all human beings in the struggle to liberate itself; 3) given the fundamental and ultimately unresolvable opposition between exploiting and exploited classes which lies at the heart of the structure of oppression, *class struggle* must be the principal motor of this emancipatory transformation; and 4) the working class is the one social force that has a strategic social power sufficient to permit its development into a revolutionary force. Underlying this analysis is an emancipatory vision which looks forward to the *disalienation of power* at every level of human endeavour, from the creative power of labour to the political power of the state.

To displace the working class from its position in the struggle for socialism is either to make a gross strategic error or to challenge this analysis of social relations and power, and at least implicitly to redefine the nature of the liberation which socialism offers. It is significant, however, that the traditional view of the working class as the primary agent of revolution has never been effectively challenged by an alternative analysis of social power and interest in capitalist society. This is, of course, not to deny that many people have questioned the revolutionary potential of the working class and offered other revolutionary agents in its place: students, women, practitioners of various alternative 'life styles', and popular alliances of one kind or another, more recently the 'new social movements'. The point is simply that none of these alternatives has been supported by a systematic reassessment of the social forces that constitute capitalism and its critical strategic targets. The typical mode of these alternative visions is voluntaristic utopia or counsel of despair — or, as is often the case, both at once: a vision of a transformed society without real hope for a process of transformation.

One well-known attack on the traditional Marxist view of the working class is symptomatic and worth a brief consideration to illustrate the strategic bankruptcy of these alternative visions to date. André Gorz's *Farewell to the Working Class* is both utopian vision and counsel of despair. Gorz proceeds from the premise that, since the future of society must lie in the abolition of work, it must be the objective of the socialist project to determine the particular form in which work will be abolished — whether, for example, as the degradation of mass unemployment or as an emancipatory 'liberation of time'. The goal he proposes is the creation of a 'discontinuous social space made up of two distinct spheres':[1] the realm of necessity, constituted by the demands of necessary material production to satisfy primary needs — a sphere that can never be fully escaped — and a realm of freedom outside the constraints of necessary social production, a sphere of autonomy which must be enlarged and to which the necessarily 'heteronomous' sphere of material production must be subordinated. The working class cannot by its very nature be the agent of this transformation because the abolition of work cannot be its objective. A class 'called into being' by capitalism,[2] the working class identifies itself with its work and with the productivist logic of capital. It is itself a *replica* of capital, a class 'whose interests, capacities and skills are functional to the existing productive forces, which themselves are functional solely to the rationality of capital'. It is also a class whose power has been broken by the form and structure of the labour-process itself. The transformative impulse must, therefore, come from a 'non-class of non-workers' not 'marked with the insignia of capitalist relations of production',[3] made up of people who, because they experience work as 'an externally imposed obligation' in which life is wasted, are capable of having as their goal 'the abolition of workers and work rather than their appropriation'.[4] This group includes all those whom the system has rendered actually or potentially unemployed or underemployed, all the 'supernumeraries' of contemporary social production, perhaps in alliance with the 'new social movements', such as the ecology and women's movements.

Countless questions can be raised about Gorz's analysis of the labour-process in contemporary capitalism and its effects on the working class. One critical point stands out: his whole argument is based on a kind of inverted technologism, a fetishism of the *labour-process* and a tendency to find the essence of a mode of production in the technical process of work rather than in the relations of production, the specific mode of *exploitation*. This, as we shall see, is something that he shares with post-Althusserian theorists like Poulantzas. In both cases, the tendency to define *class* less in terms of exploitative relations than in terms of the technical process of work may help to account for a very restrictive

---

[1] André Gorz, *Farewell to the Working Class: An Essay on Post-Industrial Socialism*, Boston 1982, p. 96.

[2] Ibid., p. 15.

[3] Ibid., p. 68.

[4] Ibid., p. 7.

conception of the 'working class', which appears to include only industrial manual workers. This tendency also affects his perception of the working class and its revolutionary potential, since in his account the experience of exploitation, of antagonistic relations of production, and of the struggles surrounding them — i.e. the experience of class and class struggle — play little part in the formation of working-class consciousness, which seems to be entirely shaped and absorbed by the technical process of work. There have certainly been important changes in the structure of the working class which must be seriously confronted; but Gorz does little to illuminate them, because in the end his is a metaphysical, not an historical or sociological, definition of the working class and its limitations, which has little to do with its interests, experiences, and struggles as an exploited class.

Questions could also be raised about his utopian vision itself. What is important from our point of view, however, is not simply this or that objectionable characteristic of Gorz's utopia, but the very fact that it *is* a utopia without grounding in a process of transformation — indeed, a vision ultimately grounded in despair. (It is no accident that Gorz's account of the utopia begins with citizens waking up one morning and finding their world already transformed.) In the final analysis, Gorz offers no revolutionary agent to replace the working class. It turns out that the 'non-class of non-workers', this new revolutionary lumpen-proletariat which apparently 'prefigures' a new society, holds that promise only in principle, notionally, perhaps metaphysically; it has, by his own testimony, no strategic social power and no possibility of action. In the end, we are left with little more than the shop-worn vision of the 'counter-culture', bearing witness against the 'system' in an enclave of the capitalist wilderness. This is revolution by example as proposed in various forms from the fatuous 'socialism' of John Stuart Mill to the pipe-dreams (joint-dreams?) of bourgeois flower-children growing pot in communal window-boxes (while Papa-le-bourgeois sends occasional remittances from home).

Even if the objective of the Left were to be perceived as the abolition of work — and not as the abolition of classes and exploitation — it would be the destruction of capitalism and capitalist exploitation, and their replacement by socialism, that would determine the form in which the abolition of work would take place. What is significant about Gorz's argument is that, like other alternative visions, his rejection of the working class as the agent of transformation depends upon wishing away the *need* for transformation, the need to destroy capitalism. It is a monumental act of wishful (or hopeless?) thinking, a giant leap over and beyond the barrier of capitalism, bypassing the structure of power and interest that stands in the way of his utopia. We have yet to be offered a consistent and plausible alternative to the working class as a means of shifting that barrier. Even for Gorz the question is not, in the final analysis: who else will transform society? He is effectively telling us: if not the working class then no one. The question then is whether the failure of the working class so far to bring about a revolutionary transformation is final, insurmountable, and inherent in its very nature. His own grounds for despair — based as they are on an almost metaphysical technologism which denies the working class its experiences, interests, and struggles as an exploited class — are simply not convincing. Much the same can be said about other proposals for revolutionary surrogates, including those implicit in the Eurocommunist doctrine of popular alliances.

II

The single most influential school of Western Marxism in recent years has been a theoretical current that derives its principle inspiration from Louis Althusser. The innovations of Althusser himself have been located by Perry Anderson in the general tendency of Western Marxism toward the 'rupture of political unity between Marxist theory and mass practice' occasioned by both 'the deficit of mass revolutionary practice in the West' and the repressions of Stalinism.[5] Hence the 'obsessive methodologism' that Althusser shared with other Western Marxists as questions of theoretical form displaced issues of political substance; hence the preoccupation with bourgeois culture and the 'retroactive assimilation' into Marxism of pre-Marxist philosophy, notably in its idealist forms, (in Althusser's case, especially the philosophy of Spinoza)[6] as 'bourgeois thought regained a relative vitality and superiority'[7] in the face of a retreating socialism in the West; hence,

---

[5] Perry Anderson, *Considerations on Western Marxism*, London 1976, p. 66.
[6] Ibid., p. 64-5.
[7] Ibid., p. 55.

too, Althusser's linguistic obscurity. Althusser's theoretical aca-demicism has existed in uneasy tandem with his active political involvement in the PCF, and the precise connection between his theory and practice has been a matter of hot dispute. There is in any case a certain incoherence in attempts to combine political practice, especially revolutionary practice, with a theory that acknowledges no *subjects* in history. The theoretical work of Althusser's pupils and successors has, with a few exceptions, been no less prone to scholastic abstractionism, 'obsessive methodo-logism', philosophical idealism, and obscurity of language; but their development has been much more clearly and concretely tied to the political movements of the West in the sixties and seventies and especially to the shifting programmes of Eurocommunism.

Eurocommunists insist that their objective, unlike that of social democracy, is not merely to manage capitalism but to transform it and to establish socialism. Their strategy for achieving that objective is, essentially, to use and extend bourgeois-democratic forms, to build socialism by constitutional means within the legal and political framework of bourgeois democracy. Eurocommunist theoreticians generally reject strategies that treat the bourgeois democratic state as if it were impenetrable to popular struggles and vulnerable only to attack and destruction from without, from an oppositional base in alternative political institutions. Euro-communist parties, therefore, offer themselves both as 'parties of struggle' and as 'parties of government' which, by achieving electoral victories, can penetrate the bourgeois-democratic state, transform it, and implant the conditions for socialism. More par-ticularly, their strategy is based on the conviction that, in the 'monopoly phase' of capitalism, a new opposition has emerged alongside — and even overtaking — the old class opposition between exploiters and exploited, capital and labour. In 'state monopoly capitalism', there is a new opposition between mono-polistic forces, united and organized by the state, and the 'people' or 'popular masses'. An absolutely crucial, indeed the central, principle of Eurocommunist strategy is the 'popular alliance', a cross-class alliance based on the assumption that a substantial majority of the population including the petty bourgeoisie and even elements of the bourgeoisie, not just the traditional working class, can be won over to the cause of socialism. It is precisely this new reality that makes possible a 'peaceful and democratic' tran-sition to socialism. Communist parties, therefore, cannot be *working class* parties in any 'sectarian' sense; they cannot even merely open themselves to alliances with, or concessions to, other parties or groups. They must themselves directly represent the multiple interests of the 'people'.

The general strategy of Eurocommunism, then, seems at least implicitly to be built upon a conflict other than the direct opposition between capital and labour and a moving force other than class struggle. Its first object is to rally the 'popular' forces against 'state monopoly capitalism', to create the broadest possible mass alliance, and then to establish an 'advanced democracy' on the basis of this popular alliance, from which base some kind of socialism can be gradually constructed. The force that drives the movement forward is not the tension between capital and labour; in fact, the strategy appears to proceed from the necessity — and the possibility — of avoiding a confrontation between capital and labour. Insofar as the strategy is aimed at anti-capitalist goals, it cannot simply be guided by the interests of those who are directly exploited by capital but must take its direction from the varied and often contradictory ways in which different elements of the alliance are opposed to monopoly capitalism. It can be argued, then, that the movement need not, indeed cannot, in the first instance be motivated by specifically socialist objectives.

The doctrine of cross-class alliance proposed by Eurocommunism is, therefore, something more than simply an electoral strategy. It embodies a particular judgment about the source of the impulse for historical transformation. There are two ways of looking at the extension to other classes of the historic role formerly assigned to the working class. One is to stress the *optimism* of Eurocommunism, concerning the possibility of 'democratizing' the capitalist state. The other is to stress their *pessimism*, concerning the revolutionary potential of the working class. There can be little doubt that, however optimistic its claims, Eurocommunist strategy is ultimately grounded in the same historical reality that has so profoundly shaped Western Marxist theory and practice in general: the disinclination of the working class for revolutionary politics. It must be added that the Eurocommunist solution has been deeply affected by the experience of the Popular Front. And it is even possible that there is more in this political strategy than simply pessimism about the working class. For example, the strategy for transforming the capitalist state by a simple extension of the bourgeois democratic forms, by the proliferation of representative institutions as against a system of direct council democracy, may reflect a more profound lack of interest in, or suspicion of, popular power.[8] However the doctrine of popular alliances is conceived and explained, the effect is the same: it displaces the working class from its privileged role as the agent of revolutionary change and diminishes the function of class struggle as the principal motor of social transformation.

Here is the crux of Eurocommunism. We cannot get to the heart of the matter simply by equating Eurocommunism with social democracy. It is unhelpful merely to dismiss the professions of Eurocommunists that their objective is to transform, not to manage, capitalism. To do this is to avoid the real challenge of Eurocommunism. Nor can the issue be reduced simply to the choice of *means* — revolutionary insurrection versus constitutionalism, electoral politics, and the extension of bourgeois-democratic institutions. The critical question concerns the source and agency of revolutionary change. It is this question that, finally, determines not only the means of socialist strategy but also its ends; for to locate the impulse of socialist transformation is also and at the same time to define the character and limits of socialism itself and its promise of human emancipation.

III

Two aspects of Eurocommunist doctrine have figured most prominently in post-Althusserian theory: the conception of the transition to socialism as an extension of bourgeois-democratic forms and, more fundamentally, the doctrine of the cross-class 'popular' alliance. Accordingly, the chief theoretical innovations of this Marxism have occurred in the theory of the *state* and the theory of *class*, in which the question of *ideology* has assumed an increasingly pivotal role. In the process, there has occurred a fundamental reformulation of Marxist theoretical principles in general. In the final analysis, the doctrine of cross-class alliances and the political strategy of Eurocommunism have, it can be argued, demanded nothing less than a redefinition of *class* itself and of the whole conceptual apparatus on which the traditional Marxist theory of class and class struggle has rested, a redefinition of historical agency, a displacement of production relations and

---

[8] Ralph Miliband, 'Constitutionalism and Revolution: Notes on Eurocommunism', *Socialist Register* 1978, pp. 165-7.

exploitation from the core of social structure and process, and much else besides. In particular, there has been a tendency increasingly to depart from Marxist 'economism' by establishing not only the autonomy but the *dominance* of the political, and then of ideology. The function of these theoretical devices in sustaining the strategy of popular alliances and 'democratization' should become evident as we examine some of the principal transformations in Marxist theories of the state and class at the hands of the post-Althusserians.

But the autonomy and dominance of politics and ideology has earlier roots in Maoism, which may help to explain the relative ease with which many of our new 'true' socialists travelled the route from Maoism to Eurocommunism and beyond, with the help of Althusser. To understand the logic of that journey and the ambiguous conception of democracy and popular struggle that informs it, something needs to be said about the attractions which the Maoist doctrines of 'cultural revolution', the 'mass line', and anti-economism have held for many people, especially students and intellectuals, in the European Left, something that explains the unlikely transposition of these doctrines from China to the very different conditions of Western Europe.

Faced with the 'backwardness' of the Chinese people and an undeveloped working class, the CPC asserted the possibility of 'great leaps forward' in the absence of appropriate revolutionary conditions — i.e. *class* conditions — by dissociating revolution from *class* struggle in various ways. Not only did the *masses* — a more or less undifferentiated mass of workers and peasants — replace *class* as the transformative force, but the rejection of 'economism' meant specifically that the material conditions of production relations and class could be regarded as less significant in determining the possibilities of revolution. It became possible to conceive of political action and ideology as largely autonomous from material relations and class, and to shift the terrain of revolution to largely autonomous political and cultural struggles. The later Cultural Revolution was the ultimate expression of this view, and of the extreme voluntarism which necessarily followed from this autonomization of political action and ideological struggle.

This conception of revolution inevitably entailed an ambiguous relation to the masses and to democracy. On the one hand, there was an insistence upon the necessity of massive popular involvement; on the other hand, the Maoist revolution was necessarily conducted by party cadres for whom popular involvement meant not popular democratic organization but rather 'keeping in touch' with the masses and constructing the 'mass line' out of the 'raw material' of ideas and opinions emanating from them. The revolution was no longer conceived as emerging directly out of the struggles of a class guided and unified by its own class interests. Instead of a class with an identity, interests, and struggles of its own, the popular base of the revolution was a more or less shapeless mass (What identity do the 'people' or the 'masses' have? What would be the content of a revolution made by them 'in their own name'?) to be harnessed by the party and deriving its unity, its direction, and its very identity from autonomous party cadres. In the later 'Cultural Revolution', when the regular party apparatus was itself set aside, the autonomization of political and ideological action was taken to its ultimate extreme.

The transportation of these principles to the advanced capitalist countries of the West, to be adopted especially by students and intellectuals, was clearly no easy matter and required significant modifications — given the existence of well-developed and large working classes with long histories of struggle, not to mention the less than ideal conditions of intellectuals in China itself. Nevertheless, it is not difficult to see the attractions exerted by this view of revolution, with its delicately ambiguous synthesis of democratic and anti-democratic elements. On the one hand, Maoist doctrine, with its insistence on keeping in touch with the masses, its attack on bureaucratic ossification, its mass line, and its Cultural Revolution, seemed to satisfy the deepest anti-statist and democratic impulses. On the other hand, (whatever its actual implications in China), it could be interpreted as doing so without relegating declassed intellectuals to the periphery of the revolution. The dissociation of revolution from class struggle, the autonomization of ideological and cultural struggles, could be interpreted as an invitation to them to act as the revolutionary consciousness of the people, to put themselves in the place of intrinsic class impulses and interests as the guiding light of popular struggles. After all, if there is any kind of revolution that intellectuals can lead, surely it must be a 'cultural' one.

Maoism, never more than a marginal and incoherent phenomenon in the context of advanced capitalism, could not long survive transportation; but the themes of cultural revolution, the autonomy of political and especially ideological struggles, and in particular the displacement of struggle from *class* to *popular masses* did survive in forms more appropriate to a Western setting.

At least, some of those who had been attracted to Maoism for its adherence to these doctrines seem to have found in Eurocommunism a reasonable substitute: an alternative to Stalinism which promised both democracy or popular involvement and a special place for elite party cadres and declassed intellectuals. In particular, here, too, *class* was increasingly displaced by the more flexible 'popular masses' — though, of course, in a very different form. And here, too, political and ideological struggles were rendered more or less autonomous from material relations and class. Maoist influences need not, of course, be invoked to explain Eurocommunist doctrine. European Communism has traditions of its own on which to draw — the legacy of the Popular Front with its cross-class alliances, suitably modified versions of Gramsci's theory of hegemony with its stress on ideological and cultural domination, etc. But for one important segment of the European Left, the transition from 'Maoism' (in its Western variant) to Eurocommunism had a certain comfortable logic. It is therefore not surprising to find certain continuous themes figuring prominently in the academic theoretical systems that have grown up side by side with Eurocommunism.

3

The Forerunner: Nicos Poulantzas

I

All the major themes of the NTS are present in embryo in the work of Nicos Poulantzas; and it is possible that had he lived, he might have followed the logic of his theoretical and political trajectory to the position now occupied by many of his post-Althusserian colleagues. As it is, however, he certainly never went so far; and if he is without doubt a major influence, he cannot really be regarded, theoretically or politically, as a full-blown NTS, either with respect to the theoretical detachment of ideology and politics from any social determinations, or with respect to the political detachment of socialism from the working class.

Poulantzas deserves special attention not only because he is perhaps the most important theorist of the post-Althusserian tradition, the one who has done most to ground that tradition, with its philosophical preoccupations, more firmly in the immediate political problems of contemporary socialism, but also because he has made a major contribution to directing Marxists generally to long neglected theoretical problems. The extent of his influence on the present generation of Marxist political theorists, which is the more impressive for the tragic brevity of his career, would be reason enough for singling him out as an exemplary case. But he is exemplary also in a more general, historical sense. The course of his political and theoretical evolution traces the trajectory of a major trend in the European Left, reflecting the political odyssey of a whole generation.

When Poulantzas wrote his first major theoretical work, *Political Power and Social Classes*, published in 1968, like many others he was seeking a ground for socialist politics that was neither Stalinist nor Social Democratic. There was then, on the eve of the Eurocommunist era, no obvious alternative in Europe. Poulantzas's theoretical exploration of the political ground was still abstractly critical, negative, chipping away at the theoretical foundations of the main available options without a clear positive commitment to any party line. Like many of his contemporaries, however, he seems to have leaned towards the ultra-left, more or less Maoist, option. At least, his theoretical apparatus, deeply indebted to Althusser whose own Maoist sympathies were then quite explicit, bears significant traces of that commitment. The attack on 'economism', which is the hallmark of Poulantzas's work and the basis of his stress on the specificity and autonomy of the political, was essential to Maoism and constituted one of its chief attractions for people like Althusser. The concept of 'cultural revolution' also held a strong fascination for Poulantzas, as for the many others who claimed it as the operative principle of 'revolutions' like that of May 1968. Whatever this concept meant to the Chinese, it was adopted by students and intellectuals in the West to cover revolutionary movements without specific points of concentration or focused political targets, characterized instead by a diffusion of struggle throughout the social 'system' and all its instruments of ideological and cultural integration. The theoretical implications of this conception are suggested by Poulantzas himself, for example, in his debate with Ralph Miliband. In this exchange, Poulantzas adopted the Althusserian notion of 'ideological state apparatuses', according to which various ideological institutions within civil society which function to maintain the hegemony of the dominant class — such as the Church, schools, even trade unions — are treated as belonging to the system of the state.[1] He went on to suggest a connection between the idea of 'cultural revolution' and the strategic necessity of 'breaking' these ideological apparatuses. It is not difficult to see why advocates of 'cultural revolution' might be attracted to the notion of conceiving these 'apparatuses' as part of the state and thus theoretically legitimizing the shift to 'cultural' and ideological revolt and the diffusion of struggle. Indeed, the centrality of *ideology* in post-Althusserian politics and theory, whatever modifications it has since undergone, may be rooted in a conception of social transformation as 'cultural revolution' — if not in its original Chinese form, at least in the specifically Western idiom of May 1968. There is also in the earlier Poulantzas, as in many of his contem-

---

[1] See Robin Blackburn (ed.) *Ideology in Social Science*, London 1972, chapter eleven.

poraries, much that is reminiscent (as Miliband pointed out in the debate with Poulantzas) of the 'ultra-left deviation' according to which there is little difference among various forms of capitalist state, whether fascist or liberal-democratic, and bourgeois-democratic forms are little more than sham and mystification. Strong traces of this view can be found, for example, in Poulantzas's conception of Bonapartism as an essential characteristic of *all* capitalist states.

Many of these notions were abandoned or modified by Poulantzas in the course of debate and in his later work. As his earlier political stance, with its ultra-left and Maoist admixtures, gave way to Eurocommunism, he moved away from his earlier views on Bonapartism, 'ideological state apparatuses', and so on. Most notably, his theory of the state as well as his explicit political pronouncements shifted from an apparent depreciation of liberal democratic forms toward an albeit cautious acceptance — especially in his last book, *State, Power, Socialism* — of the Euro-communist view of the transition to socialism as the extension of existing bourgeois democratic forms.

The shifts, both political and theoretical, are substantial; but there is nevertheless a continuity, a unity of underlying premises, that says a great deal not only about Poulantzas himself but about the logic running through the evolution of the European left, or an important segment of it, since the 1960s. There is a character-istic ambiguity in his own conception of democratic socialism and the means by which it is to be achieved, an ambiguity that persists throughout the journey from 'Maoism' to Eurocommunism and tends toward the displacement of class struggle and the working class.

II

Poulantzas's theory of the state, for all its scholasticism, was from the beginning motivated by strategic considerations and the need to provide a theoretical base from which 'scientifically' to criticize some political programmes and support others. In *Political Power and Social Classes*, Poulantzas constructed an elaborate theoretical argument largely to demonstrate and explicate two principal characteristics of the capitalist state: the unitary character of its institutionalized power, and its 'relative autonomy' vis-à-vis the dominant classes. Paradoxically, argued Poulantzas, the dominant classes in capitalism do not derive their 'unambiguous and exclusive' political power from actual participation in or possession of 'parcels' of institutionalized state power, but rather from the 'relative autonomy' which permits the state to provide them with the political unity they otherwise lack.[2]

The question underlying these theoretical arguments is fundamentally a strategic one: 'can the state have such an autonomy vis-à-vis the dominant classes that it can accomplish the passage to socialism without the state apparatus being broken by conquest of a class power?'[3] Poulantzas's answer is aimed at specific targets. He attacks 'instrumentalist' arguments which treat the state as a mere tool of the dominant classes. He also rejects the other side of the 'instrumentalist' coin, the view that the instrument can easily change hands and that, as an inert and neutral tool, it can be wielded as easily in the interests of socialism as it was formerly wielded in the interests of capital.[4] In short, Poulantzas is explicitly attacking the theoretical foundations of 'reformism' and the political strategy of social democracy. This strategy in effect shares the bourgeois pluralist view that the state can belong to various countervailing interests, and proceeds from there to the conviction that, once representatives of the working class predominate, revolution can be achieved 'from above', quietly and gradually with no transformation of the state itself. Indeed, to social democrats, today's state monopoly capitalism may appear as already a transitional phase between capitalism and socialism. Political and juridical forms, which are in advance of the economy, will simply pull the latter behind them, allowing a piece-meal transition to socialism without class struggle.

At this stage, Poulantzas's own political prescriptions remain largely implicit, apart from this very general attack on social democracy. Although his theory of the state could be adapted to an assault on Stalinism, as he was later to do explicitly by treating Stalinism as more or less the obverse of social-democratic 'statism', in this early work such criticism is muted; and, indeed, there is as yet little that might be construed as 'anti-statism'. To the extent that the book can be understood as containing implied criticisms of the PCF, they are entirely coded, as they are in Althusser's work of

---

[2] Nicos Poulantzas, *Political Power and Social Classes*, London 1973, p. 288.
[3] Ibid., p. 271.
[4] Ibid., pp. 273, 288.

the time. What can be said about *Political Power and Social Classes* is that it is generally intended to convey a fidelity to the Leninist tradition, in its Althusserian mediations.

There are, however, important theoretical manoeuvres in this work that have far-reaching political implications. It is here that Poulantzas begins to establish the dominance of the *political*, going further than his mentor Althusser, and Balibar, in distancing himself from Marxist 'economism'. He is here perhaps signalling the Maoist leanings which will become more explicit in his next major work, *Fascism and Dictatorship*; but he is also fashioning a theoretical instrument that will, as it turns out, continue to be serviceable in his subsequent shift to Eurocommunism.

Poulantzas begins by explaining the circumstances in which the political is 'dominant':

... in the global role of the state, the dominance of its economic function indicates that, as a general rule, the dominant role in the articulation of a formation's instances reverts to the political; and this is so not simply in the strict sense of the state's direct function in the strictly political class struggle, but rather in the sense indicated here. In this case, the dominance of the state's economic function over its other functions is coupled with its *dominant role*, in that its function of being the cohesive factor necessitates its specific intervention in that instance which maintains the *determinant role* of a formation, namely, the economic. This is clearly the case, for example, in the despotic state in the Asiatic mode of production, where the dominance of the political is reflected in a dominance of the economic function of the state; or again, in capitalist formations, in the case of monopoly state capitalism and of the 'interventionist' form of the capitalist state. Whereas in the case of such a form of the capitalist state as the *'liberal' state* of private capitalism, the dominant role held by the economic is reflected by the dominance of the strictly political function of the state — the state as 'policeman' [*l'état gendarme*] — and by a specific *non-intervention* of the state in the economic.[5]

In his later work, this same idea was to be stated more succinctly:

---

[5] Ibid., p. 55.

> ... monopoly capitalism is characterized by the displacement of dominance within the CMP from the economic to the political, i.e. to the state, while the competitive stage is marked by the fact that the economic played the dominant role in addition to being determinant.[6]

In other words, despite the separation of the economic and the political which is uniquely characteristic of capitalism and which survives in the monopoly phase, because of the expansion of the domain of state intervention the political sphere acquires a position analogous to the 'dominance' of the political sphere in pre-capitalist modes of production. Poulantzas even draws an analogy between state monopoly capitalism and the 'Asiatic mode of production' in this respect.

This analogy and Poulantzas's conception of the 'dominance' of the political in state monopoly capitalism reveals a great deal about his point of view. His argument is based on the Althusserian principle that, while the economic always 'determines in the last instance', other 'instances' of the social structure may occupy a 'determinant' or 'dominant' place. In fact, the economic 'determines' simply by determining which instance will be determinant or dominant. This is at best an awkward and problematic idea; but it makes some kind of sense insofar as it is intended to convey that in some modes of production — indeed typically, in pre-capitalist societies — the relations of production and exploitation may themselves be organized in 'extra-economic' ways. So, for example, in feudalism surplus-extraction occurs by extra-economic means since the exploitative powers of the lord are inextricably bound up with his political powers, his possession of a 'parcel' of the state. Similarly, in the 'Asiatic mode of production' the 'political' may be said to be dominant, not in the sense that political relations take precedence over relations of exploitation, but rather in the sense that exploitative relations themselves assume a political form to the extent that the state itself is the principal direct appropriator of surplus labour. It is precisely this fusion of 'political' and 'economic' that distinguishes these cases from capitalism where exploitation, based on the complete expropriation of direct producers and not on their juridical or political dependence or

---

[6] *Classes in Contemporary Capitalism*, London 1975, p. 101.

subjection, takes a purely 'economic' form. This is more or less the sense in which Althusser and Balibar elaborate the principle of 'determination in the last instance'. In Poulantzas's hands, however, the idea undergoes a subtle but highly significant transformation.[7]

In the original formula, the relations of exploitation are always central, though they may take 'extra-economic' forms. In Poulantzas's formulation, relations of exploitation cease to be decisive. For him, relations of exploitation belong to the *economic* sphere; and the 'economic' in pre-capitalist societies, and apparently also in monopoly capitalism, may be subordinated to a separate political sphere, with its own distinct structure of domination. It would, of course, be perfectly reasonable for Poulantzas to point out that the role and the centrality of the 'political' vary according to whether it plays a direct or indirect role in surplus extraction and whether it is differentiated from the 'economic'. It would also be reasonable to suggest that the expansion of the state's role in contemporary capitalism is likely to make it increasingly a target of class struggle. But Poulantzas goes considerably beyond these propositions. He suggests not only that the nature of exploitative relations can vary in different modes of production according to whether they assume 'economic' or 'extra-economic' forms, but also that modes of production — or even phases of modes of production — may vary according to whether the relations of exploitation are themselves 'dominant' at all. When he argues, therefore, that the 'political' and not the 'economic' is 'dominant' in monopoly capitalism, he is in effect arguing that the *relations of exploitation* (though no doubt 'determinant in the last instance') no longer 'reign supreme'.

III

In 1970, Poulantzas published *Fascism and Dictatorship*, which represents his most overtly Maoist work. Written in the wake of May 1968, when the largest youth current on the French left was Maoism in the form of *La Gauche Prolétarienne*, the book is punctuated with references to Mao; and, as if these markers were not enough to identify his current political stand, he provides

---

[7] It is worth noting that Poulantzas finds Balibar's approach too 'economistic'. *Classes in Contemporary Capitalism*, p. 13, n.1.

another sign-post: a characterization of the Soviet Union — quite gratuitous in the context of this book — in terms borrowed from Charles Bettelheim (whose work he had already cited approvingly in *Political Power and Social Classes*). It is also in this work, Poulantzas's most concrete contribution to political sociology, that he shows a remarkable insensitivity to the differences between the bourgeois-democratic or parliamentary capitalist state, and the capitalist state in its fascist form. On this, his view was to change dramatically over the next few years.

The next important milestone was *Classes in Contemporary Capitalism*, published in 1974. By now, Poulantzas had abandoned Maoism, and he had also begun to criticize PCF theory directly, though still from the left. The book contains some important applications of his theory of the state to the strategic problems of Communism, and even more important developments in the theory of class, which go a long way toward displacing the relations of production and exploitation as the determinants of class — with, as we shall see, significant political consequences.

A particular target of criticism in the book is the PCF 'anti-monopoly alliance' strategy and the theory of 'state monopoly capitalism' that underlies it. PCF doctrine, according to Poulantzas, contains several fundamental errors. It treats the relation between the state and monopoly capital as if it were a simple *fusion*, ignoring the fact that the state represents a 'power bloc' of several classes or class fractions and not the 'hegemonic' fraction of monopoly capital alone; it treats all non-monopoly interests as belonging equally to the 'popular masses', including elements of the bourgeoisie, without acknowledging the class barriers that separate the whole bourgeoisie from the truly 'popular' forces; and, in much the same way as the social democrats, it treats the state as in principle a class-neutral instrument, responding primarily to the *technical* imperatives of economic development, so that there appears to be nothing inherent in the nature of the capitalist state that prevents it from being merely *taken over* and turned to popular interests.

Poulantzas appears to be undermining the foundations of PCF strategy. And yet, though it is certainly true that his own position is to the left of the PCF mainstream, it nevertheless represents a criticism from within, proceeding from basic principles held in common — notably, the transfer of revolutionary agency to the 'people' or 'popular alliances', the transition to socialism via 'transformation' of the bourgeois state or 'advanced democracy', and hence the displacement of class struggle. In the final analysis, Poulantzas's theory is intended not to undermine Communist strategy but to set it on a sounder foundation. He does not fundamentally reject the notion of 'state monopoly capitalism' but rather *rescues* it. He reformulates the idea to correct its own contradictions, taking account of the incontrovertible fact that the state represents interests other than those of the hegemonic monopoly fraction. This has the added advantage of making it clear why and how the state is vulnerable to penetration by popular struggles. More fundamentally, although Poulantzas questions the unconditional inclusion of non-monopoly capital in the 'people', he retains the conception of 'popular alliance' and the focus of struggle on the political opposition between 'power bloc' and 'people' instead of the direct class antagonism between capital and labour. Poulantzas's 'left Eurocommunism' certainly diverges in significant respects from its parent-doctrine, but the shared premises are more fundamental than the divergences and have substantial consequences for Marxist theory.

Here we come to the crux of the matter and Poulantzas's contribution to the displacement of class struggle. The critical transformation in Marxist theory and practice, the pivot on which Eurocommunist strategy turns, is a displacement of the principal opposition from the class relations between labour and capital to the political relations between the 'people' and a dominant force or power bloc organized by the state. This critical shift requires a number of preparatory moves. Both *state* and *class* must be relocated in the struggle for socialism, and this requires a redefinition of both state and class. If the opposition between people, or popular alliance, and power bloc *cum* state is to become the dominant one, it is not enough simply to show how the state reflects, maintains, or reproduces the exploitative relation between capital and labour. It must be shown how the political conflict between two political organizations — the power bloc organized by the state and the popular alliance which organizes the people — can effectively *displace* the class conflict between capital and labour.

We have seen how Poulantzas, in *Political Power and Social Classes*, began to displace the relations of production and exploitation from their central position in the theory of the state by establishing the 'dominance of the political'. As we shall see, a similar displacement is carried out in his theory of class. The immediate effect is to transform class struggle into — or rather, replace it with — a political confrontation between the power bloc organized by the state, and the popular alliance. One might say that class struggle remains only as a 'structural' flaw, a 'contradiction', rather than an active practice. As Poulantzas points out, the state, together with bourgeois political parties, plays the same organizing and unifying role for the power bloc as a 'working class' party plays for the popular alliance.[8] Increasingly, the chief antagonists are no longer classes engaged in class struggle, nor even classes in struggle *through* political organizations, but political organizations engaged in party-political contests. His new theory of the state in contemporary capitalism goes a long way toward establishing a theoretical foundation for Eurocommunist strategy, but even more important to the doctrine of 'popular alliances' is a comparable transformation in the concept of *class*. If *class* and *class struggle* are to be made compatible with a strategy that displaces the opposition between capital and labour from its pivotal role, it is necessary to redefine class itself in such a way that the relations of exploitation cease to be 'dominant' in the determination of class. Poulantzas achieves this reformulation, and in the process succeeds by definition in reducing the *working class* to such minute proportions that any strategy *not* based on 'popular alliances' appears recklessly irresponsible.

The most important element in Poulantzas's theory of class is his discussion of the 'new petty bourgeoisie'. The question of the petty bourgeoisie, as Poulantzas points out, stands 'at the centre of current debates' on class structure and is of critical strategic importance.[9] Considerable debate has surrounded not only the class situation of 'traditional' petty bourgeois traders, shopkeepers, craftsmen, but most particularly the 'new middle classes' or 'intermediate strata', wage-earning commercial and bank employees, office and service workers, certain professional groups — that is, 'white collar' or 'tertiary sector' workers. These two 'petty bourgeoisies' are the main constituents of the popular alliance with the working class, those which together with the working class constitute the 'people' or 'popular masses'. To locate them correctly in the class structure of contemporary capitalism has been a major preoccupation of Eurocommunist strategists and theoreticians. Poulantzas stresses the strategic importance of the theoretical debate, the necessity of accurately identifying the class

---

[8] Ibid., p. 98.
[9] Ibid., p. 193.

position of these groups 'in order to establish a correct basis for the popular alliance ...'.[10]

Poulantzas begins by attacking two general approaches to the question of these 'new wage-earning groups', lumping together some very disparate arguments in each of the two categories. The first approach is that which dissolves these groups into either the proletariat or the bourgeoisie, or both. The second general 'tendency' is what Poulantzas calls 'the theory of the middle class', a politically motivated theory according to which both bourgeoisie and proletariat are being mixed together in the 'stew' of an increasingly dominant middle group, 'the region where the class struggle is dissolved'.[11] Most of these theories are intended to dilute the concepts of class and class struggle altogether. From the point of view of Marxist theory and socialist strategy, there is only one theory, among the several included in these two categories, which represents a serious challenge to Poulantzas's own: the theory which assimilates the new wage-earning groups to the working class, arguing that white collar workers have been increasingly 'proletarianized'. We shall return in a moment to Poulantzas's reasons for dismissing this approach.

Poulantzas then turns to the solution proposed by the PCF in its political strategy of the 'anti-monopoly' alliance. Like Poulantzas himself, the PCF line rejects the 'dissolution of the wage-earning groupings into the working class',[12] but it denies their class-specificity altogether and allows them to remain in a classless grey area as 'intermediate strata'. Poulantzas attacks this refusal to identify the class situation of the new wage-earning 'strata'. It is, he suggests, an abdication to bourgeois stratification theory and is inconsistent with the fundamental Marxist proposition that 'the division into class forms [is] the frame of reference for every social stratification'. The principle that 'classes are the basic groups in the "historic process"'is incompatible with 'the possibility that other groups exist parallel and external to classes ...'.[13]

It should be noted immediately that Poulantzas's criticism of the PCF line on the 'new wage-earning groups' does not strike at its roots either theoretically or practically. In fact, his argument pro-

---

[10] Ibid., p. 204.
[11] Ibid., pp. 196-7.
[12] Ibid., p. 198.
[13] Ibid., p. 199.

ceeds not as a rejection of PCF principles but, again, as an attempt to supply them with a sounder theoretical foundation, albeit somewhat to the left of the main party line. A truly Marxist theorization of popular alliances must, he argues, be based on a definition of class which grants these 'strata' their own class position instead of allowing them to stand outside class. The significant point, however, is that this class position is *not* to be found within the working class. In other words, Poulantzas is seeking a more clearly Marxist theoretical support for the Eurocommunist conception of an alliance between a *narrowly defined* working class and non-working-class popular forces.

Why, then, does Poulantzas, in common with the PCF, refuse to accept the theory which 'dissolves' these 'strata' into the working class? This theory, which he attributes primarily to C. Wright Mills, has been developed more recently in unambiguously Marxist ways by Harry Braverman and others. Poulantzas, however, apparently regards it as a departure from Marxism — for example, on the grounds that it makes the *wage* the relevant criterion of the working class, thereby making the mode of *distribution* the central determinant of class.[14] (It is perhaps significant that Poulantzas focuses on the wage as a mode of distribution and not as a mode of exploitation — as we shall see in a moment.) He argues further that by assimilating these groups to the working class, this view promotes reformist and social democratic tendencies. To identify the interests of 'intermediate strata' with those of the working class is to distort working-class interests, accommodating them to more backward, less revolutionary elements.[15] A political strategy based on the hegemony of the working class and its revolutionary interests, he maintains, demands the exclusion of these backward elements from the ranks of the working class.

On the face of it, then, Poulantzas' refusal to accept the proletarianization of white-collar workers appears to be directed in favour of a revolutionary stance and the hegemony of the working class which alone is 'revolutionary to the end'.[16] He even criticizes the PCF analysis on the grounds that, despite its refusal to accept this dissolution, it courts the same danger by neglecting to identify the specific class interests of the new wage-earning strata and

---

[14] Ibid., p. 194.
[15] Ibid., p. 204.
[16] Ibid.

hence their divergences from working-class interests. It is true that he fails to explain how these dangers will be averted by a 'working-class' party whose object is precisely to dilute its working-class character by directly representing other class interests, but let us leave aside this question for the moment. Let us pursue the implications of his own theory of the 'new petty bourgeoisie' to see whether it does, in fact, represent an attempt to keep exploitative class relations, class struggle, and the interests of the working class at the centre of Marxist class analysis and socialist practice.

For Poulantzas, the primary structural criterion for distinguishing between the working class and the new petty bourgeoisie at first seems to be the distinction between productive and unproductive labour. The 'unproductive' character of white-collar work separates these groups from the 'productive' working class. Poulantzas proceeds on the assumption that Marx himself applied this criterion and marked off the 'essential boundaries' of the working class by confining it to productive labour. Now it can be shown convincingly that Marx never intended the distinction to be used in this way.[17] In any case, Marx never said that he did so intend it, and Poulantzas never demonstrates that this is what he *meant*. He bases his argument on a misreading of Marx. He quotes Marx as saying 'Every productive worker is a wage-earner, but it does not follow that every wage-earner is a productive worker.'[18] Poulantzas takes this to mean something rather different: 'as Marx puts it,' he says, putting words into Marx's mouth, 'if every agent belonging to the working class is a wage-earner, this does not necessarily mean that every wage-earner belongs to the working class.' The two propositions are, of course, not at all the same, nor does Poulantzas *argue* that the one entails the other. He simply *assumes* it — i.e. he assumes precisely what needs to be proved, that 'agent belonging to the working class' is synonymous with 'productive worker'. He can then go on to demonstrate that various groups do not belong to the working class simply by demonstrating that they are not, according to Marx's definition (at least as he interprets that definition), productive workers.

Why this distinction — as important as it may be for other rea-

---

[17] See Peter Meiksins, 'Productive and Unproductive Labor and Marx's Theory of Class', *Review of Radical Political Economics*, vol. 13, no. 3, Fall 1981, pp. 32-42.

[18] *Classes in Contemporary Capitalism*, p. 210.

sons — should be regarded as the basis of a *class* division is never made clear. It is not clear why this distinction should override the fact that, like the 'blue-collar' working class, these groups are completely separated from the means of production; that they are exploited (which he concedes), that they perform surplus labour whose nature is determined by capitalist relations of production — the wage-relationship in which expropriated workers are compelled to sell their labour-power; or even that the same compulsions of capital accumulation that operate in the organization of labour for the working class — its 'rationalization', fragmentation, discipline, etc. — operate in these cases too. Indeed, the same conditions — the compulsory sale of labour-power and an organization of work derived from the exploitative logic of capital accumulation — apply even to workers not directly exploited by capital but employed, say, by the state or by 'non-profit' institutions. Whatever the complexities of class in contemporary capitalism — and they are many, as new formations arise and old ones change — it is difficult to see why exploitative social relations of production should now be regarded as secondary in the determination of class. Poulantzas's use of the distinction between productive and unproductive labour to separate white-collar workers from the working class seems to be largely arbitrary and circular, with no clear implications for our understanding of how classes and class interests are actually constituted in the real world.

In fact, it soon turns out that this 'specifically economic' determination is not sufficient — or even necessary — to define the new petty bourgeoisie. It cannot account for all the groups that Poulantzas wants to include in this class. Not only, he suggests, can it not account for certain groups which *are* involved in the process of material production (e.g. engineers, technicians, and supervisory staff), it cannot explain the overriding unity which binds these heterogeneous elements into a single class set off from the working class. Now, *political* and *ideological* factors must be regarded as decisive. These factors are decisive even for those groups who are already marked off by the productive/unproductive labour distinction,[19] and in some cases even override that division. In the final analysis, once these groups have been separated out from the bourgeoisie by the fact that they are exploited, the decisive uni-

---

[19] Ibid., p. 224.

fying factor that separates them from the working class is *ideological*, in particular the distinction between mental and manual labour. This distinction cannot be defined in 'technicist' or 'empiricist' terms, argues Poulantzas — for example, by empirically distinguishing 'dirty' and 'clean' jobs, or those who work with their hands and those who work with their brains, or those who are in direct contact with machines and those who are not. It is essentially a 'politico-ideological' division. Although this division cannot be entirely clear-cut and contains complexities which create fractions within the new petty bourgeoisie itself, it is, according to Poulantzas, the one determinant that both distinguishes these groups from the working class *and* overrides the various differences within the class, *including* the division between productive and unproductive labour with which it does not coincide. In other words, this *ideological* division is the decisive factor in constituting the new petty bourgeoisie as a class at all.

It is far from clear to what reality Poulantzas's ideological division corresponds, or why it should override the structural similarities among workers. What *is* true is that the organization of production in industrial capitalism establishes various divisions among workers within the labour process which are determined not by the technical demands of the labour-process itself but by its *capitalist* character. These divisions often constitute obstacles to the formation of a unified class — even in the case of workers who belong to the same class by virtue of their relation to capital and exploitation. But it is not clear why the divisions cited by Poulantzas should be more decisive than any others that divide workers in the labour-process or disunite them in the process of class organization. It is not clear why such divisions should be regarded *not* simply as obstacles to unity or roadblocks in the difficult process of class-organization — a process riddled with obstacles even for blue-collar workers — but rather as definitive class barriers dividing members from non-members of the working class.[20] In fact, Poulantzas's theory seems unable to accommodate any *process* in the development of classes at all. There seems to be only a string of static, sometimes overlapping, class situations (locations? boxes?). This is a view which in itself would seem to

---

[20] For a discussion of this distinction between class divisions and obstacles to class organization as it applies, for example, to the case of engineers, see Peter Meiksins, 'Scientific Management: A Dissenting View', *Theory and Society*, no. 13, 1984, pp. 177-209.

have significant political implications.

If the ideological division between mental and manual workers within the exploited wage-earning groups does not correspond to any objective barrier directly determined by the relations of production between capital and labour, neither does it correspond to a real and insurmountable division of interest between these workers. The class interests of both groups are determined by the fact that they are directly exploited through the sale of their labour-power; these interests have to do in the first instance with the terms and conditions of that sale, and in the last with the elimination of capitalist relations of production altogether, both the 'formal' and the 'real' subjection of labour to capital. The different functions of these workers in the labour-process may create divisions among them, based in some cases on differences in their responsibilities, education, income, and so on;[21] but these differences cannot be regarded as *class* divisions by any standard having to do with relations of production and exploitation. The ideological divisions between them are constituted less from the point of view of their own class interests than from the point of view of capital, which has an interest in keeping them apart. The imposition of capitalist ideology can certainly operate to discourage unity within the working class and interfere with the processes of class organization, but it can hardly be accepted as an absolute class barrier between different kinds of workers.

Poulantzas has thus presented a class analysis in which relations of exploitation are no longer decisive. This is in keeping with the fundamental principles of his theory. The relations of production and exploitation, according to him, belong to the 'economic' sphere which, as we have seen, though it 'determines in the last instance' may not be *dominant* in any given mode of production or social formation. This notion is carried over into the analysis of class.[22] It now becomes clear that there are cases in which political or ideological factors 'reign supreme' in determining class.

---

[21] Some of these factors — e.g. education — may even be purely 'conjunctural', varying in different capitalist countries at different times. Poulantzas may, for example, be generalizing from certain European cases — notably France? — in which the education of white-collar workers differs from that of blue-collar workers more markedly than is the case, say, in the United States or Canada. This would not be the first time that the historical particulars of French experience have been transformed into theoretical universals by Althusserian theory.

[22] See, for example, *Political Power and Social Classes*, pp. 62-70.

Poulantzas is saying more than simply that the formation of classes is always a political, ideological, and cultural process as well as an economic one, or that relations between classes are not only economic but also political and ideological. Nor, again, is he simply pointing to the special role of the 'political' where relations of production are themselves 'politically' organized. He is suggesting that ideological and political relations may actually take precedence over the relations of exploitation in the 'objective' constitution of classes, and that political or ideological divisions may represent essential class barriers. Again the relations of exploitation have been displaced.[23]

What, then, are the practical consequences of Poulantzas's views on class? Why is it a matter of such critical importance whether or not white-collar workers are theoretically included in the working class? Poulantzas himself, as we have seen, maintains that it is strategically important to separate out the 'new petty bourgeoisie' in order to protect the revolutionary integrity and hegemony of the working class. There is, however, another way of looking at it. We have seen that for Poulantzas the relations of production are not decisive in determining the class situation of white-collar workers. The 'new petty bourgeoisie' is distinguished as a class on the basis of ideological divisions defined from the point of view of capital. In other words, they constitute a class insofar as they are absorbed into the hegemonic ideology of capitalism; and that absorption seems to be definitive: the new petty bourgeoisie can be made to adopt certain working-class positions — that is, their political attitudes can 'polarize toward' the proletariat; but they cannot be made part of the working class. These propositions are very different from the observation that the inclinations of white-collar

---

[23] It is worth adding that Poulantzas appears to have difficulty keeping his focus on relations of exploitation even in cases where the 'economic' is clearly 'dominant', that is, social formations where the capitalist mode of production (in its simple or 'competitive' form) prevails. For example, in his statement of basic principles, where he defines the determining characteristics of modes of production, he suggests that *property relations* in all class societies are characterized by a separation of the producer from the means of labour. The particular separation from the means of production which uniquely characterizes capitalism takes place in the labour process, in the relations of 'real appropriation'. *This* separation 'occurs at the stage of heavy industry' (*Political Power and Social Classes*, p. 27). Poulantzas again attributes this view to Marx. For Marx, however, the critical factor is *wage-labour*; the crucial separation occurs long before the 'stage of heavy industry', not merely with the reorganization of the labour-process in the 'real' subjection of labour to capital,

workers to accept capitalist ideology may be stronger than those of
blue-collar workers; that these inclinations constitute a problem
for class organization, for the development of class consciousness,
and for the building of class unity; and that they must be taken into
account by any socialist strategy. For Poulantzas, it would appear
that these inclinations represent a decisive class boundary; and this
has significant strategic implications.

Despite Poulantzas's criticism of PCF theory and strategy, his
theory of class belongs to the 'attempt of the theoreticians of
Eurocommunism to reduce the weight of the Western proletariat
to that of a minority within society ...'.[24] At a stroke of the pen, the
proletariat is reduced from a comfortable majority in advanced
capitalist countries to a rump group which must inevitably place
class alliances at the top of its agenda. Poulantzas's very definition
of class in general and the 'new petty bourgeoisie' in particular displaces the focus of socialist strategy from creating a united working
class to constructing 'popular alliances' based on class differences,
even based on divisions imposed by capital. Any appeal to the
'new petty bourgeoisie', for example, must be directed not to its
working-class interests but to its specific interests as a petty
bourgeoisie.

The strategic implications become even clearer when this view
of alliances is embodied in a particular conception of 'working
class' parties as organizations which do not simply form alliances
with other groups and parties but directly *represent* other class
interests. Poulantzas insists that 'the polarization of the petty
bourgeoisie towards proletarian class positions depends on the

---

but in the earlier transformation of the *exploitative relationship* in the 'formal' subjection. This is the essential boundary between capitalist relations and other modes
of production, even though transformations in the labour-process have followed in
its train and have had profound effects on class formation. Poulantzas has shifted
the focus away from the relations of exploitation to the labour-process, which then
appears as the distinctive and essential characteristic of the mode of production at
the 'economic' level. This may help to account for certain peculiarities we have
already noted in his analysis of white-collar workers: for example, his refusal to
regard their status as wage-labourers — i.e. their exploitation through the sale of
their labour-power — as decisive in determining their class, on the rather curious
grounds that wages are simply a mode of distribution; and his tendency instead to
accord a critical role to the position of these workers in the organization of the
labour-process and its ideological expression in the division between mental and
manual labour.

[24] Ernest Mandel, *From Stalinism to Eurocommunism*, London 1978, p. 209.

petty bourgeoisie being *represented* by the class-struggle organizations of the working class themselves ... This means, firstly, that popular unity under the hegemony of the working class can only be based on the class difference between the classes and fractions that form part of the alliance ...'[25] This notion turns out to be a two-edged sword. On the one hand, it suggests that the popular forces should themselves be transformed in the process of struggle. That is why, argues Poulantzas, the alliance should be established 'not by way of concessions, in the strict sense, by the working class to its allies taken as they are, but rather by the establishment of objectives which can transform these allies in the course of the uninterrupted struggle and its stages, account being taken of their specific class determination and the specific polarization that affects them'.[26] On the other hand, the very idea that alliances must not be based merely on 'concessions' to allies 'taken as they are' also entails that working-class organizations must cease to be organizations of the working class. It now appears that it is not just the integrity of working-class interests that these organizations must protect, but also that of the petty bourgeoisie. Poulantzas now seems to be criticizing the PCF for taking the 'popular masses' too much for granted, instead of acknowledging the specificity of their various class interests. A 'working-class' party cannot simply make 'concessions' to elements outside itself from a vantage point consistently determined by working-class interests; it must actually *represent* other class interests — and this means establishing objectives addressed to these other class interests. This inevitably raises the question of the degree to which the ultimate objectives of socialism itself must be tailored to the measurements of cross-class alliances.

IV

The groundwork for a theorization of Eurocommunism was, then, already firmly laid in *Classes in Contemporary Capitalism*; but its logic and strategic implications were not fully worked out until Poulantzas wrote his last two major works: *The Crisis of the Dictatorships* (1975-76) — which may mark the critical turning

---

[25] *Classes in Contemporary Capitalism*, pp. 334-5.
[26] Ibid., p. 335.

point to the right — and *State, Power, Socialism*, published in 1978. The composition of the first of these books coincides with the official emergence of Eurocommunism and may be related to his involvement with the Greek Communist Party of the Interior. In his final book — written before the defeat of the Union de la Gauche but after the rise of the Nouvelle Philosophie, and other related anti-Marxist currents in France — Poulantzas felt obliged to confront contemporary attacks on Marxism at the same time as meeting some of the new intellectual trends — notably Foucault — at least half way. The critical development in these two books is a perception of the state and of the transition to socialism that endorses the Eurocommunist vision of that transition as a smooth process of 'democratization'. In *The Crisis of the Dictatorships*, for example in his analysis of the Portuguese Revolution, he reveals how far his thought has developed in this direction by rejecting any attack on the integrity of the state, any 'dismantling, splitting or disarticulating' of the state apparatus, as a threat to 'democratization'.

At this point, Poulantzas begins to converge in significant ways with the social-democratic theory of the state which he launched his career by attacking. He continues to criticize social democracy however, this time as a kind of 'statism'. For the first time he explicitly attacks Stalinism also. Like the social democrats, he insists that the state is open to penetration by popular forces and that there is no need for strategies — such as those implied by the concept of 'dual power' — based on the assumption that the state is a 'monolithic bloc without cracks of any kind'.[27] Indeed, such strategies are actively pernicious, leading to 'statism' and other such authoritarian deformations. The state need not be attacked and destroyed from without. Since it is 'traversed' by internal contradictions — the contradictions inherent in intra- and inter-class conflicts — the state itself can be the major terrain of struggle, as popular struggles are brought to bear on the state's internal contradictions. There is much here that is reminiscent of the inverted instrumentalism which he had earlier rejected, the social-democratic notion that the state, or pieces of it, can pass, like an 'object coveted by the various classes', from the hands of the dominant class to those of the dominated, thereby effecting the transition from capitalism to socialism. Like the social-democratic

---

[27] *State, Power, Socialism*, London 1980, p. 254.

strategy, this one too seems confident that the state can lead the transition to socialism without encountering insurmountable class barriers along the way. The difference between the two strategies is that for Poulantzas, the state cannot be simply *occupied*: it must be transformed. There must be a 'decisive shift in the relationship of forces' within the state — not simply within representative institutions through electoral victory, but within the administrative and repressive organs of the state, the civil service, the judiciary, the police and the military. The complete vagueness of these prescriptions, coupled with the injunction that the unity of the state must be preserved, makes one wonder how substantial these departures from social democracy really are; but even if we accept that there is a significant difference, this project is arguably even more optimistic than the social democratic programme about the possibilities of transforming the capitalist state into an agent of socialism with a minimal degree of class struggle.

If there was any political current to which Poulantzas's theory was now most congenial, it was mainstream Eurocommunism. At least, he now explicitly shared its most fundamental assumptions, concerning 'popular alliances' and the transition to socialism by means of 'extending' parliamentary capitalist democracy. Paradoxically, if Poulantzas's approach — and that of Eurocommunism generally — places unnecessary obstacles in the way of the struggle for socialism by erecting artificial class barriers *within* the working class, the same approach tends to underplay the real difficulties of the struggle by underestimating the barriers *between* classes. Poulantzas's analysis, for example, creates a gradual continuum of classes which blurs the sharp divisions between the working-class and clearly non-working-class elements of the 'popular alliance'; but even more fundamentally, the incorporation of a wide range of class interests within the popular alliance, together with the relegation of exploitative relations to a secondary position, tends even to narrow the gap between capitalist and socialist forces. This may help to account for the Eurocommunist tendency 'to understate the problems of [the] transition'[28] and underestimate the necessity of direct class confrontation and struggle. The whole approach is compounded of a pessimism based on the assumption that the real (potentially revolutionary) working class represents a minority,

---

[28] Ralph Miliband, 'Constitutionalism and Revolution: Notes on Eurocommunism', *Socialist Register* 1978, p. 170.

and an optimism based on the assumption that the mass constituency for a (modified) socialist programme represents a vast majority. Both assumptions have significant practical consequences which, taken together, circumscribe the socialist project: optimism limits the means, pessimism curtails the ends.

In his theory of the state, establishing the dominance of the political; in his theory of class, displacing exploitation and elevating ideology as a principal determinant (thereby also reducing the working class to a rump diluted in a 'popular alliance'); and in his growing acceptance of 'democracy' as an indeterminate concept joining together capitalist and socialist 'democracy' along a seamless continuum, obscuring the contradictions, antagonisms, and class conflicts that stand between capitalism and socialism, Poulantzas anticipated all the major themes of the new 'true' socialism. Nevertheless, he never pursued these themes to their ultimate conclusions; and it would probably be more accurate to regard him not so much as the first major exponent of the NTS, but as its last major antecedent.

4

The Autonomization of Ideology and Politics

I

Poulantzas undoubtedly exerted a great influence on the theoretical development of the NTS; but in the end, he was clearly still too 'economistic' for their purposes, and still too committed to the working class as a major constituent in the socialist project. The decisive detachment of politics from class was achieved by making ideology and 'discourse' — themselves conceived as autonomous from class — the principal historical determinants. It is, according to the NTS idealism, ideology or 'discourse' that constitutes individuals as 'subjects'. For the Left, the principal political subject is the 'people', constructed by something like a 'popular democratic' or 'national-popular' discourse.

The big theoretical move was made, most influentially, by Ernesto Laclau. Beginning, like Poulantzas, as a defender of what he took to be Marxist orthodoxy and theoretical rigour — for example, against André Gunder Frank, and even against Balibar and Poulantzas himself — he went on to surpass Poulantzas in privileging 'ideological determinations' and establishing their social indeterminacy. In his latest work, written with Chantal Mouffe, he has, as we shall see, taken the final step not only by detaching ideology from social determinations but by dissolving the social altogether into ideology or 'discourse'. This book, *Hegemony and Socialist Strategy: Towards a Radical Democratic Politics*, is worth examining at some length, not because it represents a particularly cogent case for the NTS, but because it is beautifully paradigmatic, summing up and taking to their ultimate conclusions all the NTS themes, revealing with particular clarity all the slippages and contradictions, both theoretical and political, inherent in its logic.

The first major step in the autonomization of ideology was

taken in Laclau's criticism of Poulantzas's book on fascism.[1] The purpose of this theoretical move was clearly a political one, to criticize Poulantzas for rejecting nationalism as a suitable weapon in the fight against fascism. It was this 'national-popular' or 'popular democratic' 'interpellation' that, according to Laclau, was missing, for example, in the German labour movement during the 1920s. In opposition to Poulantzas, he in effect endorses those aspects of KPD policy, notably the 'Schlageter line', which played on German chauvinism. We should remember that the 'Schlageter line' encouraged certain transactions with fascism — for example, when the KPD called for a general strike in memory of a proto-Nazi militant killed in action against the French in the Rhineland. Laclau admits that there was an element of 'opportunism' in this line and that it had the effect of weakening the working class against Nazism; but he argues that these effects were not inherent in the nationalistic current. They were rather produced by its 'sporadic application' and by the 'class reductionism' which compelled the KPD to conceive of this policy as a *concession* to the petty-bourgeoisie.[2]

In order to theorize this defence of nationalism, Laclau proposes a more generally applicable set of theoretical principles concerning the indeterminacy and class-neutrality of 'national-popular interpellations', and indeed of ideology in general. There is no doubt that this argument is informed by his attitudes toward the political situation of his native Argentina and by his sympathy for the 'popular interpellations' of the Peronist tradition, which in his view had a strong 'popular democratic' potential that was simply derailed as the regime collapsed, preventing any liberalization and 'any stable form of articulation between popular interpellations and bourgeois ideology.'[3]

The theory of ideology that emerged from this debate is worth exploring especially for its more general applications and its 'articulations' with the main theoretical trend associated with Eurocommunism, before we go on to examine in greater detail the final outcome of Laclau's theoretical and political odyssey in *Hegemony and Socialist Strategy*. Already in the earlier work —

---

[1] Ernesto Laclau, *Politics and Ideology in Marxist Theory*, London 1979, pp. 81-142.

[2] Ibid., p. 130.

[3] Ibid., p. 191.

although the working class still retains a prominent role in Laclau's conception of socialist strategy — the struggle for socialism is becoming not so much a class struggle as an indeterminate 'democratic' struggle conducted by a popular alliance constructed by essentially class-neutral ideology. The ground is already being prepared for the shift from Eurocommunism to the new 'true' socialism.

Viewed from the Eurocommunist perspective, as we have seen, the chief task of the 'working-class' movement is to win the hearts and minds of the 'middle sectors'. Since this battle must be fought on the ideological and political terrain, the strategy of popular alliances places a particularly heavy burden on ideological struggle and attaches a very special theoretical importance to the question of ideology. In his article 'Fascism and Ideology', Laclau clearly formulates the theoretical demands imposed by the strategy of class alliances: 'Today, when the European working class is increasing its influence and must conceive its struggle more and more as a contest for the ideological and political hegemony of middle sectors, it is more necessary than ever for Marxism to develop a rigorous theory of ideological practice which eliminates the last taints of class reductionism.'[4] Accordingly, Laclau introduces important innovations into Marxist theories of ideology, with the specific purpose of meeting these strategic needs.

To lay the foundation, however, he must first tie up certain loose ends in the theories of class presented by both Eurocommunist strategists and Poulantzas. Again the question is where to locate the 'middle sectors'. Laclau, too, is dissatisfied with the standard PCF notion of 'intermediate wage-earning strata' as fundamentally classless, but he concludes that this position may be less mistaken than Poulantzas supposes.[5] The difficulty with Poulantzas's position, suggests Laclau, is that by making *ideological* factors the primary determinant of class in these cases, he effectively denies the very basis of Marxism because he defines class apart from production relations.[6] The problem for Laclau, then, is to acknowledge and explain the ideological unity of these groups (which he accepts) *and* to give that ideological unity the priority it deserves, without contradicting the fundamental premises of Marx-

---

[4] Ibid., pp. 141-42.
[5] Ibid., p. 114.
[6] Ibid., p. 113.

ist class analysis. In his analysis, class retains its theoretical purity but loses its historical significance.

Laclau concedes, in contrast to Poulantzas, that the 'new petty bourgeoisie' is a fraction of the working class; he simply goes on to argue that, whatever the objective class situation of these groups in terms of production relations, that situation is secondary in determining their position. For them, the primary 'contradiction' with the 'dominant bloc' is not a *class* contradiction. In their case, the important contradictions 'are posed, not at the level of the dominant relations of production, but at the level of political and ideological relations ...'.[7] In other words, the 'identity as *the people* plays a much more important role than their identity as *class*.'[8] The fact that Poulantzas' old and new petty bourgeoisies are two different classes, and that the latter technically belongs to the working class, is overridden by the political and ideological unity which binds them together and separates them from other classes; and their location between the two principal classes allows them to 'polarize' either way. The class struggle between bourgeoisie and proletariat, then, is increasingly an ideological battle over these groups as the two contenders seek to win them over by ideological means.

This clearly represents an important innovation in the Marxist conception of class and class struggle. It should be emphasized, however, that all three attempts to revise Marxist theory to accommodate the 'middle sectors' — the PCF theory of classless intermediate wage-earning strata, Poulantzas's theory of the new petty bourgeoisie, and Laclau's displacement of class contradictions by ideological divisions — represent an in-house debate, a dispute about which theory of class is best suited to support the strategy of popular alliance and the 'power bloc versus people' opposition on which that strategy rests. All three depend in one way or another on displacing the relations of production and exploitation and the direct opposition between capital and labour from the centre of Marxist theory and practice, though Laclau goes much further than Poulantzas.

Laclau then presents a theory of ideology that extends the *autonomy* of ideology by dissociating it as much as possible from class relations. The argument begins with a distinction between

---

[7] Ibid., p. 114.
[8] Ibid., p. 114.

ideological expressions ('interpellations') that are determined by *class* contradictions and struggles, and those that are generated by other kinds of contradictions, especially 'popular-democratic' struggles in which the 'people' (a category that cuts across classes) is counterposed to a dominant 'power bloc', notably in the form of the state. Such non-class ideologies always appear in association ('articulated') with class ideologies; but because they are in principle autonomous, neutral, not class-specific, they can be detached or 'disarticulated' from one class ideology and assimilated to another. For example, the hegemony of the dominant class rests to a great extent on its ability to neutralize opposition by appropriating popular-democratic ideology to itself.

Here, then, is the crux of the argument. These detachable, class-neutral popular-democratic 'interpellations' are 'the domain of ideological class struggle par excellence'.[9] Indeed, since a great deal of importance is attached here to ideology, these autonomous ideological elements can be said to represent the central arena of class struggle. The significance of this argument is that, 'although the domain of class determination is reduced, the arena of class struggle is immensely broadened'.[10] A theoretical basis has thus been provided not only for political alliances that transcend class — one might say a 'theorization' of the Popular Front — but apparently also for locating the principal agents of class struggle *outside class*. Laclau gives us certain hints about who such agents might be. By putting the burden of class struggle so much on the 'articulation' and 'disarticulation' of autonomous ideological 'interpellations', he makes class struggle appear to be in large part an 'autonomous' intellectual exercise in which the 'autonomous' intellectual champions of each class compete in a tug-of-war over non-class ideological elements, victory going to that class whose intellectuals can most convincingly redefine these elements to match its own particular interests.

According to such a view, the appropriate theoretical strategy to adopt toward an ideological system like liberal democracy would appear to be first to detach its non-class — especially popular-democratic — 'interpellations' from their (temporary and arbitrary) class associations. This can be accomplished by *abstracting* them, emptying them of their specific social and historical content. They

[9] Ibid., p. 109.
[10] Ibid., p. 110.

can thus be reduced to more or less formal propositions of more or less universal application, which can then be reconstituted for articulation with a new set of socio-historical interests. If the hegemony of the bourgeoisie rests on its ability to claim popular-democratic 'interpellations' for itself, the counter-hegemonic task of the socialist political theorist is, first, to 'disarticulate' these ideological elements from bourgeois ideology by demonstrating their non-class character.

It should be noted that Laclau goes beyond the argument that not all social conflicts are class struggles and that not all ideologies are class ideologies, even when they are implicated in class struggle. He also goes beyond the observation that a particular class ideology — such as bourgeois-democratic ideology — can achieve a certain appearance of *universality*, and that it is precisely this appearance of universality that constitutes class *hegemony*. He is not even saying simply that such claims to universality must contain an important element of truth in order to be hegemonic. All this would be true, and would correctly characterize bourgeois democracy — which is both a *class* ideology and a plausible claimant to universality to the extent that it has captured the allegiance of other classes not simply by mystification but also by bringing them real benefits. Laclau, however, is saying something else. Instead of arguing that an ideology that is class-determined in origin and meaning may acquire an appearance of generality and thus contribute to the hegemony of its parent-class, he argues essentially the reverse: that such an ideology should be recognized as having 'no precise class connotation',[11] and that class hegemony depends upon claiming and seizing these essentially class-neutral 'interpellations'. To judge the 'democratic' aspects of bourgeois democracy in these terms, for example, is quite different from acknowledging that bourgeois-democratic forms, however 'bourgeois' they may be, cannot be dismissed as mere sham and mystification. It is, in effect, to argue instead that they are not 'bourgeois' at all. Laclau insists in a footnote that by 'democratic interpellations' he has more in mind than the ideology of liberalism and parliamentary democracy,[12] but it is clear that his argument is calculated to bridge the gap between bourgeois and socialist democracy and to conceptualize away the radical break between them.

---

[11] Ibid., p. 111.
[12] Ibid., p. 107, n. 36.

The strategic implication of this argument seems to be that socialism can be built simply by extending these essentially class-neutral democratic forms. Again we encounter no class barriers along the way. If, in contrast, we were to look upon these forms as class-specific, we could acknowledge their value and even the plausibility of their claims to a certain generality; but we should also have to acknowledge the break, the 'river of fire', between bourgeois and socialist democracy, as well as the difficulty of proceeding from one to the other. For Laclau, the appropriate strategy is not to stress the specificity of socialism, not to reclaim democracy for socialism by challenging the limits of bourgeois democracy with alternative socialist forms, and, finally, not to pursue the specific interests of the working class, but to dilute them in an intermediate 'stew'. We now have a theory of ideology to accompany the theories of class and the state which are needed to underpin the strategy of popular alliance and the building of socialism by the extension of bourgeois-democratic forms, all by-passing the direct opposition between capital and labour.

II

Laclau has not, however, stopped with these already substantial departures from traditional Marxist theory and practice. In his latest work, the theoretical and political logic of his earlier writings has worked itself out to the end: he says what amounts to a final farewell to Marxism, and more particularly to the working class — indeed, it must be said, to anything recognizable as socialism. His earlier remarks about the increasing influence of the European working class, and his prescriptions for socialist struggle as an effort to establish working class hegemony over the 'middle sectors', would be inconceivable from him today. The working class has now been completely displaced by the 'people', and socialism by something called 'radical democracy'. Above all, autonomous ideology — or, more precisely, discourse — has now swallowed up the whole social world. It is no longer simply a matter of detaching ideology from any social foundation; now society itself is constituted by ideology or 'discourse'. There remain no social relations or identities; there are only fields of discursivity. He has taken the logic of the NTS to its ultimate extreme, to an open downgrading of socialism itself — now at best a 'component' of radical democracy — which few of his comrades have yet been willing to emulate.

In *Hegemony and Socialist Strategy*, Laclau and his co-author, Chantal Mouffe, set out to undermine the very foundations of the Marxist view that the working class will be the agent of socialist transformation, and to replace it with a political project whose object is 'radical democracy' and whose subject is a popular alliance constituted not by relations of class, nor indeed by any determinate social relations, but rather by discourse. This theoretical project requires that Marxism be challenged in its very first premises. Laclau and Mouffe, then, launch an assault on what they take to be the 'last redoubt of orthodox essentialism', the fundamental assumptions of Marxist 'class reductionism': that the 'economy' is a 'self-regulated' mechanism, operating strictly by 'endogenous' laws with no 'indeterminacy resulting from political or other external interventions'[13]; that this mechanism, by means of its own laws of motion, automatically constitutes social agents; and that these social agents, by virtue of their positions in the relations of production, will possess 'historic interests' which will be reflected at other 'social levels' — in particular, in political manifestations, and specifically the 'fundamental interest' of the working class in socialism.[14]

This theoretical project founders spectacularly at the very first step. It begins with such an egregious misunderstanding of Marxism as to put in question the entire argument. Their summary of Marxism's first principles, its conception of the 'economy', is worth quoting at length, especially since it illustrates an interpretation of Marxism not uncommon among the NTS. Beginning with the proposition that the idea of the 'laws of motion of the economy corresponds to the thesis of the neutrality of productive forces', the exposition proceeds:

For Marxism, the development of the productive forces plays the key role in the historical evolution towards socialism, given that 'the past development of the productive forces makes socialism possible, and their future development makes social-

[13] Ernesto Laclau and Chantal Mouffe, *Hegemony and Socialist Strategy: Towards a Radical Democratic Politics*, London 1985, p. 76.

[14] Ibid., pp. 76-7.

ism necessary.' They are at the root of the formation of an ever more numerous and exploited proletariat, whose historical mission is to take possession of, and collectively manage, highly socialized and developed productive forces. At present, the capitalist relations of production constitute an insurmountable obstacle to the advance of these productive forces. The contradiction between bourgeoisie and proletariat is, therefore, the social and political expression of a primal economic contradiction, one which combines a general law of development of the productive forces with the laws of development specific to the capitalist mode of production. According to this view, if history has a sense and a rational substratum, it is due to the general law of development of the productive forces. Hence, the economy may be understood as a mechanism of society acting upon objective phenomena independently of human action.[15]

Let us pause here for a moment to highlight the critical points. Although there is much that could be said about the crude technological determinism which is here mistakenly attributed to Marx, about how this conception of history as the neutral development of productive forces begs the essential questions posed by Marx concerning the specificity of capitalism and its unique drive to revolutionize the forces of production, these issues need not detain us here.[16] It is enough for the moment to note that Laclau and Mouffe attribute to Marx the view that productive forces are 'neutral' and their development a 'neutral' process (what that means we shall see in a moment); that the proletariat is simply a reflex of this fundamentally technological process of development, as is the opposition between bourgeoisie and proletariat (the notion of class exploitation does not figure in this account at all); that the 'historic mission' of the proletariat is reducible to obeying the technological imperative by collectively appropriating the 'neutral' forces of production developed by capitalism, in order to permit their further development (again, the 'historic mission' of abolishing class exploitation does not figure in this account, which

---

[15] Ibid., pp. 77-8. It is worth noting that Laclau and Mouffe are quoting from G.A. Cohen, not from Marx. This practice of interpretation by proxy is followed consistently throughout their account of Marx.

[16] I have discussed these issues at greater length in 'Marxism and the Course of History', *New Left Review* 147, September/October 1984, pp. 95-107.

cannot accommodate anything as 'indeterminate' and 'exogenous' as class struggle).

This is, of course, not the first time Marx has been read as a technological determinist — though perhaps this reading is more uncompromising than most. What is important about this particular account is that it underwrites one fundamental assumption: according to Laclau and Mouffe, Marx's conception of the working class as a political agent, the privileged agent of the socialist transformation, presumes that the working class will emerge automatically as a unified political force in mechanical response to technological imperatives, and Marxism stands or falls according to whether this simple determinism holds true — which it clearly does not. The full force of this argument — and the extent to which it is based on a gross misunderstanding — becomes clear in what follows:

> Now, in order that this general law of development of the productive forces may have full validity, it is necessary that all the elements intervening in the productive process be submitted to its determinations. To ensure this, Marxism had to resort to a fiction: it conceived of labour-power as a commodity. Sam Bowles and Herbert Gintis have shown how this fiction would make Marxism blind to a whole series of characteristics of labour-power as an element of the process of capitalist production. Labour-power differs from the other necessary elements of production in that the capitalist must do more than simply purchase it; he must also make it produce labour. This essential aspect, however, escapes the conception of labour-power as a commodity whose use-value is labour. For if it were merely a commodity like the others, its use-value could obviously be made automatically effective from the very moment of its purchase. 'The designation of labour as the use-value of labour-power to capital obscures the absolutely fundamental distinction between productive inputs *embodied in people capable of social practices* and all those remaining inputs for whom ownership by capital is sufficient to secure the "consumption" of their productive services.' A large part of the capitalist organization of labour can be understood only as a result of the necessity to extract labour from the labour-power purchased by the capitalist. The evolution of productive forces becomes unintelligible if this need of the capitalist to exercise his domination at the very heart of the labour process is not

understood. This, of course, calls into question the whole idea of the development of the productive forces as a natural, spontaneously progressive phenomenon. We can therefore see that both elements of the economist viewpoint — labour power as a commodity, and the development of the productive forces as a neutral process — reinforce each other....

The fact is that once labour-power is purchased, the maximum possible labour has to be extracted from it. Hence the labour process cannot exist without a series of relations of domination. Hence, too, well before the advent of monopoly capitalism, the capitalist organization of labour had to be both a technique of production and a technique of domination.[17]

Then, after some passages intended to show that these relations of domination also entail resistance on the part of the workers, and that therefore the nature and rate of the development of productive forces is affected by working-class struggles, they conclude:

Workers' struggles, understood in these terms, obviously cannot be explained by an endogenous logic of capitalism, since their very dynamism cannot be subsumed under the "commodity" form of labour-power. But if this split between a logic of capital and a logic of workers' resistance influences the organization of the capitalist labour process, it must also crucially affect the character and rhythm of expansion of the productive forces. Thus, the thesis that the productive forces are neutral, and that their development can be conceived as natural and unilinear, is entirely unfounded. This also removes the only ground on which the economy could be understood as an autonomous and self-regulated universe. The first condition, therefore, of the exclusive privilege granted to the economic sphere in the constitution of social agents, is not fulfilled.[18]

Let us be very clear about what is being said here. First, Marx is being charged with a failure to understand — because blinded by the 'fiction' of labour-power as a commodity — that labour-power is not a commodity like any other, because it is embodied in

---

[17] HSS, pp. 78-9.
[18] Ibid., p. 80.

human beings 'capable of social practices'; that capital needs to control the labour-process in order to extract maximum surplus value; that therefore the labour process in capitalism is characterized by relations of domination; that workers resist; and that the development of capitalist production techniques and forms of organization have been shaped by working class struggles.

These accusations of ignorance levelled against Marx would be startling enough, given everything he has to say about the antagonistic character of the labour-process in capitalism; about commodity fetishism; about the specificity of that 'peculiar' commodity, labour-power, embodied in living, struggling human beings; about the 'two-fold' character of capitalist production, in which the production of use-values is inseparable from the production of surplus value; about how this 'two-fold' character distorts the organization of production, which must at the same time serve as an organization of antagonistic relations of exploitation; about the ways in which the organization of production is shaped by capital's need for control in conditions of class antagonism and workers' resistance; about the history of working class struggles and how they have affected the development of capitalist production; about the fact that the very instruments of labour and the modern 'science of technology' themselves are not 'neutral' but permeated by the relations of class exploitation, domination, and struggle. Much of *Capital* Volume 1 is devoted to precisely these themes, and to exploring the implications of the fact that capital's control of the labour-process is not simply determined by the 'neutral' requirements of 'efficiency' but is 'made necessary by the capitalist and therefore antagonistic character of that process'[19] and the antagonism of interests between capitalist and labourer, an antagonism that implies relations of domination and resistance. Even in the aphoristic short-hand of the *Communist Manifesto* it is clear that the development of productive forces is anything but 'neutral', determined as it is by the imperatives and contradictions of class.

But what makes the Laclau–Mouffe argument even more astounding is that these very themes, to which they accuse Marxism of being blind and which they present as a decisive blow to the whole Marxist project in theory and practice, lie at the very

---

[19] Marx, *Capital*, volume 1, Harmondsworth 1976, p. 450. Moscow 1971, p. 314.

heart of the Marxist case for associating the 'economic' interests of the working class with the politics of socialism. For Marx, it is precisely because the 'economic sphere' is permeated by the relations of class exploitation and the antagonism of class interest, indeed because the 'economic sphere' is constituted by those class relations — and not simply by some 'neutral' technological imperative — that there is an organic relation between the 'economy' and other social 'spheres'. For Marx, it is precisely because material production is organized in class-distorted ways that 'economic' relations are also relations of power, conflict, and struggle which play themselves out not only in the 'economic sphere' but also in other social domains and in the arena of politics. (In fact, is it not the first premise of historical materialism that material production is a *social* phenomenon?) It is, therefore, incomprehensible why the proposition that the organization of production cannot be separated from 'overall social relations'[20] should be regarded as a fatal challenge to Marxism, instead of its ultimate justification. And it is equally incomprehensible why the proposition that there is a fundamental antagonism at the core of capitalist production, and that this antagonism is inseparable from the relations of domination, resistance, and struggle at other social 'levels', should be regarded as a mortal blow to the Marxist conception of the socialist project, instead of a restatement of the very premises on which Marxism bases its view of the organic connection between socialist politics and the inherently anti-capitalist interests of the working class.

III

This, then, is the first fatal flaw in the Laclau–Mouffe attack on Marxism, and it clearly involves not only a breathtaking misreading of Marx, but a very substantial failure of reasoning. There is, however, something more fundamental at stake, which goes to the very core of their theoretical apparatus — and, indeed, to the theoretical underpinnings of the whole NTS project. The Laclau–Mouffe attack on the Marxist association of socialist politics and working class interests hinges on one proposition: Marxism must

---

[20] HSS, p. 80.

assume that working class unity and its socialist impulse is the 'simple effect of capitalist development' — i.e. the neutral and natural development of productive forces — without 'external intervention' from the 'spheres' of ideology and politics; in other words, the working class must spring full-grown, as a unified force for socialism, directly out of capitalist production — or else Marxism fails. To the extent that classical Marxism itself recognizes the need for mediations between the economic realities of capitalist production and the constitution of the working class as a unified socialist force, it undermines its own foundations. If workers are not united, without mediations, by a 'rational and necessary movement of history accessible to scientific knowledge'[21] there can be no justification for imputing 'objective interests' to a working class that is historically fragmented and subject to a plurality of historical interests other than those of class:

> Here, the alternative is clear: either one has a theory of history according to which this contradictory plurality will be eliminated and an absolutely united working class will become transparent to itself at the moment of proletarian chiliasm — in which case its 'objective interests' can be determined from the very beginning; or else, one abandons that theory and, with it, any basis for privileging certain subject positions over others in the determination of the 'objective' interests of the agent as a whole — in which case this latter notion becomes meaningless.[22]

If, in other words, the constitution of the working class as a unified revolutionary force is not entirely internal to the development of the productive forces in capitalism but requires 'external intervention' — for example, in the form of political education and organization — then it must lose its privileged status as the revolutionary agent, perhaps even its very identity as a class, and join all other social beings whose collective identity and connection to the socialist project are wholly contingent and dependent upon 'discursive construction'.

What precisely does it mean to deny the 'objective interests' of the working class or to maintain that workers are no different from other 'social agents' in the degree to which their interests coincide

---

[21] Ibid., pp. 83-4.
[22] Ibid., p. 84.

with the objectives of socialism? It must be noted, first, that this is very different from simply acknowledging that material *interests* do not spontaneously translate themselves into political *objectives*, and even less into concerted political *action*. It implies that material interests do not *exist* unless they are translated into political objectives and concerted political action. This must mean that the conditions of capitalist exploitation are no more consequential in determining the life-situations and experience of workers than are any other conditions and contingencies which may touch their lives (which probably also means putting in question the very first principle of historical materialism, concerning the centrality of production relations and exploitation in the constitution of human social life). The implication is that workers are no more affected by capitalist exploitation than are any other human beings who are not themselves the direct objects of exploitation. This also implies that capitalists derive no fundamental advantage from the exploitation of workers, that the workers derive no fundamental disadvantage from their exploitation by capital, that workers would derive no fundamental advantage from ceasing to be exploited, that the condition of being exploited does not entail an 'interest' in the cessation of class exploitation, that the relations between capital and labour have no fundamental consequences for the whole structure of social and political power, and that the conflicting interests between capital and labour are all in the eye of the beholder. (No matter that this makes nonsense out of the propositions with which Laclau and Mouffe began their attack on Marxism, concerning the relations of domination and resistance which permeate capitalist production — not to mention the whole history of working-class struggles against capital.) In short, the Laclau–Mouffe argument is that there *are* no such things as material interests but only discursively constructed *ideas* about them. For as a practical proposition, what else can it mean to say that no common 'objective interests' can be imputed to workers by virtue of their common situations in the relations of production? The ultimate conclusion of this argument must be that a caveman is as likely to become a socialist as is a proletarian — provided only that he comes within hailing distance of the appropriate discourse.[23]

---

[23] Ibid. I have borrowed this phrase from an article co-authored with Peter Meiksins, 'Beyond Class? A Reply to Chantal Mouffe', *Studies in Political Economy*, 17, Summer 1985.

And, indeed, it turns out that the conclusion drawn by Laclau and Mouffe from their attack on the 'last redoubt of essentialism' is that there are no 'fixed' social interests or identities, that all social identities are discursively constructed and 'politically negotiable'. In fact, this is the proposition on which their case ultimately rests; and it entails not only the dissolution of social reality into discourse, but a denial of *history* and the logic of historical process. A careful consideration of the 'clear alternatives' offered by Mouffe and Laclau, between a simplistic revolutionary chiliasm and a total denial of any organic connection between working-class interests and socialism — indeed, a denial of working-class interests *tout court* — reveals a remarkable conception of historical and social process, or, more precisely, the absence of any such conception at all. What it effectively means is that, where there is no simple, absolute, mechanical, unilinear, and non-contradictory determination, there is no determinacy, no relationship, no causality at all. There are no historical conditions, connections, limits, possibilities. There are only arbitrary juxtapositions, 'conjunctures', and contingencies. If anything holds the discrete and isolated fragments of reality together, it is only the logic of discourse. (It is perhaps significant that the only kind of relation 'between positions in the relations of production and the mentality of the producers' that they would acknowledge as 'proof' of the Marxist case would be a *logical* connection — whatever that means.[24])

In this, Laclau and Mouffe have followed the now familiar trajectory from structuralism to post-structuralism — though they seem uncertain whether the post-structuralist dissolution of social reality into discourse can be regarded as a general law of history (as it were) or whether it is only in the modern age, and particularly with the advent of 'industrial society', that social reality has dematerialized and become susceptible to discursive construction. They have, however, charted new territory by constructing a political programme out of this deconstructed social world.

Of course, if the discursive construction of social identities is to be the basis of a political programme, we need to know where the will and capacity to 'negotiate' — i.e. create — these identities will come from, and who will give them their political purpose and

---

[24] HSS, pp. 84-5.

direction. The silent question running throughout the Laclau–Mouffe argument is: who will be the bearer of discourse? Who will constitute the relevant social identities? Or, to put it another way, in the words of Mouffe and Laclau themselves: 'who is the articulating subject?'[25] That is, not only who will generate the 'hegemonic' discourse, but who, given the 'open and indeterminate character of the social', will be the 'hegemonic subject' around whom the political agent will be constructed by means of 'articulatory practices'?

There are two possible answers, one explicit and one largely, but ominously, implicit. The first answer is, in effect, no one — or everyone. In place of the 'essentialist' working class, Laclau and Mouffe offer us an indeterminate 'plural subject', a 'popular' force, constituted by people with either multiple social identities or no such identities at all; but since this plural subject is itself constituted by discourse, this is at best a circular answer. If it means anything at all, it means something rather trivial — and disconcertingly familiar. The modern world, we are told, no longer consists of clearly opposed social interests. We live in an increasingly pluralistic society characterized by constant flux and mobility, where people partake of multiple and changing social identities. That is why 'hegemonic politics', the politics of discursively constructed social identities, comes into its own as the dominant mode of politics only 'at the beginning of modern times'.[26] (Does this mean that the post-structuralist dissolution of social reality into discourse applies only to 'modern times', while earlier there may have existed real material conditions and social relations?) Where have we heard this before? After much theoretical huffing and puffing, has not the mountain laboured and brought forth — pluralism?

The alternative — which always lurks menacingly in the background — is a doctrine according to which some external agency, somehow uniquely and autonomously capable of generating a hegemonic discourse out of its own inner resources, will impose it from above, giving the indeterminate mass a collective identity and creating a 'people' or 'nation' where none existed before. The sinister possibilities inherent in such a view are obvious. In fairness to Laclau and Mouffe, however, it must be said that, although such

[25] Ibid., p. 134.
[26] Ibid., p. 138.

dangers are implicit in their essentially rootless politics, and although they are ready to attribute a considerable role to *intellectuals* in constituting social subjects by means of autonomous discursive activity, they seem to be unconscious of the dangers and to have the best of democratic intentions.

IV

But there, perhaps, is the rub — for what, after all, do they mean by democracy? This is a critical question because Mouffe and Laclau sum up their political project as a struggle for a 'radical plural democracy' carried out by a 'plural' subject, in place of the struggle for socialism carried out by a unified subject, the working class. So a democratic impulse and a plurality of 'democratic struggles' replace material interests and class struggle as the moving force of history, while socialist demands are merely 'a moment internal to the democratic revolution'. 'Democratic discourse', then, is the unifying thread of history and politics, and the cement that loosely binds together the disparate elements of the plural subject.

The argument proceeds from the premise that since the French Revolution there have been no clear social antagonisms which could be expressed in corresponding political divisions. After the 'people–*ancien régime*' opposition — the last opposition in which political divisions corresponded to two antagonistic forms of society — political oppositions have had to be constructed out of increasingly 'fragile' social antagonisms. The advent of modern industrial capitalism, far from producing sharper social cleavages capable of being expressed in a political opposition between socialism and capitalism, as Marxists believe, seems rather to mark the end of clear antagonisms capable 'of dividing the totality of the social body into two antagonistic camps.'[27] It is for this reason that Marx, in order to counter the increasing complexity and plurality of 'industrial society', was forced to invent a 'new principle' of social division, the confrontation of *classes*. Unfortunately for him, however, there could be no automatic correspondence between this social division and a political opposition; so the proposition that class struggle is the fundamental principle of political division

---

[27] Ibid., p. 151.

'always had to be accompanied by supplementary hypotheses which relegated its full applicability to the future'.[28] Thus Marxists have been forced to make assumptions about the future simplification of the social structure and the progressive development of class consciousness, which would eventually bring about a correspondence between political struggles and the struggles of classes 'as agents constituted at the level of relations of production'.

We must begin, according to Laclau and Mouffe, by abandoning the notion that there are any particular social antagonisms which have a privileged status in constituting political divisions, and by accepting, on the contrary, the 'plurality and indeterminacy of the social'.[29] There have been many different kinds of resistance to subordination, but only under certain conditions have they issued in struggles to end the relations of subordination as such. The creation of such *political* struggles out of the multifarious resistances to subordination is a matter of *discursive construction.* We must therefore focus on the 'discursive conditions for the emergence of a collective action, directed towards struggling against inequalities and challenging relations of subordination. We might also say that our task is to identify the conditions in which a relation of subordination becomes a relation of oppression, and thereby constitutes itself into the site of an antagonism.'[30]

It is here that the notion of a 'democratic revolution' enters the argument. Two centuries ago, with the French Revolution, there began a new era marked by 'the end of a society of a hierarchic and inegalitarian type, ruled by a theological-political logic in which the social order had its foundation in divine will.'[31] What was truly significant and new about this development was the 'invention of democratic culture', which would provide the 'discursive conditions' for transforming certain 'relations of subordination' into 'relations of oppression' and hence 'sites of antagonism'. Until the advent of modern democratic discourse, these relations of subordination could not have been regarded as illegitimate and hence oppressive, and it is only in the context of that discourse that they could be constructed as the terrain of struggle. So, for example, the critique of political inequality

---

28 Ibid., p. 151.
29 Ibid., p. 152.
30 Ibid., p. 153.
31 Ibid., p. 155.

entailed in democratic discourse permitted a 'displacement' to a critique of economic inequalities, as in socialist discourse — which is why the demands of socialism must be seen as 'a moment internal to the democratic revolution'.[32]

This truly bizarre account of modern history illustrates perhaps better than anything else the profound vacuity of this approach, with its insistence on the 'discursive construction of social reality'. For example, the characterization of European society until the moment of the French Revolution as a society 'ruled by a theological-political logic in which the social order had its foundation in divine will' is particularly empty. Let us, however, concentrate on the 'democratic revolution'.

In what sense was there a 'democratic revolution' (sometimes also called the Atlantic Revolution) in the last decades of the eighteenth century? This shop-worn idea, generally associated with the rather conservative historian, R.R. Palmer, and J. Godechot, has proved of limited value to historians and has failed to achieve much currency, largely because it must be defined so broadly as to be virtually meaningless in order to encompass the wide array of social structures, political institutions, and revolutionary movements that come within its purview.[33] If, however, we focus on the system of *ideas* that these varied cases arguably had in common and which alone might justify their characterization as a single revolution (again, provided that these ideas are rather broadly conceived), the result is not a happy one for Mouffe and Laclau.

Their argument requires that the new democratic discourse — which, as the argument progresses, they increasingly equate with liberal-democratic ideology — must 'construct' as illegitimate and oppressive social relations which would otherwise not be so perceived. The historical meaning and effects of liberal-democratic discourse, however, have been far more ambiguous. We need to be reminded, to begin with, that the idea of *democracy* has a very long history — something one would never guess from their account. There can be no doubt that modern conceptions of equality have expanded — at least in breadth if not in depth — far beyond the exclusive Greek conception which denied the democratic principle to women and slaves. At the same time, the

---

[32] Ibid., p. 156.

[33] See, for example, Alfred Cobban, *Aspects of the French Revolution*, London 1971, pp. 11-12.

changes that have occurred in the meaning of democracy have not all been on the side of delegitimizing inequality. Far from it. In fact, one of the most significant dimensions of the 'democratic revolution' is that it marks the *dissociation* of 'democracy' from its meaning as *popular power*, rule by the *demos*.[34] It is precisely for this reason — and not simply because of some general advance in democratic values — that 'democracy' ceased to be a dirty word among the dominant classes.

One need only consider the difference between the horror with which the American 'Founding Fathers' regarded 'democracy', and the overweaning pride with which their successors have claimed the name of 'democracy' for the political order established by these constitutional founders. The difference cannot simply be attributed to the progress of democratic culture. In a sense the reverse is true — or at least, the founding fathers had a stricter understanding than did later generations of what 'democracy' entailed. For them the word had the same meaning as for the Greeks: direct rule by the people, the people as *plebs* not as *populus* (to use a distinction employed by Mouffe and Laclau), or — from the vantage point of the propertied classes — mob rule. By these strict standards, the American republic was not — fortunately, in their view — a democracy (unless it was a 'representative democracy', as suggested by Alexander Hamilton, already signalling a new meaning, explicitly distinguished from popular rule.[35]) By the much diluted standards of later generations, children of the 'democratic revolution', the same republic was the most democratic country on earth, and indeed the perfect ideal of democracy. For, while the old meaning of democracy as popular power survived — especially in socialist discourse — the 'democratic revolution' that established liberal democracy also brought with it a new meaning, which had to do not with the substance of popular power but with certain procedural forms and civil liberties. Indeed, by the new standards, the direct exercise of popular power might be perceived as 'anti-democratic'.

It must be stressed that democracy in its original meaning always had class connotations — referring precisely to the dominance of the people as *plebs*. When Aristotle classified the main types of constitution then existing in Greece, he insisted on distin-

---

[34] cf. Raymond Williams, *Keywords*, Glasgow 1976, pp. 82-7.
[35] cf. Williams, p. 84.

guishing between them not simply on the basis of number but also on the basis of class: 'The proper application of the term "democracy" is to a constitution in which the free-born and poor control the government — being at the same time a majority; and similarly the term "oligarchy" is properly applied to a constitution in which the rich and better-born control the government — being at the same time a minority.'[36] His predecessor, Plato, was even more direct. Describing the class war between rich and poor which for him, as for Aristotle, was the source of civil strife, he explains the principle of democracy thus: 'And when the poor win, the result is a democracy.'[37] In its train come wild excesses of freedom and equality ending in anarchy.

The new meaning of democracy dissociated it from class connotations as rule by the 'poor'. By defining democracy in formal terms not related to the substance of class power, it had the effect precisely of *obscuring* the very oppressions which the old meaning starkly revealed. Liberal democratic discourse has ever since served not only to delegitimate certain kinds of subordination, but on the contrary, also to mystify and legitimate the relations of class domination and exploitation, indeed to deny their very existence by redefining them as relations between free and equal individuals.

What follows from all this is that the differences of meaning among various conceptions of democracy are not simply *differences* but also to a significant extent *antagonisms*. Or, to put it more precisely, although there are aspects of liberal democracy that have a general value, the two 'discourses' diverge irreconcilably at the point where they express the conflicting interests of two opposing classes. Liberal-democratic discourse — however progressive it may be in some respects, however much subordinate classes may have appropriated it and even helped to create it by means of their own struggles — serves the class interests of capital by denying the relations of subordination on which capitalist power rests, and by delimiting the sphere in which popular power may operate. The other meaning of democracy, which in its original form reflected the interests of the *demos* as against those of the propertied classes in Greece, in its modern socialist form expresses the interests of the working class against capital by

---

[36] Aristotle, *Politics*, 1290b. (Barker)
[37] Plato, *Republic*, 557a. (Cornford)

restoring the meaning of popular power and extending it to the classless organization of social production.

It is not, however, enough to say all this, as if disembodied ideas could be plucked out of the air to serve particular social interests. It must also be said that the idea of democracy itself and the changes of meaning it has undergone owe their existence to, and are firmly rooted in, specific social relations. Just as the original meaning emerged from the conflict of classes in ancient Greece, so the new meaning is grounded in the relations of capitalism and would not have been possible without them. The definition of democracy in purely formal terms, and the dissociation from popular power which has made it an ideal acceptable to dominant classes, were made possible by the formal separation between economic and political power which is determined by capitalist relations of production. Since the appropriative powers of capital do not rest on direct possession of 'extra-economic' force, there is a structurally separate political sphere in which 'rule by the demos' — or rather by their elected 'representatives' — can exist without directly affecting the exploitative relations between capital and labour. By the same token, capitalism has made possible a transformation of the *old* meaning, too, but in this case from the vantage point of labour; for it is the conditions created by capitalism that have brought into being the notion of popular power as the self-organization of freely associated producers and a vision of self-rule that encompasses a classless administration of social production.

All this is another way of saying that socialist demands cannot be conceived simply as 'a moment internal to the democratic revolution', both because the socialist vision departs from the liberal-democratic one in substantial ways having to do with the antagonisms of class interest, but also because both discourses have their roots in anterior social relations. In other words, the class struggles of capitalism are not, as Mouffe and Laclau would have us believe, simply reflexes of liberal-democratic discourse and its 'discursive construction' of class relations as oppressive and illegitimate; if anything, democratic discourse, in both its liberal and socialist variants, is constituted by class conflict.

The conflation of meanings embodied in Laclau and Mouffe's vague and indeterminate conception of democracy, in which all 'democratic struggles' and all forms of equality are reduced to sameness, has the effect of conceptualizing away the contradictions between capitalism and socialism by transforming the revolutionary transition into an unbroken continuity between one form of democracy and another. This is not an analysis of contemporary society and the conditions of its transformation; it is little more than a verbal conjuring trick.

V

There is yet another dimension to this argument. The proposition that socialism is a moment internal to the democratic revolution is used by Laclau and Mouffe to reinforce the contention that the emancipatory impulses of socialism do not arise out of the interests of the working class as 'agents constituted at the level of relations of production'; instead, that impulse is created by liberal-democratic discourse which 'constructs' various relations of subordination as oppressive. This means, among other things, that workers are capable of generating emancipatory struggles — and, indeed of perceiving their own subordination as oppressive — only insofar as they are instructed by liberal-democratic discourse, or, to put it another way, by bourgeois ideology. This is apparently demonstrated by the fact that workers in the nineteenth century, who did mount genuine struggles against capitalist relations of production, were not true 'proletarians' acting on their material class interests but artisans defending their artisanal identities against destruction by the new capitalist relations and motivated by democratic *political* ideas appropriated from without. In contrast, the later industrial proletariat, which is truly a product of capitalism, has, according to this view, ceased to challenge capitalist relations of production — 'these having by then solidly implanted'[38] — and confines itself to 'reformist' struggles over relations *in* production.

So, for example, Laclau and Mouffe's interpretation of Chartism (based on the most recent studies of Gareth Stedman Jones) suggests that it was not 'a phenomenon of a fundamentally social character, an expression of the class consciousness of the new industrial proletariat.'[39] Instead, it was an autonomously *political* movement whose character and objectives were constituted by the ideas of English political radicalism, 'profoundly

---

[38] HSS, p. 157.
[39] Ibid., p. 156.

influenced by the French Revolution.' (It is perhaps worth noting here that the radical tradition cited by Stedman Jones as the major ideological influence on Chartism predates the French Revolution and has a distinctively English character, tracing its origins to the English revolution of the seventeenth century. The Laclau/Mouffe version is simply one example of their liberality with texts and historical evidence — and perhaps also of a notable bias toward France.)

We shall consider later whether, even by Stedman Jones's evidence, there are legitimate grounds for this dissociation of Chartism as a *political* movement from its *social* character as a working-class movement determined by the development of capitalist production relations. It will be argued that to deny the social character of this political movement, and its foundation in the new realities of nineteenth century capitalism, is made possible only by the most artificial and *a priori* theoretical separation between economic and political 'spheres'. For the moment, it is enough to note that, according to Laclau and Mouffe, workers will not oppose capitalist relations of production, or even recognize their own condition as oppressive, unless they are inspired by a disembodied democratic spirit and an abstract urge for equality of some indeterminate kind, derived from someone else's political doctrines. Thus, nineteenth-century workers perceived their material conditions as oppressive only by derivation from the autonomous political ideology of the 'democratic revolution'. To see the emptiness of this proposition, one need only try to explain in these terms the long history of class struggle *before* the cataclysmic illumination of the French Revolution.

Laclau and Mouffe also require us to believe that while there is a smooth and non-contradictory continuity between the various forms of 'democratic struggle', there is a rigid boundary between class struggles on the economic 'level' and struggles in the political sphere. This means that political movements motivated by liberal-democratic discourse bring us closer to socialism than do class struggles impelled by material interests directly antagonistic to the interests of capital.

At this point, one begins to suspect that Mouffe and Laclau are not content with the simple proposition that the working class has no privileged position in the struggle for socialism. At first, they seemed to be arguing only that a rejection of 'economism' and 'class reductionism' — an insistence on the autonomy of politics — implies that the working class is neither more nor less revolutionary than any other social force, that while it is not necessarily revolutionary neither is it necessarily anti-revolutionary or 'reformist' , and that no other social group can be privileged as an agent of the socialist transformation either. There is no specific working-class interest in socialism, but neither does such an interest reside in any other social group. Nevertheless, for all the apparent class-neutrality of this argument, there are repeated hints that the working class actually has inherent disabilities which make it *less* likely than other social groups to be the bearer of socialist politics. It is, after all, according to Laclau and Mouffe, a characteristic of the modern proletariat — the class that is a *true* product of capitalism — to accept capitalist relations *of* production, while limiting their struggles to relations *in* production. This sounds very much like, say, André Gorz, who insists unambiguously that it is in the inherent nature of the modern proletariat — itself a product of capital — to be absorbed into the 'productivist' values of capitalist relations and therefore to be incapable of generating a fundamental challenge to capitalism. At any rate, Laclau and Mouffe have come a very long way toward accepting that the conditions of the working class, far from encouraging socialist politics, are actually inimical to socialism.

There is an even more fundamental sense in which their political project is based on undemocratic assumptions about the disabilities of the working class. The implications that they derive from their assault on 'the last redoubt of class reductionism' are very far-reaching indeed. The 'fall' of this 'last redoubt' apparently deprives workers of any political motivations of their own, indeed any social identity which is not constructed by others, notably by intellectuals.[40] The consequence is that even successful revolutions in which workers have played a dominant role become — perversely — evidence of their revolutionary incapacity. Anything less than an 'unmediated' spontaneous uprising of workers, without the 'exogenous' assistance of political organization, is taken to prove the case.

The point can be illustrated by considering an argument made by Chantal Mouffe in an article which, according to her, 'stems from' research conducted for the subsequent book with Laclau. She maintains, in her discussion of the principle that workers have no 'fundamental interest' in socialism, that 'It is actually an illusion

---

[40] e.g. ibid., p. 85.

of language that lies behind the belief that the "class struggle" can only be the work of determined political agents — the "social classes". The history of the social revolutions which have occurred until now strikingly proves this point, because none of them has been led by the proletariat.'[41]

Let us pursue the implications of the view that the essential character of a revolution is defined by the nature of its leadership. This is, after all, what it means to say that, if the leaders of a revolution do not themselves belong to the classes in whose name the revolution is being made, then irrespective of the people whom they lead — the social forces that give the revolution its momentum and direction — the 'class struggle' is being conducted by non-class agents. If it is not the revolutionary mass, its interests, motivations, goals, and powers that give the revolution its character as a class struggle, but rather the actions and intentions of the leadership, then must we not also conclude, in the manner of all the most conservative interpreters of social revolutions, that the 'mob' in these affairs is merely an irrational and anarchic force manipulated by its demagogic (or, depending on one's point of view, idealistic and altruistic) superiors, a rabble that possesses no rational goals of its own? Or should we say, on the contrary, that if the history of revolutions proves anything, it is precisely that there can be no class struggle and no revolution without class agents, no revolution that has been determined by the actions and intentions of its leaders except insofar as they have expressed the interests and goals, and harnessed the active power, of certain classes organized into a potent social force?

In the case of the Russian Revolution, for example, should we say that it was the Bolshevik leadership who conducted the class struggle; or was it rather the workers and peasants who constituted the revolutionary force, the force whose interests, social power, and capacity for collective action determined the nature and course of the revolution? Should we accept the interpretation of the Russian Revolution offered by conservative historians like, for instance, Leonard Schapiro, who dismiss the mass as an anarchic mob manipulated by the Bolsheviks for purposes of their own? Or should we instead accept the analysis proposed by a critic of Schapiro in the *Sunday Times*?

---

[41] Chantal Mouffe, 'Working Class Hegemony and the Struggle for Socialism', *Studies in Political Economy* 12, Fall 1983, p. 23.

It is precisely the myth of the workers as an 'anarchical mob ... with no thought but destruction', of the political naiveté of the soldiers, of the peasantry's 'total lack of understanding of what was happening' that has now been exploded.

American, French, and British scholars ... have begun to examine the revolution 'from below', to analyse the aspirations and actions of the masses — the workers, peasants, soldiers, and sailors. In so doing they have found that the goals of the masses were clear, rational and very much their own.

No Bolshevik propaganda was required to conjure up the workers' demand for bread and employment, the soldiers' yearning for peace, or peasant land hunger. Nor were the methods the masses used to attain their ends either blind or wild. Appeals to the moderate politicians were succeeded by direct action and mounting pressure for a new government which would sanction peasant land seizures, stem the economic breakdown and halt the war.

What brought the Bolsheviks to power was their success in articulating the demands welling up from below.[42]

Surely something is amiss when the *Sunday Times* is obliged to teach Marxists about class struggle and the nature of revolutionary forces. This reading of the Russian Revolution may not require us to view the working class — or any other class — as necessarily revolutionary; but what can it possibly mean to maintain that the Russian Revolution proves that the class struggle need not 'be the work of determined political agents — the "social classes"'? Such an interpretation comes perilously close to the classic reactionary principle that the 'mob' has no reason of its own and cannot itself be the source of any constructive political impulse.

In the end, however, it is not just the working class that is rendered impotent as a political force by Laclau and Mouffe. Not only is the working class no privileged agent of socialism, there are no historical conditions and no social interests conducive to the development of socialism. This means that no *other* 'social agents' exist whose collective identity, interests, and capacities might replace those of the working class as the basic materials of socialist struggle. In fact, there is no social basis for *any* kind of politics. Discourse is all. And, indeed, Laclau and Mouffe emphasize that

---

[42] Edward Acton, *Sunday Times*, April 8, 1984.

the various social struggles which are now taking place could as easily be 'articulated' with anti-democratic as democratic discourses. In the final analysis, everything depends upon the success of intellectuals in conducting a 'complex set of discursive-hegemonic operations'.[43] And so here we have it: In the beginning (and the end) was the Word, and the Word was with God, and the Word was God, the ultimate Subject made incarnate in ... Laclau and Mouffe?

---

[43] HSS, p. 174-5.

5

The Randomization of History and Politics

Since Laclau made his first major break with Marxism by establishing the autonomy of ideology and politics, others have gone before him in developing the characteristic themes of the NTS which he and Mouffe have simply brought together in their latest work: the dissociation of politics from class; the establishment of the non-correspondence between the economic and the political; the dissolution of the social into discourse; the replacement of the working class by a 'discursively constructed' plural subject; the subordination of socialist struggle to a plurality of 'democratic' struggles in which 'democracy' is indeterminate, abstract, and loosely defined so as to conceptualize away the differences and the antagonisms that separate socialism from capitalism.

One general principle may be said to underlie all these themes: what might be called the *randomization* of history and politics. In Mouffe and Laclau, we already noticed that the rejection of Marxism and its conception of the working class as revolutionary agent depended in the final analysis on a curiously ahistorical view of the world according to which, in the absence of a simple, mechanical, and crude determinism, there apparently remains nothing but absolute contingency. In practice, what this dualism implies is that history is pure contingency — or rather, that there *is* no history, no determinate historical *conditions, relations, processes.*

This principle had already been firmly established long before *Hegemony and Socialist Strategy.* In fact, a false dualism between absolute determination and absolute contingency, and the characterization of history as irreducibly contingent, has arguably always been implicit in Althusserian structuralism. The critics of 'Althusserianism' often attack it for its subordination of 'subject' to 'structure' and the eviction of human agency from history; but while this charge is undoubtedly well-founded, it may tend to obscure the fact that 'structure' itself has a questionable status in the Althusserian view of history. It is not at all clear — and in 'post-Althusserianism' increasingly less so — that structure has any empirical status at all, or any implications for the constitution of historical reality. The world of structure, of determinate structured relations, belongs to the realm of autonomous theory, while the empirical world, the object of historical knowledge, is a world of contingency and arbitrariness.

The duality of 'mode of production' and 'social formation' as conceptualized by Althusserianism illustrates the point. The 'mode of production' as a structure of determined relations does not exist empirically. In the 'social formation' which *does* exist empirically, structural *relations* are replaced by 'conjunctures' and juxtapositions, an arbitrary configuration of 'over-determined' elements (the potentially useful concept of over-determination has increasingly become a cover for absolute contingency). In the historical world of the social formation there are no relations to be explained, only juxtapositions to be described — even if description can be given an air of theoretical 'rigour' and determinacy by means of classification in an endless proliferation of taxonomic categories. The structural determinations of the mode of production have no explanatory status, since they do not reflect the logic of any actually existing historical and social processes. At best, they provide the necessary taxonomic categories. The paradox of structuralism, then, is that, having expelled the subject from history, it has gone a long way toward expelling the structure as well.

The final step has been taken by the post-structuralists, and with them what Perry Anderson has called the 'randomization of history' has been made complete. As language becomes the model, and the principle, of all human order, 'the notion of ascertainable cause starts to undergo a critical weakening.'[1] The result is a paradoxical synthesis of absolute determinism and absolute contingency. On the one hand, the social world is permeated by an absolutely determined structure, which reproduces itself in all empirical manifestations (just as every speech act in a sense reproduces and is determined by the invariable structure of language);

---

[1] Perry Anderson, *In the Tracks of Historical Materialism*, London 1983, p. 48.

on the other hand, that structure reproduces itself in an infinite number of irreducibly contingent, unpredictable, and arbitrary ways which are completely accidental and inexplicable (just as every speech act is a unique and unpredictable combination of linguistic possibilities). Structure is treated as if it were the cause of events (as if language were the 'cause' of every particular speech act), which effectively means that they are subject to no specific causality at all; and history becomes the sphere of 'irreducible contingency' or 'legislated accident'.[2] Finally, the ultimate paradox of structuralism works itself out when language is detached altogether from social reality: as structure disappears after subject, leaving behind it 'absolute chance', the result is a complete subjectivism, but a 'subjectivism without a subject'.[3]

Perhaps Laclau and Mouffe have not travelled the whole distance from structuralism to post-structuralism, but the basic premise of their politics — and arguably of the NTS in general — is certainly post-structuralist in spirit: social reality is constituted by autonomous discourse, and all social identities are discursively negotiable. On the face of it, the post-structuralist evacuation of both subject and structure is not a promising foundation for constructing a political programme. With no subject interior to history, no human purpose or agency, and with no intrinsic order or direction, no logic of process, no social identities or structural constraints, what would be the impulse, the objective, and the modalities of political action? Perry Anderson has noted the 'striking political heteronomy' and 'lability' of both structuralism and post-structuralism, their protean adaptability to current political fashions; and it is true that no specific 'political connotation', except precisely a subordination to prevailing political fashions, is entailed by their subjectless unstructured world — a world without *vantage point* and unshaped by human purpose or by the logic of historical process and social relations. But in Mouffe and Laclau — and in some of their NTS colleagues — we have found something very close to post-structuralist subjectivism transformed into a specific political programme.

The ease with which the structural determinism of Althusser can give way to a conception of social processes and politics as random and contingent is nowhere more vividly illustrated than in

---

[2] Ibid., p. 51.
[3] Ibid., p. 54.

the theoretical development of Paul Hirst and Barry Hindess. And nowhere are the political implications of this theoretical trajectory more baldly and openly stated. These two, together and separately, were notable first for the ludicrous extremes to which they took the Althusserian preoccupation with autonomous theory and the denigration of 'historicism' and 'empiricism'. They are now equally notable for what might be called a metaphysical empiricism, which dissolves all causality and all determinacy into irreducible specificity. From the rigidly determined mode of production to the purely contingent social formation; from structure to conjuncture.

Although their most recent conception of social process can be distinguished from the pure randomization of post-structuralist theory, and one might instead attribute to them an extreme causal *pluralism* rather than a total rejection of any causality at all, they have taken great pains to dissociate themselves from any such pluralist interpretation of their views:

> Let us be clear that the terrain of the criticism of classical Marxism we are engaged in is not that of the debate between monism and pluralism. That debate is a contest of opposed but theoretically equivalent positions, both are general doctrines of causality. What we are challenging is *not merely* the economic monist causality of Marxism, *but the very pertinence of all such general categories of causality and the privilege they accord to certain orders of causes as against others.*[4]

This seems to be a rejection of causality in principle; but even if this ambiguous disclaimer still smacks of causal pluralism, the essential point is that their rejection of Marxism, like that of Laclau and Mouffe, is based on a crude dualism that requires us to choose between simple, mechanical, and absolute determination, on the one hand, and absolute indeterminacy on the other. In practice, this leaves social processes and history in the realm of pure contingency and randomness.

If this seems a remarkable departure from their earlier dogmatic structuralism, it must be emphazised that the apparent U-turn executed by Hindess and Hirst is nothing more than a flip of the structuralist coin. Again, their empiricism is itself entirely

---

[4] Antony Cutler, Barry Hindess, Paul Hirst, and Athar Hussain, *Marx's Capital and Capitalism Today*, vol. 1, p. 128. Italics in the original.

theoretical. The insistence on particularity, and the weak or non-existent determinacy in their conception of history and social processes, are not supported by empirical investigation or historical evidence. They are theoretically constructed and a prioristic. In fact, the whole apparatus of the NTS is notable for its lack of historical evidence (and in the one significant exception, the case of Gareth Stedman Jones, we shall see that the 'non-correspondence' principle which he, like Hindess and Hirst and Mouffe and Laclau, constructs theoretically is contradicted by his own historical evidence.)

There is no need to follow the tedious journey of Hindess and Hirst in detail, since that job has already been done with great skill by Gregory Elliott in 'The Odyssey of Paul Hirst'.[5] It will be enough to note the highlights of the transition from the abstract theoreticism of their first book, *Pre-Capitalist Modes of Production*, published in 1975, whose object was 'rigorously' to construct theoretical concepts of various modes of production uncontaminated by historical considerations, to the abstract empiricism of their next major work (with Antony Cutler and Athar Hussain), *Marx's Capital and Capitalism Today*, published only two years later, in which the very idea of a capitalist mode of production was effectively rejected, its structural determinations to be replaced by the irreducible specificity and contingency of 'national economies' and particular 'conjunctures'.

It is true that the theoretical distance between these two apparent extremes is not as great as it may seem. In both cases the historical world is in effect relegated to the sphere of contingency and irreducible particularity, and in both cases politics and ideology are conceived as undetermined by the mode of production. While in *Marx's Capital and Capitalism Today* the mode of production disappears altogether, in *Pre-Capitalist Mode of Production* a similar effect was created by insisting that the ideological and political 'conditions of existence' of any mode of production are not themselves determined by that mode of production — in other words, they are (relatively?) autonomous. The flip of the coin is not, however, insignificant, because it marks an important political shift.

In the earlier work, these theoretical principles were meant to underwrite the importance of class struggle as the primary deter-

---

minant of history — or, at any rate, class struggle conceived in a very particular way. Remaining true in this respect at least to Hirst's political past, Hindess and Hirst were still conceptualizing the transition from capitalism to socialism in apparently Maoist terms. We have already noted the extreme voluntarism of the Maoist programme, its rejection of 'economism', its focus on political and ideological struggles as more or less autonomous from material conditions. All of these characteristics, in their original form, were shaped by the particular circumstances of China with its 'backward' material conditions and its undeveloped working class. These principles, as we have seen, were transplanted to the West and were reflected in various Althusserian preoccupations. In Hindess and Hirst, they took the form of an insistence that class struggle is an essentially autonomous force in the transition from one mode of production to another. Class struggle is not to be conceived as the effect of the mode of production to be transformed, but rather as the unmoved mover which stands apart from and above the mode of production and brings into being new modes of production by depriving the old of their 'conditions of existence' through ideological and political struggle. They insisted on detaching history from the structural determinations of the mode of production in order not to 'denegate the effectivity of the class struggle and the specificity of the concrete conditions in which it takes place.'[6]

In their later work, the object is exactly the reverse. In this case, where the detachment of historical contingency from the mode of production has been carried to its logical conclusion in the virtual disappearance of the mode of production altogether — and with it *any* notion of causality — the intention is *precisely* to 'denegate the effectivity' of class struggle and its essential role in history. This object is achieved by a procedure very similar to that of Laclau and Mouffe. Here, too, the argument hinges on the proposition that there is nothing in the logic of capitalism which determines the development of a united working class; and here, too, there is no consideration of the sense in which the structure of capitalism and the situation of the working class within it, if they do not automatically produce a united political force for socialism, nevertheless create the conditions in which such a force is possible.

---

[6] Barry Hindess and Paul Q. Hirst, *Pre-Capitalist Modes of Production*, London 1975, p. 279.

Again, the contention is that there is no such thing as a working-class interest apart from and prior to its ideological construction.

The whole laborious theoretical apparatus constructed in *Marx's Capital and Capitalism Today* is designed above all to support one essential principle, originally outlined in Paul Hirst's article, 'Economic Classes and Politics', which appeared shortly before the book:

> ... the notion of *relative* autonomy is untenable. Once any degree of autonomous action is accorded to political forces as means of representation *vis-à-vis* classes of economic agents, then there is no necessary correspondence between the forces that appear in the political (and what they 'represent') and economic classes. It is not simply a question of discrepancy (the political means 'represent' the class more or less accurately) but of necessary non-correspondence. One cannot, despite Lenin, 'read back' — measuring the political forces against what they are supposed to represent. That is to conceive the represented as external to, as the autonomously existent measure of, its means of representation. Classes do not have given 'interests', apparent independently of definite parties, ideologies, etc., and against which these parties, ideologies, etc., can be measured. What the means of representation 'represent' does not exist outside the process of representation.[7]

In much the same way, Laclau and Mouffe have constructed an elaborate theoretical support, using similar devices to establish the indeterminacy of the social world, in order to prop up the very same principle, which has been the hallmark of their work for several years. So, for example, in an earlier article by Mouffe:

> How can it be maintained that economic agents can have interests defined at the economic level which would be represented *a posteriori* at the political and ideological levels? In fact, since it is in ideology and through politics that interests are defined, that amounts to stating that interests can exist prior to the discourse in which they are formulated and articulated. This is contradictory. ... Once we abandon the reductionist thesis

---

[7] Paul Hirst, 'Economic Classes and Politics', in Alan Hunt ed., *Class and Class Structure*, London 1977, pp. 130-1.

that paradigmatic ideological and political forms can be attributed to positions in the relations of production, there is no longer any basis for asserting the necessarily socialist character of the interests of the working class or for determining *a priori* the form that will be taken by workers' struggles.[8]

In both cases, the conclusion is that politics — and socialist politics in particular — cannot be grounded in the material interests of any class but must be discursively constructed by autonomous ideological and political means out of 'negotiable' social identities, a process in which the working class has no privileged position by virtue of its identity as an 'economic agent'. Thus Hindess and Hirst again:

> There is in capitalist social relations no necessary process that subjects this category of [economic] agents to tendencies toward homogenisation or unification *at the political level. It follows that the basis of support for socialist politics must be created by the effects of the political actions of socialists themselves.* ... We emphasise the dependence of socialist politics on socialist ideology and organisation, a point made by Kautsky and Lenin, but which we seek to emphasise in a theoretical context radically different from that of the orthodox Marxism in which they worked. There are no 'socialist' issues and areas of struggle *per se*, assigned as 'socialist' by class interests and experience. Socialism is a political ideology. The basis for support for socialist politics is whatever issues and struggles from which it can be made. These issues are diverse and always specific to the economic and political conditions of definite nation-states. ... Marxists and non-Marxist socialists have lived under the illusion that the 'working class' must ultimately be unified against capitalism by the effects of the capitalist system itself.[9]

Capitalism contains no inherent tendency toward the 'economically determined political polarisation of classes';[10] hence 'revolutionary' socialist politics, directed at the interests of the

---

[8] Chantal Mouffe, 'Working Class Hegemony and the Struggle for Socialism', *Studies in Political Economy* 12, Fall 1983, p. 21.

[9] MCCT, vol. 2, pp. 258-9. Italics in the original.

[10] Ibid., p. 240.

working class, are 'untenable'. Instead, the object of socialist politics is to construct popular alliances.

Socialist politics, and specifically the politics of the Labour Party, then, require two fundamental 'reorientations': 'The first is coming to terms with the need to concentrate on struggle *within* political organisations, rather than broadcasting an appeal to an imaginary working class-as-political subject. ... The second is coming to terms with democracy as a medium and form of political struggle. We mean this not only in the limited sense of accepting the continued dominance of parliamentary forms but in the broader sense of recognising the role popular democratic forms can play in creating the mass base and means of struggle for socialism.'[11]

And so, from Maoism to right-wing Labourism:

> The Labour Party has been an effective *party of government.* It was capable, in the period since 1965 and until the debacle of 1979, of providing efficient and stable decision-making within the prevailing parliamentary and economic system and, therefore, of commanding the respect of the leading administrators in the civil service and local government and of management in the big public and private corporations. ... It stands in clear contrast with the experience of the Tory party in the post-Macmillan era. Civil servants, local government officials and businessmen are widely resentful and critical of capricious and unpredictable Tory decision-making. The ability to make the system 'work' is a condition for electoral success *and* for its meaningful and acceptable reform.[12]

In the interests of 'realism', then, the Left must apparently abandon 'workerism' in favour of appeals to leading civil servants and corporate executives. A broad church indeed! It is difficult to believe that Hirst is serious about the absurd suggestion that such people prefer the Labour Party as the 'natural' party of government; but perhaps with a little discursive construction, bank presidents can even be made to adopt the abolition of class exploitation as their own preferred objective and become the vanguard of socialism.

---

[11] Ibid., pp. 290-1.
[12] Paul Hirst, *Marxism and Historical Writing*, London 1985, p. 152.

Here again we see the characteristic indeterminacy of 'democracy' — and of 'socialism', which appears to mean anything and everything but the end of class exploitation — as they are conceived by the NTS; and here too there are the characteristic slippages by which they proceed from the self-evident, and indeed trivial, proposition that ideology and organization are required to construct an effective political force out of 'economic agents', to the proposition that there is nothing in the logic of capitalism nor in the conditions of the working class — nor indeed in the nature of socialist objectives — which marks out the working class as the social force whose interests and struggles constitute the materials out of which a socialist movement can be built. As always, the assumption is that if the constitution of a socialist force is not a simple reflex of capitalist development, if political organization is required, then there exist no social interests and no social capacities which are more conducive to socialism than are any others. Politics, like history in general, is random and contingent. Not only is there no absolute determination, there are no determinate *conditions, possibilities, relations, limits, pressures.* Anything — or nothing — goes.

II

We shall return in subsequent chapters to the various slippages, the huge conceptual leaps, required to sustain these attempts to dissociate politics from class and socialist politics from the interests and struggles of the working class. But one more thing needs to be said about the theoretical underpinnings of the randomization of history and politics. This concerns the curious synthesis of idealism and technologism that often seems to underlie the NTS conception of history. Laclau and Mouffe, as we have seen, launched their attack on Marxist 'economism' and 'class reductionism' by first attributing to Marx a definition of the 'economy' from which social relations had been excluded, leaving behind some abstractly 'material' substratum, so that the 'economy' was in effect identified with *technology,* and 'economic laws' with a neutral, natural development of productive forces. Their answer to this straw-technological determinism was to demonstrate, as if it would come as news to Marx, that the sphere of production was not determined by a neutral technological imperative but was penetrated by social relations of domination and resistance.

What is striking about this argument, apart from its complete misunderstanding of Marx, is that the attack on his alleged technological determinism is itself based on a technicist definition of the economy. Instead of beginning, as Marx himself did, by defining production as an irreducibly *social* phenomenon, these critics of Marxist 'economism' treat the 'economic' sphere as fundamentally asocial. This may seem an odd claim, given Laclau and Mouffe's insistence that their object is 'to demonstrate that the space of the economy is itself structured as a political space',[13] shot through with social relations; yet their argument depends precisely upon treating the relations of domination in production not as constitutive principles of the 'economy' but as if they were imported into the 'economy' from a separate, autonomous, alien sphere. It is only by proceeding in this way that they can cite the social character of production relations as a fatal challenge to Marxism, instead of its very foundation. It is only by means of an artificial, *a priori* separation of the social from the 'economic' or 'material' — which is the very antithesis of Marx's own materialism and his critique of political economy — that they can sustain their attack on the 'last redoubt of essentialism' and on the Marxist case for grounding politics in the material relations of class. This detachment of the 'social' from the 'economic' or material has the further effect of uprooting history from *any* specific determinations or causality, apart from the contingent logic of 'discourse'. Hence the paradoxical synthesis.

A peculiar kind of inverted technologism may, then, help to account for the otherwise inexplicable argument which we considered at the outset of our discussion of *Hegemony and Socialist Strategy*. Laclau and Mouffe argued that the relations of domination and resistance inherent in capitalist production nullified the whole Marxist view of the revolutionary proletariat. This seemed at the time a preposterous suggestion, since this very fact about capitalist production is what makes the Marxist case so convincing. Perhaps it is because they themselves proceed from the crudely technicist conception of the economy, which they (along with other structuralists and post-structuralists) falsely attribute to Marx, that relations of domination and resistance appear to them as something other than 'economic' relations and therefore something that must be imported from other 'exogenous' spheres.

---

[13] Laclau and Mouffe, *Hegemony and Socialist Strategy*, London, 1985, pp. 76-7.

Again, ideology and politics are completely autonomous, and the 'economy' cannot, in these terms, be the source of political struggles.

A similar technicist tendency is observable in Hindess and Hirst. Again, the Marxist conception of history is perceived as the neutral, autonomous development of productive forces, which sets in train a series of necessary adjustments in the relations of production, and then, in turn, in superstructural forms.[14] The 'mode of production of material life' — understood here as productive *technique* — 'determines the forms in which the product is possessed and distributed, that is, the relations of production';[15] and these eventually find expression in the superstructural forms of ideology and politics. In this account, too, the Marxist revolutionary project ultimately depends on assuming such a transhistorical technological imperative and the ultimate determination of politics by the development of productive technique. Their answer, again, is not to replace this asocial, technologistic conception of the material base with a view of production as intrinsically social, but simply to argue, via a long and circuitous route, that there is nothing in the logic of technological development which necessarily produces any particular political effect — a proposition that is quite unexceptionable in itself but entirely beside the point.

Paradoxically, then — or not so paradoxically — the condition for the abstract idealism and the randomization of history and politics characteristic of the NTS may be a definition of the economy in crudely technicist terms. It is arguably by attributing to Marx a technological determinism, and then by appropriating this conception of the 'economic' sphere as their own, that they are able to autonomize ideology and politics, and to detach history from any material determinations.

This procedure is not unrelated to a phenomenon we have noticed before in some of our post-Althusserians: the evacuation of *exploitation* from the mode of production and class, and a tendency to treat the technical process of work as the primary determinant. The characteristic exclusion of exploitation from the economic sphere — for example, the tendency to define capitalism as a specific form of the technical labour process rather than as a

---

[14] MCCT, vol. 1, pp. 135ff.
[15] Ibid., p. 135.

specific form of exploitation — is visible in Laclau and Mouffe's emphasis on 'industrial society' rather than *capitalism* and affects their whole perception of class and its role in history. This emphasis may represent a significant development in Laclau's thought. When in his earlier work — especially in his polemic against André Gunder Frank — he insisted that the essence of a mode of production lay in the 'sphere of production', not in the 'sphere of commodity exchange', he seemed to have in mind principally the relations of surplus extraction. Since then, the 'sphere of production' seems to be increasingly identified with the technique of the labour process. One effect of this is that of obscuring both the connections between struggles over 'relations *in* production' and struggles over relations *of* production, and also the connections between different kinds of workers, such as the 'old' and 'new' workers whom Laclau and Mouffe are so anxious to distinguish from one another in their account of working class history.

In a criticism of E.P. Thompson, for instance, they argue that it is inappropriate to lump together in a single 'working class' a 'heterogeneous set of social groups ... without sufficient recognition of the profound difference between "old" and "new" workers in their objectives and their forms of mobilization.'[16] But in fact, what is remarkable about the period during which Thompson's working class was 'making itself' is precisely the extent to which apparently different kinds of workers were joined together in new forms of organization and consciousness. Thompson's analysis is notable for its ability to explain this apparently anomalous development. He shows that, despite the ostensible differences between 'pre-industrial' and 'industrial' forms of work, these different kinds of workers were subject to the same logic of capitalist expropriation and the consequent intensification of exploitation which characterized the period, creating common class interests and common experiences among workers subordinated to capital. He is able to account for these common interests and purposes because he proceeds not from a kind of bourgeois technologism but rather from a Marxist focus on relations of production and exploitation.[17]

No analysis that concentrates on the technical process of work

---

[16] Laclau and Mouffe, p. 157.

[17] This argument about E.P. Thompson is elaborated at greater length in my article 'The Politics of Theory and the Concept of Class: E.P. Thompson and his Critics', *Studies in Political Economy* 9, Fall 1982, esp. pp. 52-8.

to the exclusion of relations of exploitation as the constitutive principle of class can account for the historical record of working-class formation in the early nineteenth century. Indeed, it cannot account for the existence of a labour movement at all, because the common ground constituted by relations of production and exploitation is effectively denied. There is in these terms no way of accounting for the common struggles of disparate workers, or even the similarities among their fragmented struggles. And when it comes right down to it, have the divisions among workers, which are so critical to Laclau and Mouffe, as well as to Hindess and Hirst, really been more remarkable than their many common struggles?

It is arguably this same conceptualization of the 'economic' sphere, which displaces relations of exploitation from the central position they occupy in Marxism, that determines, or has as its correlate, the theoretical rupture between economic and political 'levels'. This mode of conceptualization militates against a proper appreciation of working-class struggles and their political resonances. It is in this perspective that the 'reformist' struggles of the modern proletariat appear more distant from the anti-capitalist objectives of socialism than do earlier radical struggles, despite the fact — or, according to Laclau and Mouffe, precisely because of it — that the latter are often backward-looking in their modes of organization, in their perceptions of the roots of their condition, and in their objectives, while the former are directly aimed at capitalist targets even when their objectives are limited and 'purely economic'. From this vantage point, there can be no perception of how the material interests of the working class might constitute the stuff of which larger, socialist struggles can be built.

It is, then, clear how it is possible for Laclau and Mouffe, or Hindess and Hirst, to impose a rigid discontinuity between economic and political struggles, or between 'relations *in* production' and relations *of* production, a discontinuity far more absolute than has ever existed in the historical record of working-class struggles. It is also clear why they are so blind to the self-evident connections between the material interests of the working class, as an exploited class, and the objectives of socialism, the abolition of class and the establishment of a classless administration of production. It must be emphasized, however, that these irreducible separations between political and economic 'levels', or between working-class interests and socialist politics, have little to do with the realities of history or contemporary capitalism. They are simply *a priori* theoretical constructions. They exist, as it were, by definition.

6

Politics and Class

If the socialist project is to be redefined convincingly, several large questions must be answered, having to do with its objectives, motivating principles, and agencies. The Marxist conception of that project — as the abolition of class carried out by means of class struggle and the self-emancipation of the working class — provided a systematic and coherent account in which socialist objectives were grounded in a theory of historical movement and social process. There was in this account an organic unity of historical processes and political objectives, not in the sense that socialism was viewed as the ineluctable end of a predictable historical evolution, but rather in the sense that the objectives of socialism were seen as real historical possibilities, growing out of existing social forces, interests, and struggles. If the social relations of production and class struggle were the basic principles of historical movement to date, socialism was now on the historical agenda because there existed, for the first time in history, not only the forces of production to make human emancipation possible, but more particularly a class which contained the real possibility of a class-less society: a class without property or exploitative powers of its own to protect, which could not fully serve its own class interests without abolishing class altogether; an exploited class whose specific interest required the abolition of class exploitation; a class whose own specific conditions gave it a collective force and capacity for collective action which made that project practicable. Through the medium of this specific class interest and this specific capacity, the universal emancipation of humanity from class exploitation — an objective which in other times and places could never be more than an abstract utopian dream — could be translated into a concrete and immediate political programme.

No revision of the socialist project can have the same force without a similarly coherent and organic conception of ends, means, social processes, and historical possibilities. A socialist project based on the autonomy of politics is no substitute. It is not an answer but a begging of the question. In the end, it simply means that anything — or, just as plausibly, nothing — is possible.

The questions can be posed this way: if not the abolition of class, then what other objective? If not class interest, what other motive force? If not class identity and cohesion, what other collective identity or principle of unity? And underlying these programmatic questions, more fundamental historical ones: if not class relations, what other structure of domination lies at the heart of social and political power? More basic still: if not the relations of production and exploitation, what other social relations are at the foundation of human social organization and historical process? If not the material conditions for sustaining existence itself, what is the 'bottom line'?

If the objective of socialism *is* the abolition of class, for whom is this likely to be a real objective, grounded in their own life-situation, and not simply an abstract good? If not those who are directly subject to capitalist exploitation, who is likely to have an 'interest' in the abolition of capitalist exploitation? Who is likely to have the social capacity to achieve it, if not those who are strategically placed at the heart of capitalist production and exploitation? Who is likely to have the potential to constitute a collective agent in the struggle for socialism? The point has been forcefully made by Francis Mulhern:

The working class is revolutionary, Marxists have maintained, because of its historically constituted nature as the exploited collective producer within the capitalist mode of production. As the *exploited* class, it is caught in a systematic clash with capital, which cannot generally and permanently satisfy its needs. As the main *producing* class, it has the power to halt — and within limits redirect — the economic apparatus of capitalism, in pursuit of its goals. And as the *collective* producer it has the objective capacity to found a new, non-exploitative mode of production. This combination of interest, power and creative capacity distinguishes the working class from every other social or political force in capitalist society, and qualifies it as the indispensable agency of socialism. To reaffirm this proposition is not to claim that socialism is assured — it is not — or that the labour movement alone is likely to achieve it. What has to be said is that 'our major positive resource' can never be other than the organized working class, and that if it cannot regenerate itself, no outside intervention can do so. If that resource should, in some calamitous historical eventuality, be dispersed or neutralized, then socialism really will be reduced to a sectarian utopia beyond the reach of even the most inspired and combative social movement.

... Creativity is a potential, not an achievement — true enough. But the potential itself is not determined by the moral and political vicissitudes of the labour movement. It is fostered by the ordinary contradictions of capitalism, whose processes of expanded reproduction have brought forth a structurally collective economic and social order and, willy-nilly, the conditions and agencies of a real 'general interest'.[1]

These fundamental issues are not resolved, or even addressed, by the self-evident proposition that there is no direct or necessary translation of material conditions into political allegiances. Still less are they confronted by the far less self-evident proposition that no material interests even exist apart from, or prior to, their ideological and political definition and articulation. They are resolved least of all by the assumption that the fate of political parties in electoral contests proves that there is no correspondence between 'class ascription' and 'political engagement', or even that there *exist* no class interests apart from political engagements. And yet, such propositions, which tend to be conflated and confused with one another, are really all that the NTS has to offer in response to the big questions about the foundations of the socialist project.

Let us look more closely at these propositions. We have already encountered the notion that class interests do not exist in advance of their political expression or 'discursive construction', as formulated by Laclau and Mouffe and Hindess and Hirst. The same principle is asserted by Gareth Stedman Jones, who summarizes as follows the Marxist conception of the relations between social conditions and political forces which he rejects: 'The implicit assumption is of civil society as a field of conflicting social groups or classes whose opposing interests will find rational expression in the political arena. Such interests, it is assumed, pre-exist their expression.'[2] His response is that 'We cannot ... decode political

[1] Francis Mulhern, 'Towards 2000, or News From You-Know-Where', *New Left Review* 148, November-December 1984, pp. 22-3.

[2] Gareth Stedman Jones, *Languages of Class: Studies in Working Class History 1832-1982*, Cambridge 1983, p. 21.

language to reach a primal and material expression of interest since it is the discursive structure of political language which conceives and defines interest in the first place.'[3]

Now let us see what these propositions mean. Let us, for the sake of argument — and neither Stedman Jones nor Laclau and Mouffe, nor even Paul Hirst(?) has yet gone so far as to deny this — assume that there exists a class without property or rights of possession in the means of production, which must sell its labour-power for a wage, etc. ..., and that there also exists another class which appropriates the surplus labour of the first class. Presumably we can also accept that this relationship is necessarily — though in varying degrees — a relationship of conflict, or at least that there is an irreducible antagonism at its heart, to the extent that the efforts of one class to maximize the value which it derives from the labour of the other will be to the relative disadvantage of the latter, in various ways having to do with wages, conditions of work, security, control of the work-process and of other activities, and the possibilities of self-fulfillment. If this relationship of conflict and exploitation is an 'economic' phenomenon, what can we say about its implications for politics?

It is, in the first place, self-evident that we cannot claim a direct empirical transposition of these conflicts from the economic to the party-political plane. The opposition between the Conservative and Labour parties, for example, does not neatly coincide with the conflicts between capitalist employers and their wage-earning employees, either in the sense that the personnel in the two cases are identical or in the sense that the political programmes of each party are entirely coextensive and commensurate with the needs and purposes of one of the protagonists in the 'economic' conflict to the exclusion of or at the expense of the other. This proposition is almost too trivial to be worth stating; but it is not altogether clear that, in the end, the fundamental theoretical tenet of the NTS amounts to much more than this.

Still, let us take it a little further. It is also self-evident that people make their party-political choices for a variety of reasons that are not always referable to their needs and purposes as actors in the 'economic' sphere, the more so as they are seldom offered a clear political choice which corresponds to these purposes and needs. It is also true that people participate in collective identities

---

[3] Ibid., p. 22.

other than class — as men and women, as members of racial or ethnic groups, as residents of a locality, and so on — which enter into their party-political choices. It is equally clear that even when they intend to make their choices on grounds directly referable to their needs and purposes as 'economic' agents, they may have varying perceptions of what such a correspondence would entail, which of the available choices would best answer those needs and purposes. It is even possible that they may be mistaken in their perceptions of which available option would best suit their needs and purposes. Finally, the available political options are necessarily historical phenomena, which never spring pristine and full-grown out of the current social conditions but are built upon historical legacies and articulated in historical languages. Likewise, the people who make political choices are not blank slates, empty vessels, but active historical beings, possessing historically determinate languages and expectations. It is therefore self-evidently true that, even when political choices reflect 'economic' purposes and conflicts, the specific form of the political response cannot be predicted from the structure of the 'economic' sphere.

In all these senses, the non-correspondence of economics and politics is more or less uncontroversial. And these propositions do not in themselves carry any fundamental implications for the Marxist conception of the socialist project. Several other major propositions, however, are entailed by the non-correspondence principle as it is conceived by the NTS, which do not follow from the ones just outlined and which are not at all equally self-evident.

One huge conceptual leap is essential to the new socialist project. As we saw in the formulations of Stedman Jones, Mouffe, and Hirst, for example, the critical point in the non-correspondence principle is that no class interests exist apart from, or prior to, their ideological or political expression. What precisely does this mean? Perhaps it means simply that material interests do not exist as objectives except in specific ideological and political forms, or that material interests must be perceived and understood in certain ways before they can become political forces. It is true that the NTS consistently seem to confuse political *objectives* with *interests*; but they clearly intend something more. They say — and presumably mean — that material interests do not exist independently but are constituted by ideology and politics, which in effect means that material interests *do not exist*, as such, at all. Indeed class and class struggle cease to have any meaning at *any* 'level', economic as well as ideological or political. If we are being told not simply

that there is no easy translation of economic interests into ideological and political forces and objectives, but that there *are* no
economic interests apart from their translation into ideological or
political forces and objectives, then there is no such thing as class
at all, except as an ideological or political construct.

Let us return to our two classes, capitalist appropriators and the
workers whose surplus labour they appropriate. Let us assume that
no political programme or language, no ideology, even no conceptual categories exist which clearly articulate the interests of the
workers as the objects of surplus-extraction as against the interests
of the capitalists who appropriate that surplus. Would this change
the exploitative nature of the relationship or its fundamentally
antagonistic character? Would it change the fact that, on the
whole, it is better not to be exploited than to be exploited? Would
it change the relative advantages and disadvantages derived from
the relationship by the two parties? Would it negate the power and
domination exercised by one over the other? Would it alter the
fact that on this 'economic' relationship of power and domination
rests a whole structure of social and political power? If the proposition that 'interests' do not exist independently of their modes of
representation implies an affirmative answer to any or all of these
questions, we are in the realm of absolute idealism, where nothing
exists but Idea. But if it means none of these things, then what can
it possibly mean to say that material interests do not exist 'prior to
the discourse in which they are formulated and articulated'?

If material interests do 'exist', there still remains the problem of
how — or whether — they can be translated into political terms.
Several distinct questions arise here: do material interests tend,
and have they historically tended, to produce political forces?
And, whether or not such a tendency exists, *must* there be a
'correspondence' between political forces and material interests —
either in the sense that these material interests cannot be adequately served without creating an 'appropriate' political force, or,
conversely, in the sense that certain political objectives (such as the
construction of socialism) cannot be achieved without the creation
of a political force which 'corresponds' to specific class interests?

The NTS seem to imply that there has been little historical connection between material conditions and political forces, and that
any connection that has existed has been largely 'conjunctural'. So,
for example, Gareth Stedman Jones suggests that Marxist assumptions about the connection between class conditions and political
engagements — indeed the whole theoretical apparatus of histori-

cal materialism and its conception of social determination — represent unwarranted generalizations from one unique and relatively short-lived historical experience. Only in England, and even here only temporarily, has there ever been a close correspondence between class and politics, for reasons entirely specific to English history. On the shaky foundations of this contingent correspondence — or rather, on a misreading of its meaning — the whole mistaken Marxist theory of social determination is based.[4]

The new 'true' socialism further implies that there *need* be no connection between material conditions and political forces. On the one hand, since there *are* no independently existing material interests, there is clearly no question of material interests which, if they are to be properly served, require the creation of an appropriate political force. On the other hand, there would seem to be no political objectives — not even the building of socialism — that require the mobilization of political forces grounded in class, since the necessary forces can be constructed on the ideological and political planes.

It should be emphasized that none of these very large assumptions follows from the simple and uncontroversial proposition that there is no easy and mechanical translation of material conditions into political terms and no single political form to match every 'economic' circumstance. Yet it is largely by means of a conceptual slippage from the smaller to the larger propositions, rather than by means of evidence and argument, that the NTS generally make their case for the detachment of socialist politics from class. From the fact that 'political struggles do not occur in the form of direct contests between classes'[5] — for example, the contest between Labour and Conservative parties does not correspond to a struggle between workers and capitalists over the relations of production, in which the issue is socialism *versus* capitalism — and from the fact that workers sometimes vote Tory, we should, by Paul Hirst's logic (for instance), be able to conclude a great many things about the absolute autonomy of politics from class. It should follow that any connection between politics and class is more or less accidental and 'conjunctural'; that wherever political organizations and contests do not neatly correspond to class organizations and class

---

[4] Ibid., pp. 2-4.
[5] Paul Hirst, 'Economic Classes and Politics', in *Class and Class Structure*, ed. Alan Hunt, London 1977, p. 126.

conflicts, material conditions and class relations are clearly not significant determinants; that political organizations and programmes cannot be said to represent certain class interests well or badly, since there *are* no independently existing class interests. Hence, one can judge the effectiveness of these organizations and programmes only in relation to one's own ideological commitments.[6] In other words, since 'classes do not have "interests" and are not political actors,'[7] a socialist strategy can be constructed without reference to class interests and struggles. Does it really need to be said that this argument is a series of slippages compounded by *non sequiturs*? Just consider the logic of Hirst's proposition that 'relative autonomy' really entails necessary noncorrespondence: if workers are free to vote Tory, then there is no such thing as a working-class interest, and socialism can be built without class struggle.

Class conflicts have historically structured political forces without necessarily producing political organizations which directly correspond to class formations. It should hardly need to be said that workers have an interest in not being exploited, that this interest is in conflict with the interests of those who exploit them, that many historic struggles have been fought over this conflict of interest, and that these struggles have shaped the political 'sphere'. The absence of explicit class 'discourses' does not betoken the absence of class realities and their effects in shaping the life-conditions and consciousness of the people who come within their 'field of force'.[8] If these class situations and oppositions have not been directly mirrored in the political domain, it can hardly be concluded that people have no class interests or even that they have chosen not to express these interests politically. It is especially dangerous to generalize about the relation, or lack of it, between 'economics' and 'politics' or about the conditions of socialist struggle — as the NTS tend to do — from the mechanisms by which electoral parties are formed or from patterns of voting behaviour.

But perhaps most important of all, it is ludicrous to proceed, explicitly or implicitly, from the 'autonomy' (relative or otherwise) of political affiliations to very far-reaching conclusions which seem

---

[6] Ibid., p. 131.
[7] Ibid., p. 153.
[8] This phrase is borrowed from E.P. Thompson, 'Eighteenth-Century English Society; Class Struggle without Class?' *Social History* 3, May 1978.

to suggest, among other things: that the relation between capital and labour is no longer (if it ever was) the fundamental relation upon which the structure of capitalism is built; that the working class, which stands in a direct relation to capitalist exploitation, has no more interest in the abolition of that exploitation than does anyone else, or that such interests as it has (purely 'economic') can be adequately served without being translated into political terms; that because people partake of collective identities other than class, class conditions are no more important in determining their life-situations than any other social fact; that class is not available as a principle of unity and a motivation for collective action, or at least that any other collective identity will do just as well; that the working class is no more likely — indeed perhaps less likely — than any other social collectivity to adopt the socialist project as its own, and to do so effectively; and that an effective struggle for socialism — that is, a struggle for the abolition of class — can be mounted by appealing to any number of collective motivations other than class interests and by mobilizing political movements which correspond to no class forces. In short, we should demand a good deal more historical evidence and far more convincing arguments to persuade us that socialism can be achieved without the construction of a political force which does 'correspond' to particular class interests and without a confrontation between political forces which does 'correspond' to the class opposition between capital and labour.

The proposition that there is no simple or necessary corres-pondence between 'economic' or 'social' conditions and politics, in the particular senses in which it is obviously true, still leaves unchallenged the principle that the road to socialism is the self-emancipation of the working class by means of class struggle. The critical questions remain: who has a specific interest in socialism? If no one in particular, why not everyone? If everyone, why not capitalists too, and why need there be *any* conflict and struggle? If 'interest' is not the relevant principle, what is? And with or without interest, what about *capacity*? What kinds of people are strate-gically placed and collectively defined in such a way as to make possible and likely their constitution as a collective agent in the struggle for socialism? If no one in particular, why not everyone? But if some people and not others, on what principle of historical selection? If the analysis of history as class struggle, and the under-lying materialist principles which accord centrality to relations of production, are wrong, or if they do not entitle us to conclude that class struggle is the most likely path to socialism, what alternative

principle of historical explanation should we adopt, or what different connections should we draw between our emancipatory
project and our understanding of history?

At one extreme, the non-correspondence principle simply
stands for the rather trivial proposition that 'economic' or social
conditions do not mechanically produce any specific corresponding political forces. At the other extreme, the principle
implies that a political movement whose object is a fundamental
social transformation requires no roots in material conditions. All
the NTS mentioned so far have moved substantially toward the
latter extreme; but it is still not entirely clear how far all of them
want to go. It is not clear which of the following propositions each
of them would want to accept, though it is clear that they would
have to accept at least some of them in order to sustain the NTS
programme:

1) The 'economic' sphere has no essential bearing on the political, in the sense that relations of production and exploitation have
no essential bearing on the whole structure of social and political
domination.

2) The destruction of this structure of domination is not an
essential condition for human emancipation.

3) The specific relation on which the capitalist social order rests
is not the exploitative relation between capital and labour (or perhaps there *is* no such exploitative relation).

4) Since the 'economic' sphere (specifically, relations of
exploitation) has no essential relation to any other sphere or to
the whole structure of domination, the historical struggles of the
working class in the economic sphere against the effects of
capitalist accumulation and exploitation have no possible bearing
upon, and are completely discontinuous from, struggles against the
capitalist order in any other sphere.

5) Socialism does not require the abolition of class exploitation;
and/or socialism as a political project need not be a struggle for
the abolition of the 'economic' relation between capital and labour.

6) Capitalist exploitation and accumulation have no tangible
effects on the working class, or no more than on anyone else;
capitalism's cycles and crises of accumulation have no significant
consequences for the work and life conditions of those whose
labour sustains capitalist accumulation.

7) People who are the direct objects of capitalist exploitation
(on the assumption that such exploitation exists) have no funda-

mental interest in the abolition of that exploitation — i.e. would derive no fundamental benefit from abolishing it.

8) If there is such a thing as an 'interest', all human beings have an interest in the abolition of class and exploitation, and that interest is not mediated by their particular situation in the existing structure of class exploitation. For practical purposes, it makes no significant difference whether people do or do not suffer exploitation, whether they are or are not directly affected by the process of capitalist accumulation, or perhaps even whether they themselves are the exploiters. In other words, these purely 'economic' factors have no essential effect, and cannot be expected to have an effect, on the disposition or capacity to engage in the struggle against capitalism and for socialism.

Or alternatively:

9) The more people are exploited, the less likely they are to struggle against exploitation.

10) No social group is better situated than any other to undermine the structure of capitalist accumulation and exploitation, and all have an equal capacity to constitute a collective agent in this project (unless, again, the working class is *less* well situated and *less* capable).

If the non-correspondence principle implies some or all of these things, a massive reconsideration of the nature of capitalism, and even a thorough rewriting of history, would be required to make the principle convincing. But if it does not imply some or all of these things, it is difficult to see precisely what it does mean or how it can be used to support the NTS vision of the struggle for socialism.

If the non-correspondence principle raises any serious questions, they lie somewhere between the vacuity of its trivial meaning, and the solipsistic idealism of its more extreme implications. The critical questions have to do with the difficulties and modalities of mobilizing class interests and organizing class forces into an effective political movement. But then, that has always been the question for Marxism. What serious Marxist, beginning with Marx himself, has ever assumed that no efforts of political organization and education would be required to transform the revolutionary potential of the working class into an actuality? Who would deny that there have always been divisions within the working class, that the development of capitalism has created new divisions which require new theoretical advances to apprehend them and new practical means to overcome them; that the capitalist class has always, with varying degrees of success, sought to exacerbate those divisions and impose still others; that the material successes of capitalism, changes in its structure, and the ideological efforts of its proponents have affected the process of class formation; and that the first task of a socialist movement is to overcome these divisions and obstacles?

There are also, of course, critical questions having to do with the relation between working-class movements and other social movements. Although this is the preferred terrain of the new 'true' socialism, the non-correspondence principle is used precisely to evade the issue, to turn it into a non-problem, to conceptualize away the difficult questions. For example, what is the relation between the specific objectives of the new social movements and the objectives of socialism, indeed, what are the relations among the varied objectives of these movements themselves? What social interests and forces do these movements represent, and are these interests and forces capable of being organized into a coherent and stable political force, let alone a force for socialism? Such questions simply do not arise if one proceeds from the premise that social interests and forces are constructed autonomously on the ideological and political planes, and if the problems of class formation and political organization are replaced by the problems of discourse-construction. Paradoxically, the NTS 'realists' who find it necessary to dismiss as utopian (on the grounds of the non-correspondence principle) the 'essentialist', 'economistic', 'class-reductionist' Marxist view of the working class as a potentially revolutionary class, apparently see nothing fanciful or utopian (on the grounds of the same non-correspondence principle) in the belief that the role of transforming society can be played by an amorphous 'people', bound together and bound to the objectives of socialism by nothing more than the gossamer threads of 'discourse'.

7

The Non-Correspondence Principle: A Historical Case

Gareth Stedman Jones, who alone among NTS notables has put the non-correspondence principle to the test of historical investigation, provides an especially illuminating example of its theoretical and political logic. Proceeding from his own historical studies of Chartism, he draws certain far-reaching conclusions about the lack of connection between social conditions and political forces, and then applies these insights to an analysis of the Labour Party and how its recent disastrous electoral fortunes might be reversed.

It must be stressed that Stedman Jones represents a very different case from the new 'true' socialists we have examined up to now. Unlike any of the others, he has actually undertaken significant historical work which evinces a completely different attitude toward evidence and argument from anything displayed by Laclau and Mouffe, or Hindess and Hirst. His earlier work certainly falls well within the materialist historiographical tradition and sets him apart from the abstract theoreticism that marks even the most 'empirical' work of the others. These differences, however, serve to emphasize the magnitude of the break between his earlier work and the more recent theoretical and political approach exemplified by his rejection of materialism, quoted in the previous chapter, and his subordination of social reality to discourse. If, in hindsight, there was much in his earlier work, with its Althusserian leanings, that might have prepared us for the subsequent shift, it is nevertheless a remarkable trajectory that he records in his own account of his career.

In the introduction to *Languages of Class: Studies in English Working Class History 1832-1982*, a collection of essays written over a period of several years during which his views underwent these significant changes, Stedman Jones tells us that it was his study of Chartism which finally led him to disown the traditional Marxist conception of the relations between material conditions and political forces, between class as a 'structural position within production relations' and class as a 'political force'. The lack of correspondence between Chartist arguments and the particular conditions of any specific social group compelled him, first, to question the 'ideological' approach, according to which political ideology reflects material conditions, and finally to declare the *autonomy* of Chartist politics. It is worth following the trajectory of his discovery to see what it is that appears to him as compelling evidence in support of the non-correspondence principle.

Stedman Jones seems to begin with the assumption that a Marxist conception of class requires a belief that there are 'simple rules of translation from the social to the political,'[1] and, even more specifically, that party affiliations and allegiances can be predicted from class positions, or, conversely, that material conditions can be 'read off' from political programmes. He easily disposes of this straw man by means of reasonable and uncontroversial propositions, such as that inherited political languages help to shape consciousness, so that there is no simple and unidirectional formula by which material conditions produce consciousness (or ideology) and politics. Unfortunately, he then proceeds by leaps and bounds from the limited proposition that no simple correspondence exists between social conditions and politics to an endorsement of the far more comprehensive non-correspondence principle and the autonomy of politics. Furthermore, he executes this leap by generalizing from one example, which, as we shall see, is of dubious service to his case.

There was, Stedman Jones argues, no simple relation between Chartist ideas and the social conditions of the Chartists. Their programme was a specifically political rather than a social one, and it drew upon earlier radical traditions not rooted in, or answering to, the specific interests and experiences of artisanal classes. We are therefore compelled to conclude that the politics of Chartism were 'autonomous'. In particular, he has in mind the Chartists' 'attribution of evil and misery to a political source,'[2] and their perception of class oppositions in political terms, as an opposition between represented and unrepresented rather than between employer and employed — a perception inherited from traditional radicalism.[3] If

---

[1] Gareth Stedman Jones, *Languages of Class: Studies in Working Class History 1832-1982*, Cambridge 1983, p. 242.

[2] Ibid., p. 105.

[3] Ibid., p. 106.

the political language of Chartism was not the language of their own social experience but that of earlier radicals with very different social roots, it follows, according to his argument, that the political demands of Chartism were not merely symbolic of or derivative from their social grievances but were themselves primary demands, independent of any specific material or social determinations. Those 'social' interpretations of Chartism which treat it as a social movement whose political character was tangential, or regard its political demands as merely the effects of social causes, or see a contradiction between its fundamental social character and its political expressions, are therefore mistaken. The political character of Chartism is the 'centre of the [Chartist] story,'[4] autonomous from the social conditions of its adherents.

The remarks below are not intended as an attack upon Stedman Jones's account of Chartism. Indeed, there will be little attempt to go beyond his own historical evidence. What is at issue here are the conclusions he draws from that evidence and the political programme he proposes 'in the light of' these conclusions. Above all, it is not at all clear why he believes that his account represents a challenge to the traditional Marxist conceptions of the relations between politics and class, between consciousness and social being. He asks us to recognize that language 'is itself part of social being,'[5] and that we 'cannot peer straight through' political languages to an independently existing social reality, as if the former were simply an 'evanescent' reflection of the latter — since that reality is itself constituted for us through our languages. It may be true that we cannot simply 'peer straight through' political languages, but what precisely does this mean; how far are we meant to take it; and — unless he wants completely to dissolve reality into language, to dissociate language from any referent outside itself (as, for example, the French post-structuralists have effectively done) — how does it represent a fundamental challenge to historical materialism?

Several points implied by Stedman Jones's argument can be granted as more or less uncontroversial: political ideologies are not created in an historical vacuum; the consciousness of living human beings is shaped by historical legacies; people create their ideological responses to their own lived experience with the linguistic

---

4 Ibid., p. 105.
5 Ibid., pp. 21-2.

and conceptual instruments available to them; and they are capable of more than one response. How much more than this does he want to claim, and how much more is he entitled to claim, on the strength of his favourite historical example?

Granted that Chartism is notable for the political character of its perceptions and programmes, that there are discrepancies between these programmes and the social conditions of the groups represented by Chartism, and that there are significant affinities between Chartism and the traditions of pre-industrial radicalism, what are we to conclude? Does it follow that these political perceptions and demands were 'autonomous'; that they did not, and were not intended to, express grievances fundamentally social in origin and character; that Chartism as a political force was not traceable to, and conditioned by, any 'structural position within production relations'? And are we to conclude that the success or failure of this political movement did not depend on the degree to which it measured up to the social realities of class?

One thing should be noted immediately. Stedman Jones does not deny that Chartism was a movement constituted by people with a common class identity, or even that this social identity preceded the ideological unity derived from the Chartist political programme.[6] The social identity of the people represented by Chartism did not, in other words, depend upon the language or politics of Chartism. On the contrary, the existence of Chartist politics depended upon the prior existence of a particular social class. Stedman Jones does not, in fact, deny that the political language of Chartism expressed the aspirations of a particular social group, even a class constituted by relations of production. It was clearly a class movement, a political expression of a social class. Even if the politics of Chartism did not mechanically reflect (whatever that might mean) the social conditions of its adherents, it was nevertheless the political language of a social collectivity whose collective identity was constituted by social conditions. Although Stedman Jones insists — less controversially than he perhaps thinks — that social conditions 'are only endowed with particular political meanings so far as they are effectively articulated through specific forms of political discourse and practice,'[7] he is compelled to acknowledge at least that there must be some affinity between a

---

[6] See, for example, ibid., p. 95.
[7] Ibid., p. 242.

political language and the people to whom it is addressed if it is to be successfully implanted, and that such a language can become 'inapposite' as circumstances change.[8]

In fact, his whole analysis of Chartism belies his insistence on a 'non-referential conception of language',[9] since the burden of his account is precisely that Chartist language gained currency just because it did refer to — indeed reflect — certain real conditions, and that it ceased to be 'apposite' as those conditions changed. His narrative is peppered with references to how 'ideally suited' the rhetoric of Chartism was to certain specific historical circumstances and how 'ill-equipped' it was to deal with others[10]. He talks about the 'staleness and anachronistic flavour' of Chartist language as the relationship between the state and the working class changed and deprived Chartist assumptions of their plausibility. Furthermore, the circumstances to which Chartist rhetoric referred were precisely the political manifestations of 'class oppression';[11] and its political radicalism could remain successful as an ideology only as long as historical conditions allowed economic oppression to be plausibly perceived as politically determined:

> ... the success of radicalism as the ideology of a mass movement would depend upon specific conditions, those in which the state and the propertied classes in their *political and legal capacity* could be perceived as the source of all oppression. The programme of Chartism remained believable so long as unemployment, low wages, economic insecurity and other material afflictions could convincingly be assigned political causes.[12]

One might want to argue that Stedman Jones has thus conceded as much as any reasonable historical materialist could ask. He offers us a case in which people, belonging to a social class constituted by relations of production, produce an ideology that expresses their aspirations as a social class. Their political language and the needs to which it answers presuppose their existence as a social class.

---

[8] Ibid., p. 22.
[9] Ibid., p. 21.
[10] See, for example, ibid., pp. 175 and 177.
[11] See, for example, ibid., p. 177.
[12] Ibid., p. 106.

And if that political language is not commensurate with their conditions as a class, if their political solutions do not adequately answer to their social needs, it clearly does not follow that this language and these solutions do not express social grievances and are not intended to resolve social problems. It is, for example, possible that the Chartists were mistaken in their perceptions of what was required to meet their social needs, and that they could have adopted a political discourse and practice better suited to their social conditions. Alternatively, the social conditions may themselves have restricted the possibilities of an adequate response; and, within the prevailing historical limits, the Chartist programme, however inadequate to the interests of its adherents, may nevertheless have been a reasonable response, which measured up to the prevailing conditions. In either case, we have not strayed very far from the orthodox materialism of Marx himself.

Let us look more closely at those characteristics of Chartism to which Stedman Jones attaches the greatest importance: the *political* character of the Chartist programme, its attribution of social evils to political causes, and its perception of class oppositions in political terms — not as employer *versus* employed, but as represented *versus* unrepresented. The question is whether these characteristics betoken a sharp separation between social realities and political forms.

First, the social realities. Chartism coincided with a period in the development of English capitalism when (to use Marxist language that Stedman Jones himself applied in his earlier work[13]) the formal subjection of labour to capital was already well established — that is, when production relations substantially took the form of wage-labour employed by capital — but when the real subjection, the transformation of the labour-process and the establishment of capital's direct control over it, was still in progress and far from complete. The decline of Chartism, as Stedman Jones has demonstrated, more or less coincided with the accomplishment of 'real subjection', as the process of 'industrialization' effectively settled the issue of control over the labour process in favour of the capitalist at the expense of direct producers. It is at this point that the much-debated transformation of working-class struggles took place, sometimes described as a decline in working-class militancy, or, less pejoratively, as a shift from the political to the economic

---

[13] Ibid., pp. 45-7.

terrain. Chartism was, in effect, the last major working-class movement in Britain to perceive its interests and articulate its grievances
in predominantly political terms.

It appears, then, that the transformation of working-class
struggles, the shift from the political focus of Chartism to the
directly 'economic' concerns of subsequent working-class movements, corresponds to a significant change in social conditions.
While it may not be fair to assume a direct causal connection
between these social and political changes, it seems reasonable
to suppose that the political perceptions of Chartism were
encouraged, or at least made possible, by certain social conditions;
that whatever permitted or encouraged the Chartists to perceive
their interests in political terms, those conditions were no longer
present thereafter; and that the change had to do with the definitive establishment of 'real subjection'. We might then ask what in
the social situation of the Chartists conditioned their 'autonomously' political response, or what encouraged them to treat their
social problems as if they were purely political.

There is, however, probably a better, and more historical, way
of looking at the problem. It must be noted, first, that the conditions of class exploitation in *pre*-capitalist society had been such
that social grievances arising from the relations of class exploitation would inevitably encroach on the juridical-political sphere.
To the extent that the exploitative powers of the dominant classes
rested on juridical status and direct possession of coercive political
and military power — that is, to the extent that economic and
political power were inextricably united — the 'economic' and the
'political' tended also to be inseparable in the struggles of exploited
classes. An attack on the appropriative rights of lordship, for
example, was by definition a challenge to its juridical and political
privileges. Indeed, as has often been noted, the clear separation of
economic and political spheres is a distinctive attribute of capitalism, determined by its specific mode of surplus extraction. By the
same token, the differentiation of distinctly 'economic' struggles,
detached from the political sphere, is a characteristic specific to
capitalism, possible only in conditions where surplus extraction is
carried out by purely 'economic' means, that is, the appropriation
of surplus value by capitalists from juridically free and propertyless
wage-labourers. In the case of pre-capitalist movements of protest
and resistance, then, we would not be obliged to assume that a
political focus, however apparently 'autonomous', betokens a
detachment from the material conditions of class exploitation.

Since Chartism, however, was the movement of a class already subject to capital, clearly there is more to be said. If 'the attribution of misery to a political source' was based on a social reality marked by the unity of the 'economic' and the 'political', then clearly Chartism was anachronistic in continuing to express economic grievances and to perceive class relations in political terms, at a time when that unity no longer prevailed. And yet this certainly does not mean that Chartist grievances were not 'economic' in character and origin, nor that the political concerns of the Chartists were not firmly rooted in their social conditions. What it does mean is that the Chartists, like all human beings, were historical creatures, and that history does not proceed by means of clean breaks or in discontinous pieces, but by transformations of inherited realities, changes within continuities. We should not be surprised if ideological changes proceed by means of alterations in available traditions to suit new social conditions, rather than by the pristine invention of new ideologies without antecedents to match every stage of social change. The moment we treat history as a continuous process and not a series of discontinuous 'structures', the continuities between Chartism and earlier radical traditions become less important than the ways in which that unbroken tradition was *changed* by the social realities confronting the Chartists.

In fact, we can refer to Stedman Jones himself for evidence that the class conditions of the Chartists, while they did not lead to an abandonment of the old radical political focus, gave that political focus a distinctive character rooted in their own specific class experience:

What was peculiar to the Chartist phase of radicalism, therefore, was neither the abandonment of an inherited radical ambition to construct a broad popular alliance, nor a novel and class-specific way of looking at recent history in terms of what later historians were to describe as industrialization. In both these areas there existed a strong continuity between Chartism and preceding versions of radicalism. What was specific to Chartism was, firstly, the equation of the people with the working class as a result of 1832 and, secondly, a corresponding shift of emphasis upon the relationship between the state and the working classes, dramatized by the Whig legislation which followed 1832. As a result of this shift, less emphasis was placed upon the state as a nest of self-interest and corruption — 'old corruption' in Cobbett's phrase; instead, it increasingly came to be viewed as the tyrannical harbinger of a dictatorship over the producers. As the 1830's progressed, the predominant image was no longer merely of placemen, sinecurists and fundholders principally interested in revenues derived from taxes on consumption to secure their unearned comforts, but was something more sinister and dynamic — a powerful and malevolent machine of repression, at the behest of capitalists and factory lords, essentially and actively dedicated to the lowering of the wages of the working classes through the removal of all residual protection at their command, whether trade societies, legal redress, poor relief or what survived of the representation of the interests of the working classes in local government. As a conjunctural phenomenon, Chartism represented the rapid upsurge and gradual ebbing away of this specific vision of the state.[14]

Surely these adaptations and modifications of the radical tradition are at least as significant as the continuities, and surely they tell us at least as much about the social determinations of political forces. To speak, as Stedman Jones does, of the 'Chartist phase of radicalism' — as if it were simply another stage in the disembodied History of Ideas — disguises the fact that Chartism, for all its backward-looking debt to radicalism, represents a *transformation* of traditional radical ideas in accordance with the realities of a growing industrial capitalism. It occupied a brief moment, during which the social conditions of capitalism required changes in older ideological traditions without yet clearly demanding their abandonment.

The social transformations that made necessary the modification of radical ideas to suit the conditions of a capitalist working class were soon to submerge the tradition of political radicalism altogether in the 'economic' struggles of the modern working class. Although the relations between capital and wage labour had from the beginning meant that the old political relationship between exploiting and exploited classes no longer applied, the perception of that relationship in the traditional political terms may have continued to seem plausible as long as the rule of capital did not extend completely and irrevocably to the process of labour itself. The act of appropriation, of surplus extraction, was still to some degree apparently separate from the process of production, as it had been in pre-capitalist forms of exploitation. In

---

[14] Ibid., pp. 173-4.

other words, exploitation was still visibly a coercive act, not inseparable from and intrinsic to the process of production, and it was reasonable to regard the exploitative relationship between appropriator and producer as an 'extra-economic' one.

But once the subjection of labour to capital was complete, once the struggle over control of the labour process was definitively settled in favour of capital — or, to put it another way, once the act of appropriation became completely inseparable from the process of production — the relationship between exploiters and exploited began to appear purely 'economic'. This perception both reflected and obscured the real nature of capitalist exploitation. On the one hand, it reflected capitalism's specific separation of the economic and the political; on the other hand, it tended to obscure the exploitative character of capitalist appropriation, to make it invisible, as something inherent in the process of production itself. So, for example, where earlier producers might perceive themselves as struggling to keep what was rightfully theirs, the structure of capitalism encourages workers to perceive themselves as struggling to get a share of what belongs to capital, a 'fair wage', in exchange for their labour.

The formal separation of the economic and political also, of course, tends to obscure the ways in which capitalist appropriation is sustained by the state, since there is no longer any obvious unity between political and appropriative powers. This is especially true because capitalism is capable of extending formal juridical equality and political rights to producing classes, even to the point of universal suffrage, without directly challenging the appropriative and exploitative powers of the capitalist. It is also precisely this structural characteristic of capitalism that made possible the reforms 'within the unreformed system' which Stedman Jones credits with depriving Chartism of its 'purchase over large parts of its mass following', as the actions of the state no longer seemed to 'wholly correspond to the radical picture'.[15]

The concentration of struggles 'at the point of production', then, accurately reflected the realities of capitalism in a way that the political struggles of Chartism did not — but it reflected those realities only partially. In a sense, the weakness of Chartism, with its anachronistic political focus, had also been its strength; and, while it is certainly true that the realities of capitalism demanded

---

[15] Ibid., p. 106.

struggles 'on the economic plane', it is also true that the labour movement lost a great deal when the focus of its struggles shifted to the 'economic' sphere. Nevertheless, that shift was indisputably determined by the material conditions of capitalism. The political perceptions of the Chartists had simply become untenable. From the point of view of the connections between social conditions and political forces, what is significant is not so much that the Chartists expressed economic realities in political terms, but that they were the last working-class movement to do so, because thereafter the social realities became too clearly incompatible with perceptions grounded in the pre-capitalist unity of the economic and political. If working-class struggles were again to acquire a political force, it would have to be on very different terms.

What, then, can we learn from the Chartist example about the relation between social conditions and political forces, insofar as we are entitled to generalize from this example at all? First, it undoubtedly testifies to the historicity of ideology and politics. No ideology is constructed in a historical vacuum, completely anew. Historical development generally takes place by means of changes within continuities, not by means of clean breaks but by trans-formations of inherited realities. Second, Chartism testifies to the construction of politics and ideologies by living, conscious human beings, and to the creative flexibility of human responses (which also entails the possibility of making mistakes). In these ways, Chartism undoubtedly belies any simple, mechanical reflection of 'base' in 'superstructure'. There is no such thing as a single political or ideological form to match every set of production relations.

At the same time, Chartism also provides a striking example of how interests and grievances articulated in political programmes are constituted by production relations and class, how historical legacies and traditions are shaped and transformed by changing class relations, and how the reception of political languages depends upon their plausibility as means of apprehending existing social conditions and articulating existing social grievances. Finally, Chartism is also a dramatic illustration that political strate-gies will prove inadequate to the fulfilment of their own objectives, as well as short-lived, to the extent that they are not commensurate with the prevailing social realities. This historical example, then, inspires little confidence in the non-correspondence principle, either as a theoretical precept or as a political strategy.

Here we come to the pay-off. Gareth Stedman Jones applies the insights derived from his study of working-class struggle, and of

Chartism in particular, to a new interpretation of the Labour Party, its history, and the conditions for restoring its electoral fortunes. The principal objective is to construct a social alliance that builds upon and enhances what Stedman Jones perceives as a growing 'non-coincidence of class ascription and political engagement'[16], an alliance transcending the material interests of class and based upon new, potentially common interests which concern 'the distribution of non-material goods (knowledge, democratic control, environment, quality of life) of interest to all its potential constituencies.'[17] The new socialist politics would involve the creation of a new social collectivity constituted and held together not by common social conditions or class situations, but by a new political language addressed to these 'non-material', universal goals. The hallmark of this political strategy, then — and what distinguishes it in particular from the traditional socialist perspective — is that the 'non-coincidence of class ascription and political engagement', the incommensurability of political forces with social conditions, is treated as a *solution*, not a problem, a circumstance to be nourished, not an obstacle to be overcome.

The whole argument leads to one conclusion: there must be a reconstruction of an 'alliance between the working and professional classes', the alliance on which Labour's past successes were based.[18] In fact, it may be that the hopes of socialism should always have resided rather in the latter than the former, since at least a third of the working class can apparently be written off as permanently Tory,[19] and, more fundamentally, because the class-consciousness of the British working class in the twentieth century has been essentially conservative, while the 'professional classes' have had a tradition marked by 'the ethic of service, of intelligence and expertise in pursuit of humanitarian ends, of a civilizing mission both at home and abroad.'[20] Although the old professional ethic has declined and there have been great changes in the 'professional classes' in the past three decades, which have been of 'equal importance' to the fate of the Labour Party as have changes in the working class,[21] there is hope for a reconstitution of the old

---

[16] Ibid., p. 252.
[17] Ibid., p. 256.
[18] Ibid., p. 254.
[19] Ibid., p. 243.
[20] Ibid., p. 247.
[21] Ibid., p. 247.

alliance on new terms. That hope is to be found in a shared commitment to certain 'non-material goods' — a commitment to which the intelligent and rational professional classes are apparently by nature predisposed, and to which the working class is becoming more susceptible as its old exclusive class-, or caste-, consciousness wanes and it becomes 'far more permeable to practices and ideas from outside its own political and cultural inheritance'.[22] This is really old news: socialist politics must be constructed out of an alliance between right-minded people and a working class that abandons its divisive class-consciousness and learns from its betters.

This insistence on finding the best hope for socialist politics in the 'non-coincidence of class ascription and political engagement' perhaps more than anything else reveals the extent to which the new 'true' socialism is intended not as a strategy for transforming society but as a programme for creating a parliamentary majority. The whole theoretical apparatus of the NTS begins to make sense if it is perceived as a theorization of electoral principles: how, within the limits of certain very broadly defined objectives (the more broadly defined the better suited to incorporate a plurality of interests and obscure the incompatibilities between them) — for example, democracy, the quality of life — can a political party become, if not all things to all people, at least as many things as possible to as many people as possible? More particularly, how can a political rhetoric be devised which will draw together a disparate collection of people at least once every four or five years?

If the non-correspondence principle tells us little either about historical processes or about effective strategies for transforming society, it may be illuminating as a much more limited statement about the formation of electoral parties, the constitution of electoral constituencies, the construction of cross-class alliances, and the function of language and rhetoric in abstracting political perceptions from material conditions and antagonisms for the purpose of creating electoral identities. How these identities can be harnessed to a socialist struggle remains an open question. Since, as in the case of Stedman Jones, historical analysis cannot be made to justify the theoretical conclusions or the proposed political strategy, at least as a socialist strategy, perhaps we ought to read

---

[22] Ibid., p. 252.

back to the theoretical conclusions from the political strategy and consider to what extent the theoretical apparatus has been determined not so much by historical investigation or social analysis as by the logic of electoral politics.

8

Platonic Marxism

I

The new 'true' socialism leaves us with no account — or at best a profoundly inadequate one — of the social forces that will motivate the transition to socialism. If we can no longer rely on class interests, needs, and powers to generate the necessary impulse and capacity to act, what social motivations and forces will impel the socialist project? Is socialism in the specific and immediate interest of any social group, or does everyone equally have such an interest? And if we must jettison the concept of class 'interest' altogether — as some NTS suggest — what shall we put in its place? So far, we have little to be getting on with except the vaguely benevolent impulses of 'right-minded' people, and perhaps more specifically, the rational humanitarian concerns of the charitable, thinking middle classes.

Perhaps what I have called 'Platonic Marxism' can now spring to the rescue, to fill the gaps in NTS strategy. Although some NTS might recoil from the bold and uncompromising language in which Gavin Kitching has stated the principles of this creed, Laclau and Mouffe, or Hindess and Hirst, might gladly embrace it. While his own theoretical formation differs from the others in that his roots are not Althusserian, his assumptions are strikingly similar. Here too socialist politics cannot be grounded in material interests but must be constructed by *persuasion*, by means of autonomous values and ideas directed at right-minded people who are open to the higher, rational ideal of life offered by socialism. In any case, until we are offered alternative answers to the many questions raised by the NTS programme, Kitching's statement remains the most systematic and fully theorized attempt to tackle them and to provide a foundation for this 'relatively autonomous' socialism by identifying the forces and motivations that will bring it into being.

Kitching states his 'central thesis' with admirable candour: 'that the construction of socialist societies and a socialist world will take

a very long time (probably centuries) and that an essential pre-
requisite of such a world coming into being is a high degree of
material prosperity and a citizenry of considerable skill, knowledge
and intellectual sophistication.'[1] He goes on to argue that capitalism itself — and only capitalism — can provide the conditions of
general prosperity 'which may be conducive to socialist construction in the long term.' Socialists therefore have a real interest
in sustaining capitalist prosperity and promoting capitalist development, until the happy day of general 'sophistication' arrives.
Indeed, 'the central task of the Left in the current situation is to
help restore boom conditions as quickly as possible....'[2] The Left
has generally been wasting its time and isolating itself from the
political mainstream by clinging to outdated and unpopular values
and ideas. Above all, it has been cultivating the wrong constituency. Kitching proposes to identify the *real* constituency of
socialism, the particular qualities which the socialist movement
must cultivate and to which it must direct its appeal, and the
objectives most likely to mobilize the relevant audience.

Kitching does not — at least on the face of it — abandon the
notion that the working class will be the principal agent of social
transformation. While many Marxists might find his definition of
the working class too inclusive, encompassing as it does all those
'who earn their living by selling their "labour-power" (i.e. their
physical and mental abilities) for a wage or salary',[3] it is not the
breadth of his definition alone that gives a very particular political
significance to his conception of the working class and its role in
constructing socialism. In fact, political conclusions very different
from his could be drawn from a broadly inclusive definition of the
working class.[4] What makes Kitching's conception distinctive is
that he uses his broad definition not simply in order to include in
the socialist project those — for example, 'white collar' workers —
who might be excluded, or rendered secondary as class 'allies', by a
definition confined to the 'traditional' working class or manual
industrial workers; on the contrary, he employs his definition
effectively to exclude the *latter* from any central role (because they

---

[1] Gavin Kitching, *Rethinking Socialism*, London 1983, p. 1.
[2] Ibid., p. 29.
[3] Ibid., p. 13.
[4] See, for example, Peter Meiksins, 'The Boundary Question and Beyond: A
Critique of Recent Debates on the "New Middle Class"', *New Left Review*, forth-
coming.

are 'politically regressive'[5]), shifting the focus to 'mental' workers, on the principle that the greater one's 'intellectual sophistication' the greater one's susceptibility to socialist ideals. In other words, the broad definition of the working class serves here largely as a conceptual cover for completely shifting the focus of the socialist project without appearing to abandon the centrality of the working class. It is also worth noting that the groups in whom Kitching invests his hopes seem to be very similar to the 'professional classes' to which Stedman Jones attaches so much strategic import-ance — though now they are simply absorbed into the working class.

The argument runs something like this: It is a mistake to look to the material interests of the working class as the moving force of socialist struggle. In fact, the more people are tied to material interests, the less suitable they are to receive the socialist message. The adoption of radical positions requires imagination and self-confidence, which are restricted in proportion to the degree of oppression people suffer;[6] and 'the most imaginatively limiting and self-confidence sapping forms of oppression are often those which are closely related with (but not necessarily reducible to) crude material deprivation. For such deprivation places a premium on simple physical survival and allows little time or energy for wider reflection, either upon oneself or upon society.'[7] The exploitation suffered by the British 'working class' (Kitching's inverted commas indicate that he is here referring to the 'traditional' working class), though no longer necessarily associated with 'crude material deprivation', has been such as to produce a purely 'defensive', 'economistic', and anti-revolutionary consciousness. Conversely, 'the most imaginative and self-confident groups and individ-uals, and thus those most likely to adopt radical positions, are those who objectively are the least oppressed. One may even risk a generalization to the effect that consciousness of oppression and the desire to transform the world so as to be rid of oppression are inversely proportional to the 'objective' degree of oppression suffered.'[8]

The *real* constituency of socialism, then, consists of people with the necessary degree of intellectual and spiritual freedom, imagin-

---

[5] Kitching, p. 19.
[6] Ibid., pp. 24-5.
[7] Ibid., p. 25.
[8] Ibid., p. 25.

ation, self-confidence, and self-discipline to be receptive to the rational and humanitarian ideals of socialism, qualities that can come only with liberation from crude material concerns. Within the working class, this means 'mental labourers' — though Kitching fails to make it clear why *any* part of the working class should be privileged as the major constituency of socialism in preference to other social groups that may possess these qualities. It is also for this reason that socialists should encourage the development of capitalism, for its effect will be to expand the new elements of the working class, highly skilled and 'intellectually sophisticated' mental workers, while hastening the decline of the 'politically regressive' elements. It is, furthermore, useless to appeal to the material class interests of these potentially progressive elements, since they are above such crude considerations — that is, they should not be appealed to on the grounds that they belong to an exploited class. 'If it is to build upon its real constituency,' argues Kitching, 'the Left must also utilize the characteristic which gives it its greatest appeal amongst these people — its capacity for analysis and coherent argument. For if all the sections of the working class identified as the Left's real (rather than mythical) base have one characteristic in common, it is of course that they are involved in "mental labour" of various kinds'; and these are the characteristics 'which predispose these workers to the kind of rationalist humanitarian politics which, at its best, the Left can offer.'[9]

Similar principles apply, incidentally, to the question of whether democratic socialism can be established in poor or underdeveloped countries, as distinct from the prosperous nations of the capitalist West. It is, of course, commonly argued that democratic socialism is difficult, if not impossible, to implant in circumstances where economic development and primitive accumulation have yet to take place. Clearly, in conditions where rapid development, which almost inevitably occurs at the expense of the producing classes, takes place under the auspices of the state, the relations between the state and the people, especially the working class, are bound to be problematic. But Kitching's argument is a different one: again, the point is that the problem lies in the intellectual and moral failings of the poor and labouring classes themselves and the absence of the 'self-conscious' and 'informed' political activity which only material prosperity can produce.[10] It is precisely the material

---

[9] Ibid., p. 21.
[10] Ibid., pp. 54-5.

motivations of their mass base, their concern with extreme deprivation, that has been the ruin of modern revolutions: 'For whilst
mass movements of the distressed have often been led by socialists
and revolutionaries, I am arguing here that it was precisely the
motivation of their mass base which rendered them fatally flawed
as socialist movements.'[11] The 'distressed', the masses whose
support for the revolution is born of 'desperation', are too easily
'bought off'. Revolutions are safer in the hands of the more prosperous elements who do not enter the movement primarily in
order to obtain material improvements.[12]

'To be a socialist,' Kitching concludes, 'is not to support the
working class's economic interests against those of the capitalist
class. It is to believe in a particular conception of the general
interest — a conception which involves transcending class self-
interest through abolishing classes themselves. Thus, the less
pressing questions of sheer economic survival and increasing consumption to the working class, the more that class can involve itself
(on political and ethical grounds and not simply out of economic
self-interest) in a debate about the "real" general interest.'[13]

To replace the narrow impulses of class interest with a concern
for the 'real' general interest, Kitching proposes to revive the traditions of 'republican virtue' and the 'civic ideal'. 'I have wanted,'
he writes, 'to remarry socialist ideas with much older concepts of
civitas, or republican "virtue", of the duties and powers as well as
the passive "rights" of the citizen',[14] 'the concept of a truly human
life as a public as well as a private life in which a citizen has
duties as well as rights, and in which the performance of civic
duties is the primary safeguard of liberty. This civic ideal, born in
Periclean Athens, beloved of the Machiavelli of *The Discourses*
and reasserted by Rousseau, exercised a profound influence on
Marx (who after all began life as a classical scholar) and is, in my
view, at the heart of his fragmentary vision of the communist
society.'[15] It is, then, above all to the identity of its constituents as
citizens, and not as members of a class, that socialism must appeal.

Before we take a closer look at all this, one final point in
Kitching's argument is worth noting because of its implications for
the larger theoretical questions associated with the NTS and its

---

[11] Ibid., p. 36.
[12] Ibid., p. 37.
[13] Ibid., pp. 62-3.
[14] Ibid., p. 131.
[15] Ibid., p. 33.

insistence on the autonomy of politics from economics and class. Kitching does not accept this principle without qualification — or rather, he would formulate it more precisely. He certainly accepts the non-correspondence principle, but he wants to defend Marx's political economy from those who have been over-zealous in rejecting its 'economism' and 'reductionism'. He accomplishes this rescue of Marx's political economy, however, by insisting on the narrow limits of its explanatory value: 'I have tried to demonstrate that Marx's political economy is capable of generating a small number of important but quite narrow propositions even about contemporary capitalism, which however carry no necessary (i.e. logically necessary) political consequences, or consciousness consequences.'[16] What Kitching does, in short, is to localize and contain 'economic' phenomena within their own appropriate sphere and to insulate political forces and conflicts from them. So, for all his 'defence' of Marx, Kitching has taken us emphatically back to the non-correspondence principle.

At the same time, Kitching's dismissal of the traditional working class as revolutionary agent is based on what might be regarded as a highly deterministic view of the pressures exerted by material conditions upon consciousness. The more 'oppressed' people are, the less capable they are of freeing their minds for civic virtue and socialism. Again, however, the critical point is that this extreme economic determinism, this rigid correspondence between economic and political forces, is not universal but specific to particular material conditions. The degree to which ideology and politics are determined by material class concerns varies according to material conditions themselves. In other words, the extent to which 'base' determines 'superstructure' varies, so that, for example, 'in poor capitalist and socialist societies the material "base" determines the "superstructure" of politics in a relatively crude way....'[17] In prosperous countries, by contrast, politics can achieve a greater autonomy — precisely in proportion to the larger numbers of people capable of freeing their minds from crude material concerns. Similarly, the traditional working class is relatively unfit for socialism because the consciousness of such workers is materialistically determined, while mental workers are more free to pursue rationalistic and humanitarian goals, republican and civic virtues.

---

[16] Ibid., p. 164.
[17] Ibid., p. 55.

In other words, the autonomy of politics and ideology once again seems to mean that anything is possible — *except* that the 'traditional' working class might act as the agent of social transformation. Only the material conditions of 'oppressed' classes are binding, determining particular ideologies and politics — ideologies and politics that are *anti*-socialist. Other people are free to be persuaded by rational discourse, ethical debate, and a concern for the general interest.

With his conception of 'civic' or 'republican' virtue, and the rationality, restraint and concern for the general interest that these virtues entail, Kitching has at last supplied a collective motivation to replace class interest in the struggle for socialism. In fact, it can be argued that this is the only coherent account of social motivation which is compatible with the NTS, its detachment from class, its amorphous constituency, and the abstraction of its universalistic goals. And *citizenship* is perhaps the most appropriate social category to describe the collective identity of a constituency not bound together or motivated by material conditions or class; whose identity, objectives, and propensity to act collectively are constructed 'at the ideological and political levels'; which is moved by some abstract impulse for 'democracy'; and whose interest in socialist goals depends upon civic virtue, self-restraint, discipline, and a rational commitment to the 'general interest'. If Kitching's 'civic ideal' does not accurately represent the essence of socialism as it is understood by the proponents of the NTS orthodoxy, they have yet to give us a better account.

II

The most striking thing about Kitching's argument is its affinity to older, non-socialist traditions of political thought. There are, of course, important similarities between his views and the liberalism of J.S. Mill, who toyed with a kind of socialism which depended upon the long-term education of the labouring classes, the elevation of their moral standards and the level of their intellectual sophistication. And Mill too proposed that, in the meantime, capitalism must be allowed to hold sway, 'until the better minds succeed in educating the others into better things. ... While minds are coarse they require coarse stimuli, and let them have them.'[18]

---

[18] John Stuart Mill, *Principles of Political Economy*, Harmondsworth 1970, p. 114.

But there are even more remarkable affinities between Kitching's argument (and, for that matter, Mill's) and a very long tradition of deeply conservative and anti-democratic thought. Since Plato first launched his bitter attack on Athenian democracy, one of the central tenets of conservative political philosophy has been that the life of true citizenship is available only to those whose conditions of life render them free of material necessity. Plato's so-called philosophical idealism was, in fact, profoundly materialist in its insistence that specific social conditions determine the ability of people to free their souls from the bondage of the material world, the world of necessity and appearances, to reflect on higher things. Or, to put it another way, it was idealism for the rich, materialism for the poor. Virtue is knowledge, and both presuppose material freedom. The good life, the moral and rational life — and hence the life of philosophy and even citizenship — depend on such freedom, which comes only with a condition free of necessary labour and crude everyday material concerns. Plato attacked democracy on the grounds that it accorded political rights to the 'banausic' classes, the base mechanics and traders, the peasants and craftsmen, who constituted the majority of the Athenian citizen body, whose life of drudgery 'warped and maimed' their souls and rendered them incapable of moral and political judgment. The just *polis* was one in which the lower classes, driven by their baser appetites, submitted to rule by those whose souls and appetites were governed by reason.

Later historians have often echoed these sentiments, blaming the 'decline' of Athens on a vulgar materialism which invaded Athenian society at the expense of civic virtue, as the banausic multitude gained ascendancy over its natural superiors. One particularly notable theme in this historical literature has been a distinction between 'political' and 'economic' man, the one driven by motives of civic honour and glory, the other by crudely material concerns. Typically, the dominance of 'political' man is identified with the period when Athenian society and culture were dominated by the traditional aristocracy, to whom the *demos* deferred (the suggestion here is that non-labouring classes who are free of material concerns because they live on the labour of others have no crude material or class interests). The triumph of 'economic' man came after the death of Pericles and the advent of the radical democracy, which brought to the fore the lower sorts whose lives of labour and trade determined their narrow, selfish, materialistic outlook, and elevated their 'demagogic' leaders, men 'of their own stamp'.[19]

Similar themes have run throughout the whole history of Western political thought, in which most of the 'classics' take it for granted that the poor and labouring classes, the 'multitude', and particularly the propertyless, who 'have no interest but the interest of breathing' (to quote Cromwell in the Putney Debates), are too irrational and irresponsible, and/or too servile and easily bought off, to be entrusted with political rights — in contrast to the propertied classes (at least forty-shilling freeholders) who have a 'fixed' or 'permanent interest' in the community and can therefore be expected to take their responsibilities seriously.

Needless to say, the same reasoning has affected interpretations of modern revolutions. The masses, driven by the crude imperatives of material deprivation, poverty, hunger, and exploitation, and with no constructive, rational purpose of their own, are easy prey to unscrupulous and power-hungry demagogues or the blandishments of material gain. One analysis of revolution which bears a striking resemblance to Kitching's is that of Hannah Arendt. For her, the American Revolution was the only true one, driven by the purely 'political' impulse to make a new beginning, to found a new political order, an order of freedom. The French Revolution, like those that succeeded it, was fatally flawed by the intrusion of the 'social question' into the autonomous realm of politics, the invasion of the public sphere, the 'political space', by the hungry mob who, impelled by raw material needs, could never be motivated by the pure desire for liberty. In the end, even the American Revolution was corrupted, 'under the impact of a continual mass immigration from Europe', as society 'fell more and more under the sway of the poor themselves, and hence came under the guidance of the ideals born out of poverty, as distinguished from those principles which had inspired the foundation of freedom.'[20] Indeed, the rot had been there from the beginning, because the country had always been not only the land of liberty and civic virtue 'but also' (in Arendt's words)

the promised land of those whose conditions hardly had prepared them for comprehending either liberty or virtue. It is

---

[19] This kind of language is used even by a widely respected and generally judicious historian like Victor Ehrenberg. See, for example, *The People of Aristophanes: A Sociology of Old Attic Comedy*, New York 1962, pp. 360-73.

[20] Hannah Arendt, *On Revolution*, New York 1965, p. 136.

still Europe's poverty that has taken its revenge in the ravages with which American prosperity and American mass society increasingly threaten the whole political realm. The hidden wish of poor men is not 'To each according to his needs,' but 'To each according to his desires.' And while it is true that freedom can come only to those whose needs have been fulfilled, it is equally true that it will escape those who are bent upon living for their desires.

Nothing could be further from the Marxist principle that oppression and exploitation are the surest source of struggles for emancipation.

It is true that Gavin Kitching, unlike this long tradition of conservative thinkers, does, on the face of it, seem to treat the working class — or at least some part of it — as the agent of social transformation; and he does appear to regard some degree of oppression and exploitation — albeit the milder sorts — as a condition for belonging to the 'real' constituency of socialism. Nevertheless, by his explicit criteria, political competence — the ability to be motivated by humanitarian goals, ethical concerns, and rational principles — varies in direct proportion to freedom from oppression, from material necessity, and from a life of manual drudgery. Thus it would seem that, as for Plato, knowledge is virtue is — or at least presupposes — freedom from material necessity. Within the working class, this means that 'mental labourers' are more politically suitable than manual labourers or, worse yet, the poor; but what reason do we have for supposing that capitalists themselves, and especially educated ones, may not be even more the natural constituents of socialism than are wage-earning clerical workers, or even salaried university lecturers? Or why not adopt the truly aristocratic principle according to which even trade and commerce are vulgar and servile activities — in which case the Oxbridge-educated landed gentleman who lives the life of a leisured rentier would make the most promising recruit for the left? It is no great comfort to socialists of a more traditional stamp to know that Kitching, like Mill, believes — or hopes — that sometime in the distant future the masses can aspire to the knowledge that is virtue.

Placed against the historical background of this conservative and anti-democratic tradition, the flaws in Kitching's argument — not to mention its political implications — become painfully evident. Gross distortions of historical fact are required to sustain such reactionary judgments of popular movements, revolutions, and the moral and political capacities of the 'mob'. One might have thought, in any case, that this mode of analysing 'collective behaviour' had been laid to rest once and for all by the work of historians such as George Rudé and Edward Thompson. We have already had occasion to note how vacuous are those interpretations of, for example, the Russian Revolution — interpretations apparently accepted by Kitching — which see in the revolutionary masses little more than a blind mob, driven only by negative impulses and having to look to their declassed leaders for any rational, positive transformative purpose. While it is clearly true that the revolution failed to produce a democratic socialism, it would be perverse and fatuous in the extreme to blame that failure on the preoccupation of the masses with their own material concerns at the expense of truly revolutionary ideals.

It may be worth mentioning that the civic ideal, to which Kitching attaches such importance, was born — in Athens as he correctly says — in conditions that run directly counter to his assumptions. First, the civic ideal itself, far from originating as a 'pure', disembodied ethical principle detached from 'crude' material interests, was born out of the class relations of early Attica. Second, the elements of the Athenian population whose objectives were most directly expressed by the civic ideal were not the disinterested intellectuals or philosopher kings of Kitching's and Plato's dreams, nor yet the prosperous classes with the time, leisure, and freedom from material cares to 'reflect upon themselves and upon society', but rather the ordinary peasants and craftsmen who had most to gain from a dilution of aristocratic privilege in the common, levelling identity of citizenship and the incorporation of aristocratic property and power into the jurisdiction of the civic community. It was these classes whose material interests were most directly reflected in the civic principle, which set membership in the civic community, the *polis*, against the particularisms of kinship, clan, and friendship-group — the foundations of aristocratic property and power — and counterposed the identity of citizenship to the distinctions of blood and family connections. Who is to say that the moral worth of the civic ideal is devalued by its 'low' and 'vulgar' birth or its origin in material interests? Who is to say that the 'base' passions which gave it life were unfit to produce an ethical ideal at all?

This is worth mentioning because so much of the new 'true' socialism, with its assault on 'class-reductionism' and 'economism', tends to take the form of devaluing 'crude' material interests as a possible source of positive political impulses — perhaps in the spirit of the philosophical tradition which treats 'interest' and morality as diametrically opposed. No doubt there are a great many philosophical issues to be debated here; but for our purposes, the important thing to keep in mind is that this philosophical opposition has often been associated with the view that people driven by 'interest' (generally meaning material interest) are by definition morally bankrupt, and that the 'lower sorts', the poor and labouring classes who are most imperatively driven by material concerns, are the most morally bankrupt of all.

There has never been a significant expression of 'republican' virtues and the civic ideal which has been divorced from material interests in the way that Kitching's analysis suggests. There has never been a class-neutral civic humanism. The republican motivation has always had firm roots in the real material conditions of specific social groups and in their interests as opposed to others. The republicanism of Machiavelli, for example, which Kitching approvingly cites, represented an impassioned attack upon the Florentine patriciate on behalf of the middling merchants and craftsmen who had been the backbone of the Republic during what Machiavelli regarded as its golden age, but who had been substantially disenfranchised since. Rousseau, another of Kitching's authorities, was probably the most democratic of the major political thinkers before Marx, speaking on behalf of the small producer against oppression by the privileged classes and the absolutist state.

It is, incidentally, interesting to compare Rousseau's convictions about the relation between social conditions and civic virtue to Kitching's. Rousseau has often been charged with 'totalitarian' implications on the grounds that he allegedly demanded the subordination of particular interests to some abstract 'general will', which required the imposition of an oppressive self-denying virtue. Yet Rousseau, more than any other major thinker before Marx, recognized that there can be no 'general will', no 'common good', where there is no real community of interest, and that there can be no such community of interest where some human beings are exploited by others, so that their interests are unavoidably antagonistic. In other words, the implication of his argument was that there can be no civic virtue without foundation in the realities of material life; and to strive for the civic ideal is, in the first instance, to strive for the abolition of the social inequalities which make one person's loss another one's gain and inevitably make them enemies by interest. It would seem, then, that for Rousseau, in sharp contrast to Kitching, civic virtue is not the precondition of the good society; on the contrary, the good society alone can make true civic virtue possible. And it can be argued that for Rousseau as for Marx — again in sharp contrast to Kitching — the most reliable impulse toward the common good is not some elevated, rootless moral sense, but the passion of the exploited and oppressed to be free of exploitation and oppression.

There is a rather nice irony in Kitching's conclusions. In an appendix to *Rethinking Socialism*, he proposes to rescue the left from its tendency toward elitism. This elitism, he argues, is rooted in the isolation of socialist intellectuals, 'the increasing divorce of Left intellectuals from any effective political activity. ...'[21] The solution, he continues, 'lies not in theoretical criticism but in finding a more viable and popular Left politics,' which will bring leftist intellectuals back in touch with the 'people'. There is, of course, some justice in Kitching's strictures against the 'elitist' tendencies of many on the left and their isolation from mass popular movements. But given the logic of his argument about the 'real' constituency of socialism, the intellectual and moral incapacities of the 'oppressed', and the particular qualities to which a socialist movement must appeal, the irony of his plea for a non-elitist politics is truly exquisite. Socialists are castigated for being out of touch with ordinary people, only to be told that being in touch with ordinary people means understanding that they are intellectually and morally unfit to receive the socialist message, and that they will continue to be so until a long era of capitalist prosperity has raised the general level of 'intellectual sophistication' to the standard achieved today by only a few. What price democracy?

Clearly not all NTS would subscribe to Kitching's rather drastic view; but it can be argued that a similar contradiction lies at the heart of the whole NTS project. If socialism has no roots in material conditions but is essentially an ideological and political construct, a very heavy burden falls upon the autonomous artificers of ideology and politics. It is no longer simply a question of acknowledging — and who would deny it? — that developments in material conditions and production relations are not enough to create a revolutionary movement, and that the building of socialism

---

[21] Kitching, p. 177.

requires great efforts to organize the existing social forces and interests. We are now effectively being told that there *exist* no such social interests and forces. They must be *created* by ideology and politics. It is thus no longer even a matter of 'vanguardism', since there are no independently existing social forces which leaders can claim to lead or in whose interests they can claim to act. The social forces and interests that must be harnessed and led in the struggle for socialism have no identity, no existence, apart from what their ideological leaders impart to them. It is not even possible to speak of 'substitutionism'. What does not exist cannot be replaced or represented. It must be created, invented, contrived. This is the awesome task our new ideological and political leaders have taken upon themselves. Surely we have reached the last word in socialist elitism.

9

Socialism and Democracy

We have noted that an essential component of the NTS programme is a detachment of socialist objectives from the material goals of classes and a new emphasis on 'non-material', universalistic, humanistic ends — such as democratic control, peace, a health-giving environment, and the quality of life, or the satisfaction of 'primary human needs'. Of these objectives, the most general and the one that has been subjected to the most systematic theorization is democracy. As a political programme, the NTS can in fact be more or less identified with the strategy of 'democratization', developed most completely, but not exclusively, by Eurocommunist theorists. Tracing the programme of democratization to its roots and its basic assumptions may tell us a great deal about the NTS project in general. It will certainly put to the most rigorous test any suspicions that the project may have anti-democratic and elitist implications.

In a collection of papers entitled *Marxism and Democracy*, originally presented at a conference in December 1978 organized by the Sociology Group of the Communist Party of Great Britain, the editor, Alan Hunt, outlines a conception of democracy which might be accepted by all new 'true' socialists, stressing the 'relative autonomy' or 'indeterminacy' of democratic practices and invoking the non-correspondence principle:

> Forms of democratic action and organization do not carry an automatic class label. There is nothing specifically 'bourgeois' about parliamentary elections. Nor can they be counterposed to a system of recallable delegates as the essence of proletarian democracy. The class consequences of particular forms of democratic practices are only the result of the balance of forces at the specific time. Parliamentary democracy is thus bourgeois only in the sense that historically it has existed under conditions

in which the bourgeoisie has been the hegemonic class. ...

The project of socialist revolution must be seen as the completion, as against the destruction, of the historical stage initiated by the advent of capitalism; the essential condition of this advance is the removal of impediments imposed by the specifically capitalist organization of economic and social life. ... Thus the realization of democracy involves not the smashing of bourgeois democracy but its completion, liberated from the undemocratic framework of capitalist relations. Political competition, representative government, political rights do not bear an ahistorical capitalist essence but provide elements whose transformation makes possible the attainment of the socialist project. ...

A political perspective which emphasizes the necessity and possibility of the expansion of democracy as a precondition of socialist advance requires a radically different view of socialist strategy. First it necessitates a changed strategy of alliances in which the problem is no longer how other classes, for example the petty bourgeoisie or the peasantry, are to be limited as subordinate partners to the working class. If classes are not seen as homogeneous entities it follows that political forces do not bear a direct or necessary relationship to classes. ...

The limitations of democracy within capitalist society stem from its primarily formal characteristics. The major thrust of the argument advanced in this collection is that this is not an absolute barrier.[1]

There ought to be no dispute concerning the identification of socialism with the extension of democratic control to the very foundations of social organization. This principle in itself is not, however, what distinguishes the NTS from other conceptions of socialism. Its distinctive characteristic is the abstraction and autonomization of democracy, an insistence on the 'indeterminacy' of bourgeois democracy and its lack of any particular class character, and above all the conviction that the (relative?) autonomy of bourgeois democracy makes it in principle expandable into socialist democracy. Socialism is thus merely the completion of capitalism, and the progression from one to the other can be conceived as a seamless continuum.

---

[1] Alan Hunt ed., *Marxism and Democracy*, London 1980, pp. 16-18.

All this further implies that, if the class opposition between capital and labour remains critical in the 'economic' sphere, this is not necessarily the relevant opposition at the political level. Indeed if it were, we could no longer conceive of the transition from capitalism to socialism as an unbroken passage, since the process would be interrupted at the point where antagonistic class interests intervene. Instead of class, the central categories at the political level are politically constituted entities, often called 'power blocs' or even 'officialdom' on the one hand, and the 'people' on the other. Both these categories — but especially the latter — are in principle capable of infinite expansion, by ideological and political means. The task of socialist strategy is to constitute the 'people' out of the available forces, more or less irrespective of class, depending upon the prevailing circumstances and varying suscep- tibilities to democratic discourse on the part of existing social groups, and thereafter to lead the 'people' against the 'power bloc' or 'officialdom' in order to extend democracy beyond the formal- political limits of bourgeois democracy.

In some formulations, the 'people', though conceived as inde- pendent of class and as not itself determined by class, is still spoken of as an alliance of those classes most susceptible to anti- power-bloc sentiments. In other formulations, the detachment from class is more complete. So, for example, Barry Hindess argues that: 'The problem is not to establish the class character of democracy, to identify the class character of political forces, to construct alliances between classes and other interests, or what- ever. It is to mobilize effective support around socialist objectives out of the forces, struggles and ideologies operative in particular societies.'[2] The clear implication is that there is no necessity for the relevant forces to be constituted, directly or indirectly, by class relations. Any connection between politically relevant forces — such as the 'people' — and class forces will, it appears, be purely contingent or 'conjunctural'.

With political struggle thus detached in varying degrees from class conflict, any nostalgic adherence to the Marxist doctrine that class struggle will be the moving force in the transition from capitalism to socialism would seem to depend on the principle (ar- ticulated, as we have seen, by Chantal Mouffe) that the 'class struggle' does not require class agents. At any rate, the motivating

---

[2] Barry Hindess, 'Marxism and Parliamentary Democracy', in Hunt, p. 42.

drive in the transition is here dissociated from class interests and relocated in a disembodied democratic impulse, which, though it may 'conjuncturally' coincide with certain class interests, is autonomous from them.

The best that can be said about this approach is that what it offers as a solution is little more than a restatement of the problem. It is undoubtedly important to insist that democracy belongs to the essence of socialism, and that a major task of the socialist movement is to recapture the terrain of democratic struggle, which has too often been ceded to 'liberal' or 'bourgeois' politics. The NTS, however, with its abstraction and autonomization of democracy, does little to advance the issue. The expansion of democracy, which is here treated as a means, a strategy, for the construction of socialism, is not a means or a strategy at all but rather the very goal that must be attained. If the democratic struggle is meant not only to improve the application of bourgeois democratic political forms but also, as Bob Jessop suggests, to encompass the 'fundamental social relations' that underlie them, if, in particular, 'the realization of democracy requires the reorganization of the relations of production to eliminate class-based inequalities in political freedom,'[3] then we are really back where we started.

The reformulation of the socialist project proposed by Hunt, Hindess, Jessop, et al. simply conceptualizes out of existence the very problems that need to be solved. It is merely a theoretical conjuring trick, a play on words, that makes the strategy of extending bourgeois democracy look like a method for achieving the transition to socialism and makes the transformation of a 'popular democratic' movement into a socialist movement seem relatively unproblematic. It depends in the first instance on conflating the various meanings and aspects of 'democracy', so that the question of socialist democracy becomes merely a quantitative one, a matter of *extension, expansion.* We lose sight of the chasm between the forms of democracy that are compatible with capitalism and those that represent a fundamental challenge to it. We no longer see the gap in the continuum of 'democratization', a gap which corresponds precisely to the opposition of class interests. In other words, we are induced to forget that the struggle between capitalism and socialism can be conceived precisely as a struggle over different forms of democracy, and that the dividing line between the two

---

[3] Bob Jessop, 'The Political Indeterminacy of Democracy', in Hunt, p. 63.

forms can be located at exactly the point where fundamental class interests diverge.

Colin Mercer, in the same collection of essays, catalogues the 'multiple definitions' of democracy in order to demonstrate that Marxists have been wrong 'to assign democracy to a necessary class-belonging.' This, he argues, is 'complicit with the liberal state's own conception of it,' that is, the claim by capitalism to be the sole possessor of democracy.[4] Mercer seeks to challenge this claim by outlining the various connotations of 'democracy', many of which have no association with capitalism and are quite distinct from bourgeois democracy. His conclusion is that the concept of democracy suggests 'a complexity which denies the possibility of collapsing the word and the reality of democracy into any one of its possible meanings — its representative form, its popular form or its class form. It must in effect embrace all of these. There is no pure "bourgeois" democracy which can be posed as simply opposite to "proletarian" democracy or replaced by it in a revolutionary *fiat*. The articulation of these meanings of democracy is central to the development of a concept of transition in Marxist theory and practice which would reject the simple dichotomy of "formal" and "direct" democracy and its associated strategic models'.[5]

The flaws in this argument are obvious. The very diversity of meanings in the concept of democracy highlights the differences between bourgeois democracy and other forms; and it is precisely the conflation of these meanings that has supported the capitalist claim to exclusive ownership of democracy, encouraging us to identify democracy as such with its bourgeois-parliamentary forms. Yes of course it must be the objective of socialism to achieve democracy in all its multiplicity — including an extension of those bourgeois-democratic forms which serve as a protection against arbitrary power and not simply as a cover for capitalist domination. But, in a sense, it is this very objective that brings socialism into fundamental conflict with capitalism. It is precisely the multiplicity of facets contained in the socialist meaning of democracy that makes it impossible to conceive of the transition from capitalism to socialism as nothing more than an extension and completion of the democratic forms nurtured by capitalism. The extension of

---

[4] Colin Mercer, 'Revolutions, Reforms or Reformulations? Marxist Discourse on Democracy', in Hunt, p. 109.

[5] Ibid., p. 110.

bourgeois democracy may be important in itself; but there is a qualitative difference between democracy conceived in formal-juridical terms and democracy conceived, for example, as entailing the self-organization of freely associated producers. The fact that some institutions of the former may not be in principle antagonistic to the latter does not mean that all social interests compatible with the one are also compatible with the other. It may be that some class interests which are compatible with, and even served by, bourgeois-democratic forms are irrevocably antagonistic to democracy in the sphere of production relations. A careless insistence on the non-correspondence of politics and 'economics' and the 'indeterminacy' of democracy may obscure the fact that, while liberal democracy can be compatible with capitalism precisely because it leaves production relations intact, socialist democracy by definition entails the transformation of production relations.

In fact, the non-correspondence principle in a sense mirrors the basic presupposition of capitalist political ideology, the sharp separation between political and economic or social spheres, the very separation that makes possible the development of liberal-democratic forms while leaving capitalist production relations intact. It is this divide that confines 'democracy' to a formal political-juridical sphere and firmly excludes it from the substance of social relations. The hegemony of capitalist ideology depends upon retaining a distinction between the principles of citizenship and the rules that apply in non-political domains.

Of course an attack on capitalist hegemony must take the form of challenging this ideological division and expanding the meaning of democracy, but the problem is hardly just a linguistic one. The divide between the spheres in which capitalism can permit democracy to operate (and even here it can do so only up to a point) and those in which it cannot, corresponds to the insurmountable divisions between antagonistic class interests. Here, if not before, there must be a break in the continuum from one form of democracy to the other; here, if not before, in other words, class-determinations will become decisive — and no amount of verbal conjuring will spirit the problem away.

That bourgeois democracy is 'indeterminate' and in principle classless has been the fundamental premise of social democratic programmes, just as it is the presupposition of the NTS. Before we look at some of the inadequacies of this axiom, it needs to be stressed that its importance has been vastly exaggerated. Even if we accept that the political and juridical forms of liberal democracy are not class-specific and need not serve the interests of capital, what does this actually tell us about the transition from capitalism to socialism? Does not the character of the transition depend less on the class-associations of bourgeois democracy than on the class-specificity of socialism? Are not the NTS asking us in effect to accept not only that liberal democracy is 'indeterminate' but that socialist democracy is equally so, in the sense that it represents no fundamental challenge to any class interest and that all classes have an equal interest in attaining it? It is, of course, true that the force of socialism lies in its uniquely legitimate claim to 'indeterminacy' or, more precisely, universality — as representing the interests of all humanity against those of particular classes; but because the fulfillment of that claim presupposes the abolition of all classes and class exploitation, the socialist project must, in the first instance, represent some class interests and oppose others. So the whole NTS project, like the more traditional programmes of social democracy, to the extent that it proceeds from the 'indeterminacy' of bourgeois democracy to a view of socialism as merely an extension of bourgeois democratic forms, rests on a logical fault. Neither the classlessness of these forms nor the formal compatibility of liberal democratic institutions with socialism would tell us very much about the conditions of the struggle for socialism or the barriers that stand in its way.

The confusion of issues at the heart of the NTS project is illustrated by the following typical observation: '... once it is accepted that there is no Chinese Wall between "bourgeois" and "proletarian" democracy the Leninist idea of "smashing" the "bourgeois state" becomes unacceptable. There is bound to be a conflict between different types of institution, but not necessarily an irreconcilable contradiction.'[6] What, then, does it mean to say that there is no 'Chinese Wall'? At best, it means that the institutional forms of parliamentary democracy are not in themselves antithetical to socialism, that they need not be destroyed as a pre-condition to socialism, that they are not in themselves useless to socialists in their struggle to transform society, and perhaps even that they may still have their uses after the destruction of capitalism. With certain qualifications, these are not unreasonable propositions; at least they may serve as a useful corrective to

---

[6] Geoff Hodgson, *The Democratic Economy: A New Look at Planning, Markets and Power*, Harmondsworth 1984, p. 55.

uncritical applications of Leninist principles which treat liberal-democratic forms as if they 'correspond' to capitalism so completely and exclusively that they can be dismissed — and must even be destroyed — as the enemies of socialism. These are points to which we shall return. There is, however, more to the 'indeterminacy' argument than this. The absence of a 'Chinese Wall' between different forms of democracy means that democracy 'can grow, first within capitalism, and then beyond it', and apparently also that a focus on democracy in the struggle to transform society can transcend divisions between socialists and non-socialists. In other words, the transition from liberal democracy to socialist democracy can take place by means of more or less non-antagonisic increments, as one set of democratic institutions is imperceptibly transformed into another by extension, by supplementing inadequacies and filling in gaps.

What all this means is that, by some neat conceptual conjuring, the transition from capitalism to socialism has been transformed into a relatively non-antagonistic process of institutional reform. But does the transformation of society and the relations of production become less problematic and antagonistic simply because we call it an extension of democracy rather than a transition from capitalism to socialism? When, for example, Hodgson maintains that, although 'it is possible that future developments will lead to the erosion or end of the limited democracy that survives within capitalism', the incompatibility of capitalism and democracy 'is not predetermined or inevitable,'[7] how far does he want to go? Is *any* amount of democracy compatible with capitalism? If not, and if there is a point at which the expansion of democracy by definition means the end of capitalism, because it means the end of capitalist domination and exploitation, will that point pass unnoticed simply because we call it another incremental change in the process of extending democracy, instead of a revolutionary change in the relations of production?

It is not, in the end, the institutional forms of parliamentary democracy that are in question. A case could be made, as we shall see in the next chapter, that at least some of these forms may serve a useful purpose even under socialism. The critical point, however, is that liberal democracy entails a separation of political rights and powers from economic and social ones, as well as a limited and

---

[7] Ibid., p. 123.

formalistic conception of political democracy itself. This separation belongs to the essence of liberal democracy; it is not just a flaw in the system. Parliamentary democracy is not simply a form of representation; it is a particular delineation of spheres of power, a specific definition and isolation of the spheres in which democratic principles may be allowed to prevail. It is, in fact, a *denial*, as we have seen, of democracy in the sense of popular power. And this delimitation is the very foundation of private property and its power in capitalist society. In other forms of property and exploitation, the exploitative force of property depends upon a unity of political and economic power, so that political rights must remain exclusive. In capitalism, where exploitative power does not rest directly on the exclusive possession of political force but on absolute private property and the exclusion of producers from it, it is possible (though not necessary) to extend political rights more or less universally — but then the power of property depends upon a rigid separation between political and economic spheres. This is a structural characteristic of capitalism; and it means that any effort to reunite these separate spheres, at the point where it challenges capitalist power and property, will entail all the antagonisms and struggles which attend the decisive battle between exploiting and exploited classes. No socialist strategy can be taken seriously that ignores or obscures the class barriers beyond which the extension of democracy becomes a challenge to capitalism.

There is also another danger in this insistence on the 'indeterminacy' of democracy, as we saw in Laclau and Mouffe's conception of the 'democratic revolution'. No doubt at least some of the contributors to the Hunt volume would emphatically dissociate themselves from the extreme formulations of Laclau and Mouffe, but there is a certain logic in the detachment of democracy from social determinations that impels us toward those extremes. Stripped of its association with specific social interests, 'democracy' in the NTS becomes an abstract ideal. If as a political objective it reflects the motivations of any actually existing social being, and is not simply an abstract good with no power to sustain collective social action, it seems that we must postulate some autonomous drive for 'democratization' residing in the depths of human nature. We are given little guidance as to who in particular might want or need democracy, whether some kinds of people might want or need more — or different aspects — than others, how a social force capable of bringing it about might come into being — or indeed why there should be any difficulty or conflict about it at all. If, on the other hand, the democratic drive is not universal, or not immediately so, and yet at the same time is not constituted by material conditions and class relations but is constructed by ideology and politics more or less 'autonomously', then are we not again thrown back upon the old utopian elitism which Marx himself denounced? Must we not look to some privileged producers of 'discourse' to implant the democratic impulse from without, giving a collective identity to an otherwise shapeless mass, creating the 'people' and then imparting to them a socialist or democratic spirit which they cannot bring forth out of their own resources?

10

Capitalism, Liberalism, Socialism

I

In the NTS project, the transition from capitalism to socialism is in effect replaced by a transition from *liberal democracy* to socialism, and the problems of the socialist struggle are conceptualized away by assuming that there is a fundamentally non-contradictory continuum from one to the other. The structure of capitalism and its system of classes become largely irrelevant to the problem of transition, and the connection between liberal democracy and capitalism is treated as purely contingent or 'conjunctural'. Liberal democracy is 'indeterminate', class-neutral. The NTS is thus predicated on the very mystification that gives liberal democracy its ideological force in sustaining the hegemony of capitalism. The power of socialist thought to counter the hegemony of capitalist ideology is thereby effectively neutralized.

There is a version of this NTS argument (echoing yet again the platitudes of traditional social democracy) which suggests not only that the relation between liberal democracy and capitalism is purely 'conjunctural', or that the 'democracy' in liberal democracy is 'indeterminate', but that there is a basic *contradiction* between liberal democracy and capitalism, that their conjunctural connection has produced a 'contradictory totality' which makes it possible to transform the liberal democratic state into an instrument for effecting the transition to socialism. In fact, on reflection, the NTS project of achieving socialism by extending liberal democracy probably implies precisely this. At any rate, it is certainly the assumption underlying the analysis of the 'democratic revolution' presented by Laclau and Mouffe.

The case has been made explicitly by two Americans — not surprisingly, given the tremendously important ideological role played by the mythology of 'democracy' in the United States. (In what other country is the national self-image as a *democracy*, indeed the ultimate democracy, so assiduously cultivated and so central to the dominant ideology?) Samuel Bowles and Herbert Gintis have fleshed out the 'contradiction' between liberal democracy and capitalism by arguing that

> The juxtaposition of liberal democracy and capitalism itself introduces a contradictory element into the reproduction of the social relations of production, because of the discrepant forms of political participation supported by each. Capitalism structures practices through rights in *property*, to be exercised by owners or their representatives, while liberal democracy vests rights in *persons*, formally independent from ownership. As a consequence, popular struggles in liberal democratic capitalist societies typically attempt to apply the rules of the game based on person rights to contests within the sphere of capitalist production, where their application directly confronts and contests the power of capital. Capital, conversely, has historically attempted to apply the rules of the game based on property rights to the politics and structure of the state.[1]

In a footnote, they explain that 'By liberal democracy we mean a state characterized by generalized civil liberties and universal adult suffrage, by its substantial separation from control over the allocation of social labor and the disposition of surplus labor time, and by formal rules of participation by rights equally vested in persons.' This definition — which is reasonable enough — suggests that from the very outset Bowles and Gintis acknowledge, at least implicitly, the barrier separating the proper domain of 'democracy' in liberal democracy (the formal juridical and political sphere), from the domain in which its writ does not run (the sphere of production relations); and they acknowledge by their definition that this barrier is not an incidental by-product of the 'conjunctural' association between liberal-democracy and capitalism, but that it is inherent in the meaning of liberal democracy itself. This would seem to mean that there is *no* fundamental contradiction between capitalism and liberal democracy but that, on the contrary, they share the same essential premise on which capitalist hegemony rests, namely the formal separation of the 'political' and the 'economic' and the confinement of 'democracy' to an abstractly distinct

---

[1] Samuel Bowles and Herbert Gintis, 'The Crisis of Liberal Democratic Capitalism: The Case of the United States', *Politics and Society* 11, no. 1, 1982 p. 52.

political sphere consisting of formal procedures and juridical princ-iples. Bowles and Gintis do not, however, accept the implications of this structural compatibility, arguing instead that liberal demo-cracy is in principle inimical to capitalism because it permits the 'transportation' of discourses and practices from one sphere, where 'rights in persons' prevail, to the other, based on 'rights in property'.

Without engaging in a philosophical debate about whether 'rights in persons' as understood by liberal democracy entail the kind of opposition to 'rights in property' that this argument demands, let us examine what the 'contradiction' means in practice. Bowles and Gintis begin by suggesting that their argu-ment will rest on the ways in which the powers vested in the working class and other popular elements by the liberal democratic state have obstructed the accumulation process, effecting a 'distributional shift adverse to capital' while also weakening the capacity of unemployment, the 'reserve army', to discipline labour. At this stage, then, the argument amounts to little more than say-ing that, on the whole, life tends to be more difficult for capitalists when workers have the right to organize and vote. This is hardly a startling or objectionable proposition, but it derives much of its exaggerated force in their argument from a persistent neglect of other prominent aspects of the liberal democratic state, not least its perfectly efficient utilization as a coercive instrument for repressing recalcitrant 'persons' — as if this coercive character were somehow incidental to, or even in contradiction with, the essential character of the liberal-democratic state.

It turns out, however, that the argument about the effects of liberal democracy on the accumulation process will not quite do in any case. In spite of their elaborate statistics, Bowles and Gin-tis come to some rather lame conclusions: 'the impact of the [distributional] shift on the accumulation process as a whole has not been adequately explored, and we cannot offer a definitive analysis here,' though various popular political gains 'appear to have been costly to capital'.[2] Soon we discover that the ground of the argument has shifted, as if the authors have lost confidence in their own optimistic assessment of liberal democracy. The empha-sis is no longer on the ability of liberal-democratic institutions and practices to transform or impede capitalism, but simply on the

---

[2] Ibid., pp. 75-7.

capacity of liberal-democratic *ideology* to expose the evils of the capitalist system. Liberal democracy, it seems, has not so decisively altered the balance of power between capital and labour as to prevent capital from responding to the current crisis by clawing back the gains won by 'popular' elements, nor, for that matter, from doing so by using the existing state apparatus — though Bowles and Gintis have surprisingly little to say about the relative ease with which the 'New Right' in Britain and the United States has made use of existing state institutions to attack the structure of social welfare which these two authors apparently regard as the essence of liberal democracy, again as if the repressive organs of the state were somehow incidental to its nature and purpose. Liberal democracy has apparently not even succeeded in shifting the terrain of struggle from what we were led to believe was the less advantageous economic terrain — the home-ground of capital — to the allegedly more advantageous terrain of the state, nor has liberal democracy displaced the essential antagonism between capital and labour. It even turns out that the power of organized labour in the US has been 'in decline, not ascendancy, during almost the entire postwar boom.'[3] In fact, we now recall that we were told at the outset that 'the working class has relinquished all claims for control over production, investment, and international economic policy in return for a relatively high level of employment and a secure claim on distributional gains.'[4] In other words, we now discover that when it really matters, when capital in crisis can no longer afford its concessions to 'popular' elements, the American working class, without a strong organization or a political representative of its own, finds itself disarmed in the face of an onslaught against its 'secure' gains, launched by capital with the help of the liberal-democratic state.

What, then, is the function of liberal democracy in prosecuting the struggle against capitalism? Suddenly we find ourselves in familiar territory:

Demands posed as universal rights and movements constituted by the universal discourse of liberal democracy are prone to become class demands and class movements. ...
The crisis of capital may thus hasten the realization that the

---

[3] Ibid., p. 82.
[4] Ibid., pp. 52-3.

struggle over universal rights — the right to participate in political decisions, the right of a free press — is a class struggle. If we are correct in this conjecture, the ongoing conflict over the reconstitution of the accumulation process may starkly reveal the anti-democratic imperatives of capitalism as a system and thus unify for socialists two of the most powerful potential mass issues in the US today: the defense and extension of democracy and the defense of living standards.

Capitalism may survive the encounter. But liberal democracy may well be radically transformed — either toward a corporate authoritarianism, as a condition of capital's survival, or toward an instrument, however imperfect, of popular power.[5]

A pretty feeble conclusion, one would have thought, after all the high hopes we were urged to invest in the 'contradiction' between liberal democracy and capitalism. So liberal democracy can go either way, depending on ... what? Could it be the balance of class forces? And if so, are we not again where we started?

In the end, the argument comes down yet again to the transformative effects of liberal-democratic *discourse*. Again, we are asked to rely on the power of its 'universal' demands to 'starkly reveal the anti-democratic imperatives of capitalism.' And again, we are back where we were with Laclau and Mouffe, or Hunt and Co. It might be legitimate to make a far more limited claim: that the values of the welfare state have been sufficiently embedded in capitalist culture to make the complete dismantling of social welfare institutions no longer an easy task; but this claim is very different from treating the discourse of liberal democracy as a major force for socialism. If it is the ideological effects of liberal democracy that count above all, then what about the many ways in which it *conceals* the 'anti-democratic imperatives' of capitalism? What about the extent to which the mystifications of liberal democracy have *impeded* the development of class demands, and the ways in which its ideological apparatus has been deployed by representatives of capital for precisely this purpose? What about the effects of liberal-democratic institutions and practices in disorganizing the working class as a class by constituting them as isolated individual citizens, as against the collective identity and organization that they acquire at the 'level' of production relations

---

[5] Ibid., pp. 92-3.

and through everyday class struggles? And if the battle for socialism is to be renamed a 'democratic' struggle, will the change of
name alter the reality or transform the nature and conditions of class
struggle, with all the attendant oppositions of class interests and all
the obstacles it has to overcome?

II

Something more needs to be said about the role of liberal
democracy in sustaining the hegemony of capitalism. The question
is not an easy one; and if it is important not to fall into the very
mystifications that sustain that hegemony, it is no less important to
avoid dismissing liberal democracy as nothing more than a mystification. In what follows, therefore, the term 'liberal democracy' will
continue to be used instead of, say, 'bourgeois' or 'capitalist
democracy', if only because these terms in a sense prejudge the
issues in dispute. We are not quite ready to conflate 'liberalism'
entirely with capitalism.

The first question that should be raised has to do with the
nature of capitalist relations of production and the sense in which
they form the kernel of liberal democratic principles. This question
has important strategic implications. One could, as we have seen,
begin by assuming not only that the relation of liberal democracy
to capitalism is tangential and contingent, but even that liberal-
democratic 'freedom' and 'equality' are somehow *antithetical* to
capitalist domination and inequality. Social democratic revisionism
seems to have been based on such an assumption, with its strategy
of 'patchwork reform' and passive faith in some 'peaceful process
of dissolution'[6] which would eventually and more or less automatically transform capitalism into socialism. This strategy seems
to have been based on the premise that the liberty and equality of
bourgeois democracy were so antithetical to capitalism that the
mere maintenance of bourgeois juridical and political institutions,
assisted by reform, would produce a tension between freedom and
equality at this level and unfreedom and inequality at other levels
of society.[7] This tension would in a sense replace class struggle as

---

[6] This is how Marx describes the principles of German Social Democracy in his
circular letter to Bebel, Bracke, Liebknecht et al., of 17-18 September 1879.

[7] Cf. Lucio Colletti, 'Bernstein and the Marxism of the Second International', in
From Rousseau to Lenin, London 1972, pp. 92-7.

the motor of social transformation. At the other extreme might be a position that regards liberal democracy as so completely a mere reflection of capitalism that it must be regarded as simply a deception, a mystification. This is roughly the position of various ultra-left groups. Liberal-democratic capitalist states, according to this view, are not substantially different from authoritarian or even fascist forms of capitalism. If such radically divergent programmes are associated with different assessments of liberalism and its relation to capitalism, an attempt to situate liberalism in the capitalist mode of production cannot be an insignificant task for socialist political theory.

To determine the relation between liberalism and capitalism, one might begin with Marx's own account of juridical equality and freedom as an integral part of capitalist relations of production. Equality and freedom — of a particular kind — are, suggests Marx, inherent in exchange based on exchange values. The relation between subjects of exchange is a relationship of formal equality; moreover, it is a relationship in which the parties, recognizing each other as proprietors, 'as persons whose will penetrates their commodities'[8] and who appropriate each other's property not by force, are *free*. Capitalism, as a *generalized* system of commodity exchange, then, is the perfection of this form of juridical equality and freedom; but here, of course, freedom and equality acquire a rather special meaning since the particular exchange which constitutes the essence of capitalism is that between capital and labour, in which one party (juridically free and 'free' from the means of labour) has only his/her labour-power to sell. This means that the very object of the 'free' exchange between 'equals' is precisely the establishment of a particular social relation, a relation of unfreedom and domination which nevertheless retains, indeed is based on, the formal and juridical freedom and equality of the exchange relationship. Thus, wage-slavery, based on the commodification of labour-power, is characterized by a kind of 'freedom' and 'equality' that distinguishes this form of exploitation from all other relations between exploiter and exploited — master and slave, lord and serf — in which surplus-extraction relies more directly on relations of juridical or political domination and dependence.

Marx goes on to comment on the 'foolishness' of those socialists (specifically the French and in particular Proudhon, though he

---

[8] Karl Marx, *Grundrisse*, Harmondsworth 1972, p. 243.

might just as well be commenting on any number of modern social democrats and NTS) '... who want to depict socialism as the realization of the ideals of *bourgeois* society'[9] and argue that the freedom and equality characteristic of that society have simply been *perverted* by money, capital, etc. For Marx, the unfreedom and inequality of capitalist relations are, of course, not perversions but *realizations* of the form of freedom and equality implied by simpler forms of commodity exchange. Thus while bourgeois freedom and equality represent an advance over preceding forms, it is a mistake to regard them as antithetical to capitalist inequality and domination.

The equality and freedom of capitalist productive relations can, therefore, be regarded as the kernel of liberal democracy, insofar as the latter is the most complete form of *merely* legal and political equality and freedom. As Marx suggests, the 'constitutional republic' is as much the juridical principle of capitalist exploitation as brute force is the juridical principle of other modes of exploitation, and both express the right of the stronger:

> All the bourgeois economists are aware of is that production can be carried on better under the modern police than e.g. on the principle of might makes right. They forget only that this principle is also a legal relation, and that the right of the stronger prevails in their 'constitutional republics' as well, only in another form.[10]

A proper evaluation of liberal democracy, then, implies an appreciation of the ways in which the capitalist state is an active agent in class struggle, the ways in which political powers are deployed in the interests of the dominant class, how the state enters directly into the relations of production — not only on the higher planes of class struggle, but in the immediate confrontation between capital and labour in the work place itself; the ways in which, for example, the legal apparatus and police functions of the state are the necessary foundations of the contractual relation among 'equals' which constitutes the domination of the working class by the capitalists. An analysis of the link between liberalism and capitalism must recognize that the 'autonomy' and 'universality' of the capitalist state are precisely the essence of its perfection as a *class*

---

[9] Ibid., p. 248.
[10] Ibid., p. 88.

state; that this 'autonomy' and 'universality' (which are not merely apparent but to a significant extent real), the appearance of class-neutrality which is the special characteristic of the capitalist state, are all made possible and necessary by precisely that condition which also makes capitalism an effective form of class exploitation: the complete separation of the producers from the means of production and the concentration in private hands of the capacity for direct surplus-extraction. It must be acknowledged that the clear separation of class and state in capitalism — expressed, for example, in the state's monopoly of force, which can be turned against members of the dominant class itself — is not merely a separation but a more perfect symbiosis, in effect a cooperative division of labour between class and state which allocates to them separately the essential functions of an exploiting class: surplus-extraction and the coercive power that sustains it.

At the same time, liberal democracy, while grounded in the juridical principles of capitalist productive relations, cannot be reduced to them. The minimal form of freedom and equality intrinsic to capitalism *need* not give rise to the most developed form. If equality and freedom of a very limited and ambiguous kind are essential and common to *all* capitalist social formations, liberal-democratic political institutions have *not* been equally common and are certainly not essential to capitalism, even if they have been most conducive to capitalist development under certain historic conditions. The nature of the relation between capitalism and liberal democracy must, therefore, be further specified with due consideration not only to general structural links but to the particular realities of history. One must go beyond the function of juridical and political freedom and equality in sustaining capitalist relations of production and the position of the dominant class, and take account of the value liberal-democratic political forms have had for subordinate classes, indeed, the degree to which these political and legal forms are the legacy of historic struggles by subordinate classes. The role of liberal democracy in civilizing capitalist exploitation must be acknowledged; and this acknowledgement entails a recognition of the crucial differences among forms of capitalist state. There is a massive difference between capitalism with a liberal face and capitalism in a fascist guise. Not the least difference concerns the position of subordinate classes, their freedom to organize and to resist. The seduction of working-class movements by liberal-democratic political forms cannot be lightly dismissed as a failure of class-consciousness or a betrayal of the revolution. The attractions of these institutions have been very real in countries where the tradition has been strongest. In those countries where the tradition has been weak, recent history has surely demonstrated as dramatically as possible that the absence of these forms has serious consequences and that their acquisition and retention are worthy goals for a working-class movement. Any socialist strategy ignores at its peril the hold exercised by these political principles and institutions or underestimates the legitimacy of their claims.

To sum up, liberal democracy can neither be completely separated from nor reduced to the principles of capitalist exploitation. Any reasonable analysis must consider both the foundations of liberal democracy in capitalist relations of production and its historic role in checking the excesses of capitalism. At the same time, it must be acknowledged that the particular effectiveness of liberal-democratic institutions rests not only on their performance — in common with other forms of state power — as coercive instruments, but also on their uniquely powerful *hegemonic* functions.

The legal and political institutions of liberal democracy may be the most potent ideological force available to the capitalist class — in some respects even more powerful than the material advances achieved under the auspices of capitalism. The very form of the state itself, and not simply the ideological or cultural apparatus that sustains it, is persuasive. What gives this political form its peculiar hegemonic power, as Perry Anderson has argued, is that the consent it commands from the dominated classes does not simply rest on their submission to an acknowledged ruling class or their acceptance of its right to rule. The parliamentary democratic state is a unique form of class rule because it casts doubt on the very existence of a ruling class.[11] It does not, however, achieve this effect by pure mystification. As always, hegemony has two sides. It is not possible if it is not plausible.[12] Liberal democracy is the outcome of long and painful struggles. It has conferred genuine benefits on subordinate classes and given them real strengths, new possibilities of organization and resistance which cannot be

---

[11] Perry Anderson, 'The Antinomies of Antonio Gramsci', *New Left Review* 100, November 1976-January 1977, p. 30.

[12] For a very fine discussion of this aspect of class hegemony, see E.P. Thompson on the rule of law as the expression of ruling class hegemony in eighteenth century England in *Whigs and Hunters*, London 1975, especially pp. 262-3.

abandoned to the enemy as mere sham. To say that liberal democracy is 'hegemonic' is to say both that it serves the particular interests of the capitalist class and that its claims to universality have an element of truth.

The point is not that people are necessarily duped into believing that they are truly sovereign when they are not; it is rather that, with the triumph of representative institutions and finally the achievement of universal suffrage, the outer limits of popular sovereignty on a purely *political* plane really have been reached. Thus, the severe restrictions imposed upon popular power by the character of parliamentary democracy as a *class* state may appear as the limitations of democracy itself.[13] At least, the full development of liberal democracy means that the further extension of popular power requires not simply the perfection of existing political institutions but a radical transformation of social arrangements in general, in ways that are as yet unknown. This also means putting at risk hard-won gains for the sake of uncertain benefits. A major obstacle to the socialist project is that it requires not merely a quantitative change, not simply another extension of suffrage or a further incursion by representative institutions upon executive power, but a qualitative leap to new forms of democracy with no successful historical precedent.

Capitalist hegemony, then, rests to a significant extent on a formal separation of 'political' and 'economic' spheres which makes possible the maximum development of purely juridical and political freedom and equality without fundamentally endangering economic exploitation.[14] Liberal-democratic legal and political forms are compatible with, indeed grounded in, capitalist relations of production because, with the complete separation of the producer from the means of production, surplus extraction no longer requires direct 'extra-economic' coercion or the producer's juridical dependence. The coercive power on which capitalist property ultimately rests can thus appear in the form of a 'neutral' and 'autonomous' state. Not surprisingly, therefore, the separation of political and economic spheres that characterizes the liberal state in *practice* has also been enshrined in *theory*, particularly in the English-speaking world where the liberal tradition has been

---

[13] Anderson, p. 30 and n. 53.

[14] These points are discussed in greater detail in my article, 'The Separation of the "Economic" and the "Political" in Capitalism', *New Left Review* 127, May-June 1981.

especially strong. The effect has been to produce various modes of political analysis that abstract 'politics' from its social foundations: for example, in political philosophy, where concepts like 'freedom', 'equality', and 'justice' are subjected to intricately formalistic analysis deliberately divorced from social implications; or 'political science', which scrutinizes political 'behaviour' or political 'systems' as if they were devoid of social content. These procedures give theoretical expression to the abstraction of 'politics' in the liberal democratic state and to the appearance of 'universality' or 'neutrality' on which its hegemony rests; and they urge us to accept formal equality and freedom without looking too closely at the substance enveloped in the form. The NTS, with its class-neutral, 'indeterminate' democracy, is the latest contribution to this ideological tradition.

If liberal democracy is at the core of capitalist class hegemony, it is presumably the task of socialist political theory to approach liberal-democratic theory 'counter-hegemonically'. How the counter-hegemonic project is conceived, however, very much depends on what one means by 'hegemony'; and there is a way of thinking about 'hegemony' that has the effect of replacing class struggle and its chief protagonist, the working class, by intellectuals and their 'autonomous' activity as the principal agency of revolutionary change. One of the essential premises of this conception (as it appears, for example, in certain recent interpretations of hegemony in which Gramsci's notion is manipulated and grafted onto Althusser's theory of ideology) is that the hegemony of the ruling class over subordinate classes is one-sided and *complete*.[15] Such formulae tend to expel *class struggle* from the concept of hegemony. There is no struggle here; there is only domination on one side and submission on the other. 'Hegemony' thus ceases to represent a distillation of class conflict which necessarily bears the marks of the subordinate classes, their consciousness, values, and struggles.[16]

---

[15] For a discussion of some interpretations of Gramsci that suggest such a view of hegemony, see Tom Nairn's review in the *London Review of Books*, 17 July-6 August 1980, pp. 12-14. See also E.P. Thompson, 'Eighteenth Century English Society: Class Struggle Without Class?', *Social History*, vol. 3, no. 2, May 1978, pp. 162-4 and n. 60.

[16] This is arguably the effect of Althusser's conception of ideology as a kind of systems maintenance device embodied particularly in 'Ideological State Apparatuses' which ensure the reproduction of the social structure.

In this vocabulary, to speak of establishing the 'hegemony of the working class' becomes, oddly, not a way of describing the self-emancipation of the working class but precisely its opposite. It suggests that working class 'hegemony' is created by means of 'autonomous' theoretical and ideological practice — on behalf of, not *by*, the working class; and that intellectual activity can produce a counter-hegemonic 'culture', an *ideal* consciousness for a working class whose *real* consciousness, absorbed by capitalist hegemony, is 'false'. Again, we have the vision of an illuminated few who will 'bring the public mind to reason ... take culture away from [the] enemy ... and instil it, suitably transformed, into the working class'[17] — presumably by means of 'disarticulation' and the reconstruction of popular 'discourse'.

It is probably necessary to stress that I agree wholeheartedly about the need to claim democratic values for socialism (though the need is greater in practice than in theory); but even granting the importance of theoretical activity in challenging the ideological hegemony of the ruling class, the strategy of 'disarticulation' rests on a shaky theoretical foundation. Of course not all social conflicts are class struggles and not all ideologies implicated in political struggles — even in class struggles — are specifically class ideologies. It is also true that the 'democratic' elements of liberal democracy have, under certain historical conditions, been taken up by various classes. Nevertheless, an ideology that can claim the allegiance of more than one class, an ideology that has a certain *universality*, does not thereby necessarily cease to be a *class* ideology — that is, not simply a neutral element *articulated* with a class ideology but an ideology that is itself class-determined in origin and meaning. Ideology may contribute to class hegemony by giving the particular interests of one class the appearance of generality; and it may be true, as Laclau suggests, that the ideological hegemony of the bourgeoisie rests on a 'consensus' that 'many of the constitutive elements of democratic and popular culture ... are irrevocably linked to its class ideology'.[18] The success of these claims has not, however, been achieved merely by adopting popular-democratic ideologies that 'have no precise class connotations' and making them appear to be the exclusive property of

---

[17] Nairn, pp. 12-13.
[18] Ernesto Laclau, *Politics and Ideology in Marxist Theory*, London 1979, p. 110.

bourgeois class ideology. If anything, the reverse is true: bourgeois ideological hegemony rests on the ability of the bourgeoisie to present its particular class interests (plausibly and with an element of historical truth) as if they had 'no precise class connotations'. The ideology of the dominant class undoubtedly incorporates elements of popular struggles against its own dominance, and in this sense to some extent 'neutralizes' them; but to say this is to say no more than that class ideology is the product of class *struggle*, which is never one-sided.

To counter the ideological hegemony of the capitalist class, therefore, the task of the theorist is *not* to demonstrate that what *appears* universal in bourgeois ideology really *is* universal, having 'no precise class connotations' — which is, in effect, precisely to accept the hegemonic claims of the dominant class — but rather to explain how what appears universal is in fact particular; not simply to extract from liberal democratic forms a sense in which they do *not* express capitalist class interests, but also to understand clearly the sense in which they *do*; not to empty ideological formulae of their specific social content but to explicate the specificity and particularity of meaning in them; not to abstract ideology from its historic conditions in order to convert particular class interests into universal principles available for 're-articulation', but to explore the historic conditions that have made possible the generalization of a particular class interest and conferred 'universality' on the capitalist class.

This is, again, not to say that socialist political theory must, by reducing liberal democracy to class ideology, dismiss it as pure mystification or sham. The point is simply that an account must be given of liberal democracy which makes clearly visible not only its limitations but also the *discontinuity*, the radical break, between liberalism and socialism. If the defeat of capitalist hegemony rests on the reclamation of democracy by socialism (and insofar as that reclamation can be assisted by theoretical means), it cannot be achieved simply by 'disarticulating' democracy from bourgeois class ideology. New, *socialist*, forms of democracy must be defined whose specificity is clear and which represent an unmistakeable challenge to the claims of bourgeois democracy that its particular form of 'popular sovereignty' is universal and final.

III

There is another side to the relation between liberal democracy and capitalism. If liberal democracy was born out of capitalist relations of production, should it also die with them? If liberal-democratic institutions have acted to *civilize* as well as to support capitalism, is the need for such institutions dependent on the persistence of capitalist relations of production, or might a socialist society be faced with problems that demand similar solutions? In other words, has liberalism produced a legacy that can and ought to be adopted by socialism? Here again, the NTS, with its insistence on the seamless continuity between liberal democracy and socialism, obscures the issue. While it may be true to say that socialism could not have existed without liberalism, our understanding of either is not advanced by regarding one as a mere extension of the other and ignoring the fundamental ways in which they are diametrically opposed. Liberalism and socialism can be conflated in this way only by means of an empty formalism which voids them of their social content.

Let us consider what social needs are served by liberal principles and institutions, and whether similar social needs will persist in a socialist society. From this point of view, it can be argued that if liberalism is about anything worth preserving, it is about certain ways of dealing with political authority: the rule of law, civil liberties, checks on arbitrary power. This function of liberalism must be conceded even if the status of 'bourgeois liberties' is at best ambiguous in a class-divided society where they may not only obscure class oppositions with a false equality but actively serve as instruments of class power and hegemony. It is not here a question of how *democratic* 'bourgeois democracy' may or may not be. In fact, one ought perhaps to begin by again separating the 'liberal' from the 'democratic'. This coupling tends to obscure the difference between 'democracy' as *popular power*, and 'democracy' as a formal, procedural principle. It may be that the most important lesson of liberalism has little to do with democracy but is concerned with controlling state power — and here, the earlier *anti*-democratic forms of liberalism may have as much to say as does liberal democracy.

To say that liberalism has a lesson for socialism in this respect is, of course, to make a highly contentious assumption, namely that the state will persist as a problem in classless society and that the most democratic society may continue to be faced with a *political* problem analogous to that of undemocratic societies. Much of socialist doctrine is based on the assumption that, if the state will not actually wither away in a classless society, state power will at least no longer constitute a *problem*. Social democrats and NTS who have unbounded faith in the efficacy of bourgeois-democratic forms seem not to regard the state as a problem even in capitalist society. Indeed, they treat it as an instrument of salvation. More interesting questions are raised by socialists who are convinced that the state apparatus of bourgeois democracy must be 'smashed' and replaced by something radically different. As Ralph Miliband has argued, those who speak of the 'smashing' of the bourgeois state have not squarely faced the fact that they will — indeed must — replace the smashed state with yet another, perhaps temporarily even strengthened, state; that the smashing of the bourgeois state and its replacement by a revolutionary state do *not* in themselves mean the 'dictatorship of the proletariat', if that concept still carries its original democratic implications; that there is always a tension between the necessity of 'direction' and 'democracy', between state power and popular power, which has been consistently evaded.[19] So serious is the problem, suggests Miliband, that democracy can be preserved only by a system of 'dual power' in which state power is *complemented* by widespread democratic organizations of various kinds throughout civil society.

It must be added, however, that the problem is not likely to be confined to some awkward 'transitional' phase during which a strong state will undertake to fulfill the promise of the revolution by transforming society. If, for example, as Marx suggests, the central organizational problem of *all* societies is the allocation of social labour, then there is a sense in which the *political* question will be particularly important *after* the complete overthrow of capitalism. Capitalism is, after all, a system in which that central social problem is not dealt with 'politically', a system uniquely characterized by the absence of an 'authoritative allocation' of social labour. It is a system with what Marx calls an 'anarchic' social division of labour not dictated by political authority, tradition, or communal deliberation but by the mechanisms of commodity-exchange. One might say that it is capitalism, then, which in this very particular sense involves the 'administration of things and not people' — or perhaps the administration of people by things; while the new

---

[19] Ralph Miliband, *Marxism and Politics*, Oxford 1977, pp. 180-90.

society will be faced with a new and substantial organizational problem which very much involves the administration of people.

Marxist theory has not done much to clarify the issues at stake, let alone resolve the problem of the state under socialism. Marx and Engels had little to say on the subject of the state in future society, and what they did say is often ambiguous. In particular, the debate has been plagued by a vagueness and inconsistency in the use of the term 'state'. We are told that the *state* will 'wither away' in classless society. If (as is usually but not always the case) the state is defined as a system of class domination, it is a mere tautology to say that the state will 'wither away' once classes are abolished. The definition of the state as synonymous with class domination resolves nothing. It simply evades the issue. On the other hand, if the 'state' refers to *any* form of public power, it is not at all clear that the state will disappear with class — nor is it clear that Marx or Engels thought it would.

Whatever Marx and Engels may have thought about the future of the state, the real question is not whether a public power will be needed in a classless society, but whether that public power will constitute a problem. In other words, are there certain problems inherent in public power itself whether or not it is *class* power? I take it for granted that it is hopelessly naive to believe in an advanced socialist society administered completely by simple forms of direct and spontaneous democracy. It is difficult to avoid the conviction that even classless society will require some form of *representation*, and hence *authority* and even *subordination* of some people to others. That premise granted, it must be added that, whether or not one uses the term 'state' to describe political and administrative power in a classless society, it seems unduly optimistic to believe that there can ever be a case in which power exercised by some people on behalf of others does not constitute a problem. Socialist political theory must, therefore, face the dangers posed by representation, authority, and subordination, and the fact that their very existence makes possible the misappropriation of power.

These problems cannot be dismissed by the mere assertion that representation, authority, and subordination will present no danger in the absence of class. Among other things, it is necessary to consider the possibility (hinted at by Marx himself, for example in his discussions of the Asiatic mode of production and other pre-capitalist formations) that public power may be, and historically often has been, itself the *source* of differentiation between appropriators and direct producers. There is good reason to believe that public power, instituted to undertake socially necessary functions — warfare, distribution, direction of communal labour, the construction of vital public works — has often been the original basis of the claim to and capacity for surplus-appropriation. In other words, the state — in the broad sense — has not emerged from class divisions but has, on the contrary, *produced* class divisions and hence also produced the state in the narrow sense. It does not seem wise to assume that no constant and institutionalized protection will be needed in the future to prevent the similar transmutation of 'political' authority into 'economic' power, public power into something like class domination.

However much Marx or Engels may have tended toward political utopianism, the view that public power in classless society will still be a problem requiring conscious and institutionalized control is entirely consistent with the fundamental Marxist view of the world and the meaning of the socialist revolution. Marx's belief in the complete transformation of society once class domination disappears does not imply that all problems associated with class domination will automatically and forever dissolve of themselves. On the contrary, the essence of the transformation itself is that socio-historical forces will for the first time be consciously controlled and directed instead of left to chance. This is what Marx means when he speaks of man's history before the revolution as 'pre-history' and thereafter as 'human history'. The planned direction of social forces certainly does not refer simply to 'economic' planning in the narrow sense — the planning of production quotas, and so on. The 'economic' is itself a *social relation*, and the social relations of production themselves must be 'planned'. Furthermore, if 'economic' power, the power to extract surplus labour, consists in a relationship of domination and coercion, then it is also *political* power; and the planning of the social relations of production must include 'political' planning at every level of society, institutional measures to prevent the re-emergence of domination and exploitative relations.

Even in a classless society there will probably have to be organizations whose conscious and explicit object is not simply to complement but to *check* power and prevent its misappropriation. There will have to be ongoing institutions, not simply emergency measures such as the power of recall, to act to this specific end, and equally important, to maintain a *consciousness* of the dangers. Assuming that the political form of socialism will be a *repre-*

sentative system, with some kind of administrative apparatus, there will still be tension between state power and popular power. Representation is itself a problem; and to the extent that the political problem cannot be practically resolved by replacing representation with direct democracy, by further democratizing the system of political organization, the problem must still be faced on another plane. In other words, the very existence of a state — however democratically representative — necessarily places a special task on the agenda: not simply democratic organization throughout civil society, but — and this may not be the same thing — what Marx calls the *subordination* of the state to society.[20]

The debate on the future of the state ought not to be reduced to a matter of textual interpretation; but discussions of the question are bound to return to the sketchy comments made by Marx and Engels on the subject. Since it is probably easier to demonstrate that they were optimistic about the disappearance of politics than to prove that they saw the state as a continuing problem, a few remarks in support of the latter interpretation should be added here. Particularly interesting is what they have to say — or at least imply — about the legacy of bourgeois liberalism and its possible application to post-revolutionary society.

It must be said, first, that both Marx and Engels may have clouded the issue by asserting that in a classless society the *state* will disappear or that the 'public power will lose its political character.'[21] This is not the same as saying that there will *be* no public power, or even that the public power will cease to be a problem. Engels, who most often and explicitly repeated the assertion that the state 'in the proper sense of the word' would disappear, is also the man who, in attacking the anarchists, stressed the continuing need for *authority* and *subordination* and mocked the anarchists for believing that by changing the name of the public authority they had changed the thing itself. Even if, as Engels writes, 'public functions will lose their political character and be transformed into the simple administrative functions of watching over the true interests of society,'[22] the problem is not self-evidently resolved. Is

---

[20] Karl Marx, 'Critique of the Gotha Programme', in *The First International and After*, Harmondsworth 1974, p. 354.

[21] Karl Marx and Friedrich Engels, 'The Manifesto of the Communist Party', in *The Revolutions of 1848*, Harmondsworth 1973, p. 87.

[22] Friedrich Engels, 'On Authority', *Marx-Engels Selected Works*, vol. 1, Moscow 1962, p. 639.

it not possible that — even in Engels's own view — institutionalized measures will be required precisely to *ensure* that the public power, vested with authority over others and subordinating others to it, will maintain its purely 'administrative' character and continue to act in the true interests of society? In a class society, such a humane and 'unpolitical' public power would be impossible; but, if it becomes *possible* only in a classless society, it does not become inevitable.

That Marx, too, may have perceived the state as a continuing problem is suggested by the very formula, 'the subordination of the state to society.' Note, first, that he does not here speak of the *absorption* of the state by society, as he appears to do in his very early work,[23] nor does he refer to the state's dissolution. What, then, is meant by the subordination of the state to society? Other texts — for example, *The Civil War in France* where Marx discusses the Paris Commune — suggest it means that the public power will consist of officials who are the 'responsible agents of society', not 'superior to society'. The problem, however, only *begins* here. How is society to ensure that its officials will remain 'responsible' and not 'superior' to it? Marx may seem to dismiss the question too lightly and optimistically, since he has little to say about it except to speak of the subjection of officials to instant recall. It cannot, however, be taken for granted that he failed to see the problem or to recognize its magnitude.

In the *Critique of the Gotha Programme* where the 'subordination of the state' appears, Marx hints not only that the problem of the state will persist in communist society, but that the restrictions on state power instituted by the most 'liberal' of bourgeois societies may have something to teach on the score of dealing with that problem:

> Freedom consists in converting the state from an organ superimposed upon society into one completely subordinate to it, and today, too, the forms of state are more free or less free to the extent that they restrict the 'freedom of the state'.[24]

'Freedom' in bourgeois society is, of course, something very different from the complete 'subordination of the state to society'

---

[23] For example in 'On the Jewish Question', or *The Economic and Philosophic Manuscripts*.

[24] 'Critique of the Gotha Programme' p. 354.

which can occur only in the absence of class domination. On the other hand, Marx appears to see some kind of connection between freedom in the bourgeois state and the subordination of the communist state to society, a connection that has something to do with the establishment of checks on state power, institutionalized restrictions on the 'freedom of the state'. He goes on to ask: 'What transformations will the state undergo in communist society? In other words, what social functions will remain in existence that are analogous to the present function of the state?' Marx undoubtedly contributed to the optimistic notion that the state will eventually wither away; but he is here apparently suggesting that the state will persist, that it probably will have certain functions analogous to its present ones, and that it may even pose analogous problems. Furthermore, the precise nature of these analogies can only be determined 'scientifically', and, one does not get a flea-hop nearer to the problem by a thousand-fold combination of the word people with the word state.' This may mean that a democratic state is still a *state*, and will require conscious and institutional efforts to restrict its 'freedom' — which, among other things, appears to mean to restrict bureaucratization — if it is to be subordinated to society. Insofar as the most 'liberal' forms of the capitalist state represent the hitherto most advanced modes of restricting the freedom of the state, it is possible that socialists have something to learn from 'liberalism' in this regard.

What particular kinds of restrictions on the state's 'freedom' Marx had in mind is perhaps suggested by Engels's comments on the Gotha Programme — and his remarks are somewhat surprising:

> ... a heap of rather confused *purely democratic demands* [figures] in the programme, of which several are a mere matter of fashion, as for instance, the 'legislation by the people' which exists in Switzerland and does more harm than good if it does anything at all. *Administration* by the people, that would be something. Equally lacking is the first condition of all freedom: that all officials should be responsible for all their official acts to every citizen before the ordinary courts and according to common law.[25]

---

[25] Letter to August Bebel, 18-28 March 1875, *Marx-Engels Selected Correspondence*, Moscow 1965, p. 293.

The implication here is, again, that freedom lies in restricting the freedom of the state; and it is clear that this is not simply a matter of establishing more democratic legislative or representative institutions, but concerns above all the administrative apparatus. Particularly striking is the importance Engels attaches to the law and the court system in restricting the freedom of the state. There is a suggestion that certain legal systems represent a kind of *opposition* to the state — perhaps even an organization 'in society' — rather than a mere instrument of the state. The common law system, the 'independent' judiciary, judges who are not part of the administrative apparatus, the jury system, the recourse of citizens to 'ordinary courts' against state officials — characteristics more typical of the English legal tradition and of those legal systems which emanate from it — are being implicitly opposed to the continental tradition and in particular its system of administrative law. In short, Engels appears to be suggesting — in what may seem an excessively optimistic echo of English bourgeois ideology (which has an especially hollow ring in the wake of recent events in Britain, especially during the miners' strike) — that the 'rule of law' in the particular English sense can play an essential role in restricting the state's freedom. And if the efficacy of 'liberalism' in this form as a real check on the bourgeois state must certainly be questioned, such a view cannot simply be dismissed. While Engels goes on to repeat the optimistic conviction that the advent of socialism will mean the dissolution of the state 'in the proper sense of the word', it is not at all clear that for him — or for Marx — this means the disappearance of public power as a danger. It might be useful, then, to consider bourgeois legalism and other 'liberal' restrictions on the freedom of the state, and what these institutions may have to teach about the modalities of subordinating the state to society even under communism.

IV

In any case, whether or not liberalism can teach socialism anything about the post-revolutionary state, it can at least reveal something about the seductiveness of a particular political tradition, which has more immediate strategic implications. It is significant that in countries in which the liberal — not necessarily *democratic* — tradition has been strongest, working-class movements have been least revolutionary and have most consistently placed their faith in the political institutions of bourgeois democracy. Socialist movements in other countries may have *acquired* that faith; but the English, for example, have had a mainstream labour movement with an unbroken tradition of loyalty to these institutions. It seems also to be true that where liberalism has been strongest, socialist theory has been least Marxist. Even Marx himself was affected by this political tradition. He did, after all, suggest in 1872 that Britain and the United States were the countries most likely to achieve the transition to socialism by peaceful means. Addressing a meeting in Amsterdam, he said:

> You know that the institutions, mores, and traditions of various countries must be taken into consideration, and we do not deny that there are countries — such as America, England, and if I were more familiar with your institutions, I would perhaps also add Holland — where the workers can attain their goal by peaceful means. This being the case, we must also recognize the fact that in most countries on the Continent the lever of our revolution must be force. ...[26]

Without speculating on the accuracy of this judgement, it is instructive to consider why Marx made it, what factors he found operating in England and America that distinguished them from other countries which would more probably require violent revolution to achieve the transformation of society. No doubt England was the most proletarian country in the world; and Marx seems to have expected America to become 'the workers' continent par excellence', as he suggests later in the Amsterdam speech. In the relevant paragraph, however, Marx does not refer to the *class* configurations of different countries, but to their 'institutions, mores, and traditions'. As for which institutions and traditions he particularly had in mind, it seems unlikely that the crucial factor for Marx was the degree of *democracy* by itself. England in 1872 was still many years away from universal manhood suffrage, and even further removed from a system of one man–one vote, or any kind of universal adult suffrage, and had a far from democratic political tradition; while France had already experimented with universal manhood suffrage and other politically democratic institutions long before, was on the eve of establishing a bourgeois

---

[26] Karl Marx, 'Amsterdam Speech', 8 September 1872.

democratic republic, and had provided the world with its most influential democratic tradition. Considered in the context of other statements by Marx — for example, in the *Critique of the Gotha Programme*, the *18th Brumaire*, and the letter to Kugelmann of April 12, 1871 — the judgement of the Amsterdam speech appears to be singling out not so much the *democratic* elements of English and American political institutions as their '*liberalism*', particularly the degree to which they restrict the 'freedom of the state', in contrast to the more strongly bureaucratic and police states of the major capitalist countries on the Continent, which would almost certainly require violent revolution to 'smash' their rigid state apparatus.[27] In other words, the apparently less rigid British and American forms of capitalist state at least created the impression that the structure of domination, at the pinnacle of which stood the state, could more easily be shifted by peaceful, parliamentary means.

If Marx allowed himself a certain optimism concerning the political forms and traditions of liberalism, it is not surprising that such a large proportion of the working classes which have experienced them directly can be so tenaciously faithful to a political tradition that has not been notably democratic. The recourse subordinate classes have had to judicial and political institutions in their relations with dominant classes, together with the restrictions on the 'freedom' of the state itself, have created a faith — though hardly unlimited — in the efficacy of legal and political forms. How, then, should socialist theory deal with this tenacious ideology?

In confronting non-liberal regimes, particularly fascist or other forms of dictatorship, a case can be made for the principles of the Popular Front and a corresponding ideological strategy in which the continuities between liberalism and socialism take precedence over the discontinuities. Doubts must exist even here about incurring the risks of a strategy that seems to suppress class struggle, subordinate the interests and independent action of the working class, and postpone the struggle for socialism; but even if we

---

[27] Engels later showed less confidence in the flexibility of the American state. In his introduction to Marx's *The Civil War in France*, he cites the United States as the country in which the state power has most successfully made itself 'independent in relation to society', rendering the nation powerless against politicians who take possession of and exploit that power — despite the absence of a standing army and a rigid bureaucracy.

accept the necessity, in such cases, of courting these dangers, no such argument can be made in the circumstances of liberal democracy. In the liberal democratic state, where the limits of popular power consistent with a class society have essentially been reached, the struggle for socialism stands apart at the top of the agenda. An intellectual strategy is needed which goes beyond the union of liberalism and socialism in a theoretical Popular Front. There are, of course, many immediately pressing battles to be fought in all of the liberal democracies — against nuclear annihilation, for example, or, for that matter, to protect the gains of liberal democracy itself — and these require broad alliances; but in all these battles and alliances, the specificity of the socialist struggle must always remain clear.[28] An intellectual strategy must, then, be found which can, while acknowledging the value of liberal institutions, preserve that specificity and clearly define the break, the 'river of fire', between liberalism and socialism.

This is a large question, but one or two suggestions can be briefly made. We should not, to begin with, be too absorbed by the formula 'liberal democracy', so that our attention is focused on the opposition 'liberal democracy' versus 'socialist democracy', as if the major issue were the difference between two aspects of democracy. It may be useful to resituate the discussion by *contrasting* liberalism ('democratic', or 'pre-democratic') to democracy, to define democracy as *distinct* from — though not in opposition to — liberalism. If we concentrate our attention on the differences between the problems to which 'liberalism' and 'democracy' are respectively addressed, we can recognize the value of liberalism and its lessons for socialism without allowing liberalism to circumscribe our definition of democracy.

Liberalism has to do essentially with 'restricting the freedom of the state' — through the rule of law, civil liberties, and so on. It is concerned to limit the scope and the arbitrariness of political power; but it has no interest in the *disalienation* of power. Indeed, it is a fundamental liberal ideal even in its most 'democratic' forms that power *must* be alienated, not simply as a necessary evil but as a positive good — for example, in order to permit fundamentally individualistic human beings to occupy themselves with private

---

[28] See, for example, Raymond Williams, 'The Politics of Nuclear Disarmament', *New Left Review* 124, November-December 1980, for a discussion of this point as it relates to the peace movement.

concerns. This is why for liberalism *representation* is a *solution* not a *problem.*

In contrast to liberalism, *democracy* has to do precisely with the disalienation of power. To the extent that some form of alienated power or representation continues to be a necessary expedient — as in any complex society it undoubtedly must — from the point of view of democratic values such representative institutions must be regarded not only as a solution but also as a problem. It is in confronting this problem that socialism has something to learn from liberalism — not about the disalienation of power but about the control of alienated power.

Even democratic power will undoubtedly present dangers about which liberalism — with its principles of civil liberties, the rule of law, and protection for a sphere of privacy — may yet have lessons to teach; but the *limitation* of power is not the same thing as its disalienation. Democracy, unlike liberalism even in its most idealized form, furthermore implies overcoming the opposition of 'economic' and 'political' and eliminating the superimposition of the 'state' upon 'civil society'. 'Popular sovereignty' would thus not be confined to an abstract political 'sphere' but would instead entail a disalienation of power at every level of human activity, an attack on the whole structure of domination that begins in the sphere of production and continues upward to the state. From this point of view, just as the coupling of 'liberal' and 'democracy' may be misleading, the joining of 'socialist' and 'democracy' should be redundant.

This also means that there can be no simple, non-antagonistic extension of liberal democracy into socialist democracy. Even if the term 'democracy' is allowed to stand for both these cases, it must at least be acknowledged that there have throughout history existed radically different forms of democracy, and that the institutional differences that distinguish, say, the Athenian from the modern American or British form reflect their very different social bases. It is historical nonsense to deny that there is any correspondence between the institutional forms of these various democracies and the varying social foundations on which they rest. The configuration of social relations and power that will distinguish socialism from capitalism will necessarily be reflected in different institutional forms. The very heart of socialism will be a mode of democratic organization that has never existed before — direct self-government by freely associated producers in commonly owned workplaces producing the means of material life. The very existence of such democratic institutions by definition means an end to capitalist relations and the forms of democracy compatible with them.

Nor is it simply a matter of tacking 'economic' democracy onto an already existing 'political' democracy. It is not just that democracy at the level of production will require new forms of supporting institutions at other 'levels'. More immediately important is the fact that the political sphere in even the most 'liberal-democratic' capitalist society is itself constructed to maintain, bureaucratically and coercively whenever necessary, the barriers to democracy at the 'level' of production relations. To treat the transition to socialism as just an incremental improvement on liberal democracy, as if all that is required is to 'transport' its democratic principles from the polity to the economy, is to forget not only that there is no such thing as a socially indeterminate democratic principle but also that one of the essential functions of the liberal democratic state is vigilantly to police and coercively to enforce the confinement of 'democracy' to a limited domain.

11

Socialism and 'Universal Human Goods'

I

There is a way of linking socialism to 'universal human goods' which is completely different from the new 'true' socialism. Raymond Williams, a writer in another category than all discussed hitherto, exemplifies this. His work meets many of the real concerns of the NTS without denying the Marxist premise that the particular interests of the working class coincide with the general interests of humanity, that the self-emancipation of the working class entails the emancipation of human beings generally from class exploitation, and that the working class has not only a fundamental class *interest* in socialism, but also a specific collective *capacity* to bring it about. What makes his book, *Towards 2000*, especially important is that, while he addresses the issues raised by the 'new social movements' — the issues of peace, the environment, gender, cultural poverty, etc. — and acknowledges that these concerns have been too often neglected by the class-organizations of the left, the whole thrust of the book is to counter dismissals of the working class and to reaffirm the importance of class politics. The work contains a direct attack on the mystifications of parliamentary representation which clearly denies the 'indeterminacy' of democracy by firmly asserting the existence and specificity of a *bourgeois* democracy and contrasting it to specifically socialist forms.[1] Above all, the book is permeated by a deep *anti-capitalist* passion that is strikingly absent in the leading exponents of the NTS, who are prone to evading the issue by avoiding the word itself at critical moments in their arguments: so, for example, we have Laclau and Mouffe's 'industrial society', or Stedman Jones's 'the mixed economy', 'the welfare state', 'Britain's economic plight'

---

[1] Raymond Williams, *Towards 2000*, London 1983, pp. 102-127.

and 'national decline' (significantly, he refers only once to 'capitalism' in his musings on the Labour Party, and that simply in an account of Crosland's views). It is worth adding that Williams, who has professionally contributed perhaps more than any other contemporary Marxist in the English-speaking world to the study of 'superstructural' or cultural processes, and certainly far more than any of the NTS enthusiasts for language, ideology, and discourse, shows no inclination to exaggerate or hypostatize their role in social reproduction or political struggle.

Williams first identifies two strands in the traditional claim of the labour movement that it was 'more than a congeries of certain particular interests.'[2] The first argument, deriving its force from the 'culture of poverty' in which the movement was born, rested on the sheer magnitude of the poverty which industrial capitalism seemed to entail. 'It could not be right,' according to this view, 'for so many human beings to have to live like that.' With the decline of absolute poverty in the advanced capitalist countries, the successes of organized labour in improving the conditions of the traditional working class, and the growth of new relatively comfortable and privileged sectors within the labour movement, 'there is no longer any reliable basis for the claim [on the part of the labour movement] to a general interest in absolute human need.'

The second argument, however, was of a different kind: 'the capitalist system, by expropriating the common means of production, and by the private appropriation of the surplus-value of labour, is inherently hostile to the general interest, and thus incompatible with it.'[3] What bound this general interest to the particular interests of the working class, in Williams's account, was the particular capacity of the working class to bring about the destruction of capitalism. 'The familiar next step of the argument,' he continues, 'is that the organised labour movement is the only force which can end capitalism.' For Williams, the force of the argument that capitalism is contrary to the general interest has not changed with the development of the system; but the assumption that any action by the labour movement against capitalism, however particular in its targets and limited in its scope, automatically connects with the general interest, has steadily been losing its credibility. People have not only ceased — with some justification — to believe

---

[2] Ibid., p. 162.
[3] Ibid., pp. 162-3.

that struggles to advance the particular interests of the working class are necessarily anti-capitalist, but have even tended to forget the first premise that capitalism is against the general interest 'and that by industrial and political action it can be ended and replaced by a system which is in the general interest: socialism.'[4] The task facing the socialist movement, Williams suggests, is to construct a plausible and accessible conception of the general interest, and to find a way of reconnecting the labour movement to it.

It is worth noting that, while Williams is quite prepared to question whether many 'particularist' working class struggles are really anti-capitalist and conducive to the general interest, he seems to take for granted that the fundamental class interests of the working class are essentially anti-capitalist, and that it is this quality which makes it possible and necessary to think of the socialist project as a 'reconnecting' of the labour movement with the general interest — not simply in the sense that the general interest as conceived by socialists must include 'all reasonable particular interests', but apparently also in the sense that the working class has a more immediate and specific capacity than do other social groups for 'connecting' with the general interest, and therefore with socialism. In other words, he still seems to accept that the working class, through the medium of class struggle, remains the major vehicle of the struggle for socialism.

At the same time, Williams points out that the plausibility of the connection between the particular interests of the working class and the general interest has been weakened by the fact that a great many social objectives which must be regarded as essential to the general interest and to the project of human emancipation have been neglected by class organizations and have not appeared as expressions of class interest:

All significant social *movements* of the last thirty years have started outside the organised class interests and institutions. The peace movement, the ecology movement, the women's movement, human rights agencies, campaigns against poverty and homelessness, campaigns against cultural poverty and distortion: all have this character, that they sprang from needs and perceptions which the interest-based organisations had no room or time for, or which they had simply failed to notice.[5]

---

4 Ibid., p. 163.
5 Ibid., p. 172.

There is, however, a critical difference between Williams's analysis and those which treat the particularity of many working-class struggles, the complexity and multiplicity of the social identities in which people participate, and the neglect of certain vital social issues by the organs of class struggle, as a licence to dissociate the socialist project from the specific interests and struggles of the working class, and indeed from class struggle in general. It is a mistake, argues Williams, to interpret the separation of these social movements from the instruments of class interest 'as "getting beyond class politics"'. The local judgment on the narrowness of the major interest groups is just. But there is not one of these issues which, followed through, fails to lead us into the central systems of the industrial–capitalist mode of production and among others into its system of classes.'[6]

And yet, there is still an ambiguity here. Although Williams takes for granted the centrality of the working class in the struggle for socialism, and its fundamental interest in the replacement of the capitalist system by a socialist order, it is not altogether clear how, or even whether, this fundamental interest differs from that of all human beings who have a share in the 'general interest' simply by virtue of being human. True, the proposition that the class system of capitalism inevitably lies at the heart of all the major social issues and is the major obstacle which sits across the path of all efforts to achieve the human goals of peace, security, a careful economy and a caring society, seems to suggest that the class struggle between the principal classes which constitute the capitalist system will be the decisive battle in the struggle to achieve these goals. Nevertheless, Williams generally avoids the vocabulary of class struggle, urging us to reconstitute the socialist movement as a movement 'which begins from primary human needs ... bringing a wide range of needs and interests together in a new definition of the general interest,'[7] and thus also to revise and broaden our conception of the socialist constituency.

Even here, however, there is a critical difference between Williams's approach and that of the NTS. It is true that he refers to the 'predominantly middle-class leadership or membership of the new movements and campaigns' and the pressures that keep so many in the working class away from resistances to the existing

---

[6] Ibid., pp. 172-3.
[7] Ibid., pp. 173-4.

order: 'All the decisive pressures of a capitalist social order are exerted at very short range and in the very short term. There is a job that has to be kept, a debt that has to be repaid, a family that has to be supported.'[8] He even accepts that, as a consequence of that order, 'lacking the privileges of relative social distance and mobility, or of independent (often publicly funded) access to extended learning, the majority of employed people — a significantly wider population than the working-class in any of its definitions — have still primarily to relate to short-range and short-term determinations', while for the more privileged classes there is available a 'social distance, an area of affordable dissent' which may make them more open to the universal 'human needs' expressed by the new social movements. Lest, however, these observations should give comfort to the likes of Laclau and Mouffe or Gavin Kitching, it must be stressed that the thrust of his argument takes us in a political direction directly opposed to the NTS. As long as the new social movements cannot engage the 'hard social core', the working class, Williams insists, these movements will remain not only marginal but ineffective, because the working class is situated at the centre of the social order, in its 'decisive relations', in 'the strongholds of the economic order itself', where 'there are not only the dominant institutions and their shadow subordinates ... [but also], for most of the time, most of the people.'[9] 'It is significant,' he points out, 'that the new movements are active and substantial in almost every area of life except this', the economy.[10] Yet it is to this central core that every major social issue must eventually bring us back.

What is then quite absurd is to dismiss or underplay these movements as 'middle-class issues'. It is a consequence of the social order itself that these issues are qualified and refracted in these ways. It is similarly absurd to push the issues away as not relevant to the central interests of the working-class. In all real senses they belong to these central interests. It is workers who are most exposed to dangerous industrial processes and environmental damage. It is working-class women who have most need of new women's rights. ... Whatever movement there may be

---

[8] Ibid., p. 254.
[9] Ibid., p. 254.
[10] Ibid., p. 253.

on issues at some distance from these local and decisive relations, there is no possibility of it becoming fully effective until there are serious and detailed alternatives at these everyday points where a central consciousness is generated.[11]

And if 'it is at just these points, for historically understandable reasons, that all alternative policies are weakest', this does not mean that the locus of struggle must be resituated away from the arenas of 'local' working-class concerns, for 'it is in what will happen in this central economic area that the future of the social order will be determined.'[12]

Although there remain ambiguities in Williams's association of socialist politics with 'primary human needs' of a general, class-neutral kind, he seems to be telling us something that runs directly counter to the NTS project: the 'local', 'everyday' concerns that occupy the working class are closer to the heart of the social order, and to the source of those conditions that will determine the fate of 'primary human needs' and universal goods, than are the new movements which have these needs and goods as their immediate objectives. Perhaps we can also read into Williams's argument a recognition that the 'social distance', the 'area of affordable dissent' available to more privileged classes may be available to the new social movements only as long as they maintain their distance from the central core, the 'decisive relations', of the economy, only as long as these social issues are made to appear sufficiently distant from the centre of the capitalist order not to challenge it in any fundamental way — which may account for the 'active and substantial' presence of the new movements in 'almost every area of life except' the economy. In short, there are people for whom dissent is 'affordable' so long as it fails to challenge the capitalist order; and there are others who, though less able to afford resistance in the short term, are so situated that even their more 'local' and particular struggles can directly affect the 'central system' of the prevailing order where the destiny of universal human goods is determined.

---

[11] Ibid., pp. 255.
[12] Ibid., p. 260.

II

The place of 'primary human needs' or 'universal goods' in the socialist project is a critical and painfully difficult question. The socialist movement, if it is to have any credibility as an emancipatory project, must broaden its conception of human liberation and the quality of life. But even broadening socialist objectives explicitly and emphatically to include all the human goals which must be part of a truly emancipatory vision would not, by itself, resolve the question of the socialist constituency or the nature of the socialist struggle, its forms of organization and its specific targets. In particular, it would not imply that we can abandon the conception of the socialist project as a class struggle whose object is the abolition of class. If we accept a vision of socialism that includes such 'human' goals as peace, security, democracy, a caring society, and a careful economy, and if at the same time we also acknowledge that the class system of capitalism and the capitalist drive for accumulation are now the principal barriers to the achievement of these objectives, then what conclusions should we draw about the specific nature of the struggle and the social forces that are likely to carry it forward?

Two rather different conclusions are possible. One might say that, once people can be made to see that it is capitalism and its class system which above all stand in the way of their non-material, human goals, the abolition of class can become everyone's project as much as it is the specific objective of the working class. In other words, one might conclude that, even if the abolition of class is the direct and specific object of working-class 'material' or 'economic' interests, it is equally in the interests of other social groups in other respects, and that the specificity of working-class material interests does not entitle that class to a privileged role in the struggle to abolish class exploitation. Alternatively, one might say that, if the abolition of class is the core of the socialist project, even if its ultimate object is to achieve larger human goals, socialism is not likely to become the collective project of other social groups in the way that it can be for the working class, people who are the direct objects of class exploitation, whose collective identity springs directly from this class system, whose organization and strategic location are defined by it, and whose collective actions, even when they are particularist and limited in scope, are necessarily directed at the relevant target. If the latter seems more plausible, the socialist movement can still draw on other constituencies and can still connect with other social movements, but it must still be conceived and organized as an instrument of class struggle whose first strategic concern must be to serve the class interests and forge the class unity of the working class.

Here we encounter the difficulties that afflict the NTS project, with its tendency to shift the focus away from class-bound material interests to universal 'human' goals. Of course these 'human' goals must be the ultimate objective of the emancipatory struggle, and of course there is an important sense in which even the abolition of class — let alone the satisfaction of working-class interests — must be regarded as an interim objective, perhaps a means rather than an end. But what the NTS in effect proposes is that these ultimate 'human' goals can now be the immediate objectives (however long it may take to achieve them) of a political movement. This means not only that these concerns constitute the common interests around which an effective collective agent can be organized, but also that this collective agent can be directed against the very foundations of the capitalist system. To maintain this is to say one of two things: 1) that the material and social conditions for the achievement of these objectives now exist (in a way that has never been true before), in the sense that the existence of classes is no obstacle — either because the relations of production and exploitation are not, and perhaps never have been, critical in determining historical processes, or because these obstacles have already been removed. In such a case, it only remains to put the necessary instrumentalities in place to achieve those 'human' objectives. Or 2) the threat to these human interests — peace, security, the environment, the quality of life — is so much greater than ever before that an interest in their protection overrides, in unprecedented ways and degrees, all other social interests and all other historical determinants, and is sufficient to create a force capable of transforming the social and material conditions of the prevailing order.

It is tempting to think that the most ardent exponents of an 'autonomous' socialist politics must believe in the first of these two propositions, since they appear to be convinced that only 'discourse' is required to achieve the desired objectives. This is not, however, a position that needs to be taken seriously, since a massive rewriting of history would be required to demonstrate the marginality of production relations and class in determining historical processes, or at least a thorough reanalysis of capitalism to demonstrate that alone among historic modes of production this one subordinates production relations and class to other historical determinants (or perhaps to show that classes no longer exist in advanced capitalist societies in any significant sense?).

There is a somewhat weaker form of this argument, which actually has gained a certain currency: that 'welfare-state capitalism' has so completely altered the nature of the capitalist system that the old issues which made up the substance of class politics have now been resolved. Given the many new class issues created by the 'welfare state' itself, the many new burdens that have been imposed on the working class, not to mention the dismantling of the welfare state now underway in some advanced capitalist countries, and the continuing — indeed growing — salience of class issues in the politics of advanced capitalist countries, however much the nature of class forces and the 'parameters of class politics' may have been altered by welfare capitalism, this argument is almost as hard to take seriously as the stronger version. 'First of all,' as Göran Therborn has recently reminded us, 'it should never be forgotten that welfare state capitalism is still capitalism. Not only do the classical questions of capitalist politics remain, but the current economic crisis poses a threat to the achievements of welfare-state capitalism — full employment, social security, greater equality between men and women — and thereby makes of them central political issues. It would be a fundamental error to suggest that the fully developed welfare state has, even in appearance, removed the basic objects of working-class militancy, such as wages, working conditions, employment and social security.'[13] And to the extent that the (temporary?) resolution of some of these issues has apparently made inroads upon the political terrain of the left and captured parts of its traditional constituencies, new class issues, as well as new — and newly militant — class forces, have also emerged. There is, therefore, no convincing evidence to suggest that the conditions of modern capitalism have pre-empted the ground of class politics or rendered class unnecessary or unavailable as a political force.

The second argument — that the extent of the threat to basic human interests is now great enough to override other social determinations — has some force at a time when the dangers of nuclear annihilation and ecological disaster threaten not only the

---

[13] Göran Therborn, 'The Prospects of Labour and the Transformation of Advanced Capitalism', *New Left Review* 145, May-June 1984 pp. 29-30.

fulfillment of humanitarian goals but the existence of humanity itself, and when these threats have generated large popular movements even among people resistant to mobilization by other, less apocalyptic concerns. The moral force of these movements is unquestionable; but in a sense, the very qualities that give them their particular strength make them resistant to transformation into agents of a fundamental social change, the transition from capitalism to socialism. These movements do not reflect, and are not intended to create, a new collective identity, a new social agency, motivated by a new anti-capitalist interest which dissolves differences of class interest. They are not constituted on the basis of the connections that exist between the capitalist order and the threats to peace and survival. On the contrary, their unity and popular appeal depend upon *abstracting* the issues of peace or ecology from the prevailing social order and the conflicting social interests that comprise it. The general interests that human beings share simply because they are human must be seen, not as requiring the transformation of the existing social order and class relations, but rather as something *detached* from the various particular interests in which human beings partake by virtue of belonging to that social order and its system of classes. In other words, such movements have tended to rely on the extent to which they can *avoid* specifically implicating the capitalist order and its class system.

Here indeed are political programmes designed to be more or less 'autonomous' from social conditions and material interests; but it is precisely their autonomy that makes them resistant to development as programmes for socialist change. In fact, the inadequacy of the NTS formula is perhaps nowhere more vividly evident than here. One need only try to imagine the actual modalities by which such a 'popular' movement might be transformed into a socialist force. How exactly should we envisage the process whereby a movement, mobilized precisely on the basis of its abstraction from the prevailing conditions of class and class interest and a deliberate detachment of its aims from a fundamental challenge to the existing structure of social relations and domination, might be transformed into a stable collective force directed against those class conditions and that structure of domination? Unless, of course, the movement itself becomes the terrain of class struggle. Indeed, the very fact that such movements must rely so heavily upon bracketing off their objectives from material interests and class conflict tells us a great deal about the importance of material interests and class conflict in shaping political forces; for the moment these issues are allowed to surface, the very identity and unity of these popular movements is shattered. In other words, these movements can go one of two ways: they can retain their 'popular' identity and unity by foregoing the capacity to act as a strong oppositional force; or they can become more substantially effective, even in achieving their own specific ends, by harnessing their popular power to the politics of class.

These strictures apply to any notion of a socialist movement which 'begins from primary human needs', universal humanitarian goals transcending material interests and class — if by that is meant, not a movement for human emancipation and the achievement of universal humanitarian goals through the medium of class struggle and the abolition of class, but a movement that attempts to *bypass* class interests and class struggle in the hope of creating a transformative collective agent simply by means of an 'autonomous' universalistic 'discourse'. What, after all, would it mean to organize a political movement around 'primary human needs' in this sense?

Again, the problem can be illustrated by asking ourselves why, in a socialist movement so conceived, capitalists themselves might not be as much a part of the collective revolutionary agent as anyone else. Since they are 'people', with the same *human* interests as everyone else, what is to prevent socialist discourse from including them? If, however, we concede that capitalism is contrary to human interests, and that therefore capitalists cannot be among the natural constituents of socialism, then we are also conceding that capitalist production relations are the relevant target of the socialist struggle, the structure of power which must be attacked in order to achieve human goals, and also that people — or at least some people (only capitalists, and possibly the 'traditional' working class?) — put their class interests before their 'human' interests. And if this is so, under what specific circumstances could we organize a political movement around a commitment to 'primary human needs'? Do we really want to say, for example, that while some people — indeed, whole classes, and particularly the principal antagonistic classes of capitalism — are bound by their material conditions to put class interests before human goals, there is a vast middle ground of social groups not bound in this way, and that it is they who will conduct the struggle for socialism? If so — and above all — *how*? From what strategic vantage point, and with what collective power, will this 'autonomous' mass launch its attack upon the points of concentration of capitalist power? Indeed, by what means will it retain its identity and unity?

None of this is to say that people are incapable of being motivated by altruism, compassion, or a selfless concern for the 'general interest', or that these motivations have no role to play in the socialist project. But a transformative struggle cannot be organized by these principles, least of all in a society structured by class, with the irreducible antagonisms of interest and the configuration of power this entails.

Neither can we usefully conceive of socialism as simply a 'rational' goal which any creature of reason would adopt, once having attained the requisite level of 'intellectual sophistication'. Of course the anti-intellectualism of certain socialist tendencies is stupid and dangerous, and of course an effective socialist movement requires education. But there is nothing in education or 'rationality' as such that conduces to socialism or democracy. History offers ample evidence that there is no incompatibility between 'intellectual sophistication' and a commitment to exploitative and oppressive social relations. What *is* fundamentally and irreducibly incompatible with such social relations is the interests of the exploited class; and it is to this social principle that 'intellectual sophistication' must be harnessed if 'reason' is to be a force for socialism.

Nevertheless, if the pursuit of working-class interests is still the indispensible vehicle of socialism, still the only form in which 'universal human goods' can constitute a practicable political programme, there remains a need to link those interests explicitly with those universal objectives. The democratic impulse of socialism, its commitment to human emancipation and the quality of life, must always be kept clearly in sight if the class struggle is to stay on course as a struggle for socialism. There is, then, an important sense in which the language of 'universal human goods' is the language of translation from working-class consciousness to socialist consciousness. And it may also be the language of appeal which most effectively spells out the better quality of life offered by socialism to those so-called 'intermediate groups' who may be torn between their exploitation by capital and the benefits they derive from their service to it. The mistake of the new 'true' socialism lies not in the belief that there must be ideological mediations between the material interests of the working class and the ultimate objectives of socialism, but rather in the conviction that the need for such mediation means that there is no organic or 'privileged' connection between working-class interests and social objectives.

Either we maintain that, because all human beings qua human beings have an interest in socialism — or in freedom from exploitation, in democratic control, peace, security, and a decent quality of life — they are all equally candidates for socialist commitment through persuasion; or else we have to admit that, even if at bottom and in the long run all human beings have such an interest, there are more immediate structures of interest and power standing massively in the way of its realization. If the latter is so, then socialism must still be conceived, in the first instance, not simply as an abstract moral good but as a concrete political objective, which mobilizes the social forces most immediately directed against the capitalist structure of interest and power. Socialism takes the form of such a concrete project, with identifiable targets and agencies — yet one which is at the same time capable of 'connecting' with the 'general interest' — only insofar as it is embodied in the interests and struggles of the working class.

12

Conclusions

I

Work on this book coincided almost exactly with the duration of the 1984-85 miners' strike in Britain, and this conclusion was completed shortly after the workers' return to the pits without an agreement. By the time this book is published, the strike will be history — but it will indeed be *history*, because the strike represents one of the most important episodes in the record of the British labour movement in the twentieth century. This historic event marked a significant test for the new 'true' socialism, the first major working-class action to occur with the entire NTS theoretical apparatus already in place and available to apprehend it. It goes without saying that this was a time when the question of class politics intruded itself more insistently than ever. At the time of writing, it is perhaps too soon to judge what lasting effects the strike will have on NTS perceptions of class and its political resonances, or on their views of the relation between the working class and socialist politics; but one or two things have already emerged. No doubt there are people whose belief in the non-correspondence of politics and class will have been deeply shaken by these events and who will feel obliged to think again; but so far the most remarkable results have been the pronouncements issuing from some NTS quarters that the strike has sounded the death knell of class politics. Nowhere is the perversity of NTS logic more vividly evident than in these funeral orations.

A particularly revealing example of this genre can be found in Michael Ignatieff's 'Strangers and Comrades'. This article represents something like the last word in the politics of discourse. In its own way it is a remarkable expression of the linguistic socialism outlined earlier by Ignatieff's *History Workshop* comrade, Gareth Stedman Jones. Gazing sorrowfully at the labour movement from the heights of his wisdom and refined sensibilities, Ignatieff writes in the pontifical yet soulful mode which has made him the darling of the British literary press, their favourite repentant socialist and resident progressive:

> There are those on the Left who maintain that the miners' strike is a vindication of a class-based politics after decades in which the agenda of the Left was defined by cross-class campaigns like feminism and CND. Yet the strike demonstrates the reverse: a labour movement which is incapable of presenting a class claim as a national claim, which can only pose its demands in the language of total victory, which takes on the State and ends up on the wrong side of the law cannot hope to conserve its support and legitimacy among the working class public. The miners' strike is not the vindication of class politics but its death throes.
>
>   ... The trouble with Arthur Scargill's politics is not that it doesn't have justice on its side, but that it utterly lacks a conception of how competing classes, regions, races and religions can be reconciled with each other in a national community.
>
>   What the Left needs is a language of national unity expressed as commitment to fellowship among strangers. We need a language of trust built upon a practice of social comradeship.[1]

In what sense, then, is class politics dead? By Ignatieff's criteria, the measure of success for class politics is the extent to which a class can submerge itself in a 'national community' and join in fellowship with its opposing class. Whatever else this notion is, it can hardly be a recipe for socialist struggle — unless socialism is no longer to be conceived as the abolition of class, or unless we are being asked to imagine that the final dissolution of class will take place by mutual agreement, a general reconciliation in which exploiters and exploited will join hands in comradely fellowship. If 'what the Left needs is a language of national unity', in the sense intended by Ignatieff, it is certainly not for the purpose of advancing the cause of socialism, whatever else its purpose might be — the construction of an invincible parliamentary party without socialist pretensions, or whatever (though — leaving aside the more sinister resonances in the idiom of 'national community' — it is difficult to imagine even an electoral success built upon this

---

[1] Michael Ignatieff, 'Strangers and Comrades', *New Statesman*, 14 December 1984.

fatuous appeal to the language of national fellowship). Indeed by Ignatieff's standard, the real death of class politics would be signalled by the emergence of a truly united and militant class movement, openly and effectively opposed to the interests and power of capital, with a good chance of success in the struggle for socialism.

The first thing that strikes one about an argument like Ignatieff's is the extent to which it echoes the rhetoric of the right, its appeals to law and order and its characterization of 'Scargillism' as a blind subordination of the national good to selfish sectional interests. On closer consideration, however, what is even more striking is the particular way in which this argument — and indeed the whole of NTS doctrine — while caught up in the 'national popular discourse' of Thatcherism, *departs* from the Thatcherite view of the world.

The supreme irony is that, while many on the left have been busy announcing the death of class politics and denying the 'privileged' position of the working class in the struggle for socialism, the Conservative government has been conducting a policy whose first — and last — premise is that an organized working class represents the greatest threat to capitalism. If the 'New Right' in Britain has a single overriding characteristic, it is a perception of the world in terms of the class opposition between capital and labour and a willingness to prosecute class war with no holds barred. Among the decisive moments in the creation of this newly militant class consciousness and spirit of determination were the miners' strikes of 1972 and 1974. In the words of one of the Right's most popular journalistic spokesmen: 'Old fashioned Tories say there isn't any class war. New Tories make no bones about it: we are class warriors and we expect to be victorious.'[2]

And so, one project has dominated — obsessively so — the Thatcherite programme: the use of the state to destroy the power of organized labour. To this end, all the weapons of the state have been deployed, from the law and the police, to economic policy, to the system of welfare and social security.[3] The 1984-85 miners' strike was the fruit of this obsession and its most notable product to date.

---

[2] Peregrine Worsthorne, quoted in Huw Beynon ed., *Digging Deeper: Issues in the Miners' Strike*, London 1985, p. 88.

[3] See Chris Jones and Tony Novak, 'Welfare against the Workers: Benefits as a Political Weapon', in *Digging Deeper*, pp. 87-100.

The irony, too, is that even in their favourite arena of ideology and discourse the NTS have given the game away. Having chosen first to neglect — indeed, in effect to deny — the front line of battle, the real political class war being waged by the 'new Tories', they have elected to meet Thatcherism on its purely rhetorical terrain. But having already conceded the central political battle by effectively denying its existence and by confining their opposition to the ideological periphery, they have gone on to cede the rhetorical ground as well. Although the 'New Right' has been unusually open in its declaration of class war, it has used the rhetoric of class-lessness, appealing to the 'people' precisely in order to weaken class-consciousness among its class adversaries, disguising the language of class in the ideological cover of national security, honour, glory, and community. Instead of joining battle in the ideological arena of class, the NTS have for all intents and purposes been swallowed up in this discourse of mystification. They have effectively reduced the socialist struggle to an ideological battle between left and right 'discourses'. In this battle, the principal adversary is an *ideological* bogey-man called 'Thatcherism'. This ghostly being — which has thoroughly mesmerized the British NTS — apparently has no material foundation and must be conjured away by incantations of 'populist' discourse, a 'democratic' discourse often laced with large doses of patriotism and jingoism to charm the 'people' away from the Thatcherite magic.

The New Tories have had far less difficulty than the NTS in assessing the significance of the miners' strike and its antecedents, even if they have misjudged the tenacity and unity of the workers and underestimated the tremendous costs which would be incurred by provoking the dispute. At least they have understood the strategic importance of working-class organizations and have recognized that the principal arena of political struggle is in the conflict of interest between capital and labour. Other aspects of the strike and what it tells us about the connection between class and politics are no doubt beyond the ken of Thatcherite analysis, though one might have expected the NTS to be more receptive. The strike has demonstrated — as the labour movement has done so often before — how 'merely economic' class struggles, even when their objectives are limited, have a unique capacity to alter the political terrain and to unmask and confront the structure of capitalist power, the state, the law, the police, as no other social force can do. It has demonstrated yet again how the experience of 'economic' struggle nourishes consciousness — few intimate observers expect the miners and their families ever to see the world again as they did before the strike; how it teaches new skills and reveals hidden resources; how it fosters new attitudes, relationships, solidarities, and modes of organization;[4] and how it expands the horizons of struggle, repeatedly breaking through the barriers between the 'economic' sphere and the political.

The incongruity between NTS perceptions and the realities of class conflict as they are constituted by the participants on both sides is curious. To deny the existence of working-class interests and to deny that these interests have repeatedly found expression in political terms, when the experience of struggle has revealed its own limits and exposed the obstacles standing in its way, is to deny the whole long and painful history of working-class struggle. How is it possible to ignore the many major advances of the labour movement that have been achieved in precisely this way? As 'economic' struggles have reached their limits, the battle has moved to the political arena, and the pursuit of working-class interests has overflowed its 'economic' boundaries into political movements whose aims were often explicitly socialist. Not the least significant example, of course, is the creation of the Labour Party itself.

There has never been a time when organized labour has not, in one form or another, challenged capital, even if in some countries at various times there have been moments of quiescence. Often, it has been in the limited form of pressing for terms and conditions of work better suited to the interests of the workers and less to the imperatives of capital accumulation, but repeatedly the battle has moved to the wider political front. What is especially remarkable about the history of working-class struggle is, in fact, not how seldom the working class, in pursuit of its 'narrow' material interests, has created political forces with a socialist impulse, but on the contrary, how often workers have returned to professedly socialist movements in the face of repeated betrayals — from Blum to Mitterrand, from Attlee through Wilson to Callaghan. And we should not underestimate the number of instances in which the capitalist order as a whole has been powerfully challenged by workers' movements, even if the challenge has ultimately failed — as in Italy or Germany after the First World War.

Our judgment of the oppositional impulse in the labour move-

---

[4] See, for example, *Digging Deeper*, Part Two, 'Digging in for Coal: the Miners and their Supporters'.

ment, and its socialist potential, cannot be based on the view that the only significant challenge to capitalism will be the last and successful one. It is absurd to proceed as if anything short of the final assault represents an accommodation to capitalism and a refusal of socialism. Nor can the depth of opposition between labour and capital be measured by the degree of insurrectionary violence. It is one of the many paradoxes of the NTS position that, while its adherents vehemently reject revolutionary violence as a viable option in advanced capitalist democracies, they tend, at least implicitly, to recognize as genuine challenges to capitalism on the part of the working class only those which take this form. Equally paradoxical is the fact that the very people who decry what they take to be demands for instant socialism, and who envisage the transition in the most gradualist terms, also seem to dismiss as inconsequential any working-class challenge to capitalism that does not issue in the immediate establishment of socialism. At the same time, social movements that are far from attacking the foundations of capitalism, either in their aims or in their consequences, are hailed as the stuff of which socialism will be made. And, finally, it is profoundly misleading to impose a rigid discontinuity between the 'lesser' forms of 'merely' economic struggle and more directly political assaults on the capitalist order, not only because the larger struggles have always grown organically out of the smaller oppositions, but, more fundamentally, because both are rooted in the essential antagonism of interest between capital and labour. There is, in other words, no clean caesura, either historically or structurally, between these forms of opposition.

No one can seriously maintain that any other social movement has ever challenged the power of capital as has the working class, even with its often severely limited objectives and its woefully inadequate modes of organization. It should, however, be added that, for all its limitations and institutional conservatism, the labour movement has more consistently than any other social collectivity stood on the side of the various causes which the left regards as valuable and progressive — not only those causes that have directly to do with the material class interests of labour, but those that pertain to 'universal human goods', peace, democracy, and a 'caring society'. This is, on the whole, true even in the 'worst case', the United States. If working-class movements still have much to learn about the full dimensions of human emancipation, and if they have yet to create forms of organization adequate to their task, there has been no historically identifiable social force that has even come close to their record of emancipatory struggles, either in the breadth of their visions, the comprehensiveness of the liberation they have sought, or in their degree of success.

II

Both the historical record and the structural antagonism between capital and labour tell a story very different from the one we are offered by the NTS. One cannot, then, help wondering what exactly we are being told when the NTS deny the connection between the working class and socialism, or even between economic conditions and political forces in general. Again, we are reminded that the NTS has come to fruition not at a time when the opposition between labour and capital has receded into the background, but rather when the antagonisms of class have been especially urgent and visible. It would be interesting to speculate about the historical and sociological reasons for this curious detachment from reality — for example, about whether it is the ideological representation of a specific social interest in its own right; at any rate, we can at least expose its faulty theoretical foundations.

The NTS is based on a profound misunderstanding of what it means to say, as Marxists traditionally have done, that capitalism has laid the foundation for socialism and that the working class is the revolutionary class. According to the straw-Marxism conjured up and then knocked down by the NTS, there will be an automatic, mechanical, and non-contradictory transition from capitalism to socialism. More specifically, this Marxism is a crude technological determinism according to which the development of productive forces — conceived as a natural, neutral process — will inevitably and mechanically produce a united and revolutionary working class. In other words, Marxism stands or falls according to whether a unified working class immediately committed to socialism is directly given by capitalist production relations and the development of productive forces. Since history has clearly denied any such mechanical determination, say the NTS, the whole Marxist project collapses. There is no sense here of Marx's own complex and subtle understanding of the ways in which capitalism creates not the mechanical inevitability of socialism, but the possibilities and contradictions which put it on the historical agenda as it never could have been before. Missing too is his conception of the working class not as a mechanical reflex of technological development, whose 'historic task' is nothing more than (automatically) to appropriate collectively the forces of production created by capitalism, but rather a class which contains the possibility of a classless society because its own interests cannot be fully served without the abolition of class and because its strategic location in the production of capital gives it a unique capability to destroy capitalism.

The problem, however, lies not simply in a faulty interpretation of Marx, but more fundamentally, in a thoroughly inadequate, indeed non-existent, conception of history as a determinate process — indeed as a process at all, as distinct from an arbitrary series of contingencies, at best held together by the logic of discourse. For underlying this interpretation of Marxism is the crudely dualistic view, which we have already noted as a characteristic of the NTS (and which is part of its structuralist legacy), that where there is no absolute determination there is absolute contingency. There is little room here for historical *relations, conditions,* or *possibilities*; there are only contingent juxtapositions or 'conjunctures'.

There is perhaps yet another element in the NTS rejection of the working class as revolutionary agent. Somehow the notion has gained currency, even on the left, that the very idea of a collective historical agent is a metaphysical abstraction, and one of the more pernicious Hegelian legacies surviving in Marxism, fraught with dangers of despotism and oppression. There is no crime so heinous that it cannot, according to this view, be justified by those who claim to act 'in the name of' the 'universal class', that mythical collective agent, the revolutionary proletariat.

But why should this be so? Consider the alternatives. Failing a collective agent, history must be made by individuals acting independently, or by Great Men and/or Great Women, or else there are no human agents in history at all — in which case *any* political movement is clearly a delusion and a waste of time. Even the most limited political intervention, even the most 'moderate' political programme which presupposes that people can deliberately intervene in the shaping of social arrangements, however modestly, inevitably assumes the possibility of a collective agent, even if only a political party. There is nothing metaphysical about this assumption, nor is it fanciful to assume that people can be joined by some principle of unity, some common purpose and commitment, in the pursuit of certain common goals.

It is not even unreasonable, or metaphysical, to assume that such common purposes and commitments are likely to be grounded in certain common social circumstances and experiences. In fact, the assumption that political movements need *not* be grounded in existing social identities and interests would at best be highly fanciful, and at worst profoundly dangerous. Is it conceivable that a political programme could be devised in complete abstraction from the immediate social conditions and interests of any living human being, without any presuppositions about the kinds of people that are likely to congregate around it? And is it possible to imagine a political movement constructed simply by announcing a programme and sitting back to wait while it exerts its own magnetic force? It is probably safe to say that political movements generally draw upon existing collective identities and appeal to existing collective interests — that is, interests in which people partake by virtue of belonging to identifiable collectivities. Political movements without a sound basis in existing social collectivities and not firmly guided by existing social interests have tended to go one of two ways: at best, for lack of their own social roots they have become instruments of the dominant interest — as social-democratic parties have more than once, whether willingly or not, become the agents of capital when they have uprooted themselves from their working-class foundations. At worst, political movements without firm social roots have degenerated into precisely the despotic arbitrariness which critics have wrongly attributed to the Marxist conception of the revolutionary proletariat. In fact, it can be argued that the most metaphysical — and potentially dangerous — view of historical agency is that historical agents are constituted by nothing but Discourse or Idea. If the threat of despotism is to be found anywhere, it is surely here, in the notion of Idea incarnate in the bearers of discourse, who will create social collectivities — such as the 'people' — where none existed before, out of a shapeless mass with no social identity of its own.

What, then, is specific to the Marxist conception of the collective agent, the revolutionary working class? The first premise, of course, is that production is essential to human existence and the organization of social life. (It cannot be emphasized enough that the NTS rejection of Marxism begins here, with an effective denial of this elementary fact and everything that follows from it.) On the assumption that political movements must be grounded in social relations and interests, the critical question for Marxism is, what social relations and interests are commensurate with, and provide the surest grounding for, a political project that has as its object the transformation of production relations and the abolition of class? Marxism's answer is that there is such a thing as a working class, people who by virtue of their situation in the relations of production and exploitation share certain fundamental interests, and that these class interests coincide with the essential objective of socialism, the abolition of class, and more specifically, the classless administration of production by the direct producers themselves.

This is not to say that the condition of the working class directly determines that its members will have socialism as their immediate class objective. It does, however, mean that they can uniquely advance the cause of socialism (though not completely achieve it) even *without* conceiving socialism as their class objective, by pursuing their material class interests, because these interests are by nature essentially opposed to capitalist class exploitation and to a class-dominated organization of production. Since the material interests of the working class cannot be satisfied within the existing framework of social relations, and since a pursuit of these interests will inevitably encounter the opposing interests of capital, the process of struggle will tend to expose its own limitations, spill over into the political arena, and carry the battle closer to the centres of capitalist power. Furthermore, since the working class itself *creates* capital, and since the organization of production and appropriation place the collective labourer at the heart of the whole capitalist structure, the working class has a unique capacity to destroy capital. The conditions of production, and of working-class struggle, are also such as to encourage the organization of workers into a collective force potentially suited to carry out this project. This does not mean that the working class is immediately available as a political organization ready-made to prosecute the struggle for socialism. It simply means that the organizational and political efforts of socialists will most fruitfully be devoted to unifying the working class and serving its interests, while the boundaries of class struggle are pushed forward. To say — as the NTS repeatedly do — that *classes* are never political agents, while undoubtedly true in its limited way, is therefore quite beside the point.

There is one unique characteristic of socialism which adds an even greater force to the Marxist argument that the revolution must come by the self-emancipation of the working class: although the struggle between exploiting and exploited classes has been a major force in every transformation of production relations, no other social revolution has ever placed the exploited class of the old social order in command of the new one. No transformation of production relations has had as its principal object the interests of the exploited class, however much those interests may have moved the revolution forward. Even more specifically, socialism alone presupposes both a continuity between the direct producers of the old order and the new, and a social organization of production administered by those direct producers themselves. The Marxist project is based on the premise that the collective labourer of advanced industrial capitalism will be the direct producer of the socialist order, and that socialist democracy will be constituted by the self-organization of freely associated producers. This places the collective labourer in capitalism at the centre of the socialist project as no exploited class has ever been in any other social revolution. Thus, unless the class interests of the working class themselves direct them into political struggle and to the transformation of the mode of production, the socialist project must remain an empty and utopian aspiration. This does not mean that socialism is inevitable, only that it will come about in this way or not at all.

III

There is, then, a powerful case on both structural and historical grounds for connecting the working class organically to the socialist project, and this case has yet to be answered by the new 'true' socialists. Yet perhaps we are debating at cross purposes; for in the final analysis, the theoretical and political touchstone for the NTS is not socialism at all, but simply electoral victory. Once we understand that the logic of their argument is an electoralist logic, once we accept that their standards of success and failure have little to do with the conditions for establishing socialism and everything to do with constructing victorious electoral alliances, we may be no more satisfied with the non-correspondence principle as a theory of history, but it will at least make some kind of political sense.

If, however, we continue to measure the vital signs of politics not simply by electoral statistics but by the standard of socialist objectives, the experience of working-class struggle must lead us to very different conclusions. The point here is not that electoral politics are in essence inimical or at least unnecessary to socialist transformation, but rather that electoral victory, or even the seizure of power by other means, is not itself the goal of the socialist struggle and therefore cannot be the standard by which we judge the success of working-class politics. Here is the failure of logic that lies at the heart of the NTS programme: it purports to advance the cause of socialism by adopting a politics whose criterion is not socialism but electoral victory.

Two very different political logics flow from these different criteria, which have little to do with the opposition between parliamentary reformism and revolutionary insurrectionism. The logic of the NTS suggests that we will come closer to socialism by moving further away from it. It castigates the left for demanding 'instant socialism' when people are not ready for it, and insists that the failure of (say) the Labour Party results from its adherence to the outmoded politics of working-class interest. It manages to suggest at one and the same time that working-class politics must be abandoned as inimical to socialist objectives, and that these objectives will be advanced by appealing to political interests even less congenial to socialism.

The other logic implies that, if people are not 'ready' for socialism (though how often have they really been offered the choice?), it is perverse to adopt positions that lead *away* from socialism rather than toward it. The question then becomes: how can a socialist movement pursue more immediate, 'non-revolutionary' goals without straying irredeemably from the path to socialism, while at the same time expanding the horizons of struggle and constructing a unified and effective political force to carry it on? In other words, the question is not simply how best to construct a parliamentary majority — or even to seize power — by the shortest and easiest route, but rather what short-term political goals are realistic in the prevailing conditions which are also desirable from the perspective of socialist values and conducive to advancing the struggle for socialism? The most obvious answer would seem to be that, since working-class interests are inherently opposed to the interests of capital as no other social force is in the same immediate way, since the structure of both capitalism and socialism rests upon the same working class, and since no socialist movement has ever existed that has not emerged from the articulation of political forces with working-class interests, a consistent pursuit of those interests, which will also lay a foundation of trust, is the immediate political programme most likely to keep us on course in the struggle for socialism.

On this score, ultra-left criticisms of social democracy, reform-ism, and 'trade-union consciousness' have tended to be nearly as misleading as the NTS criticisms of Marxism, and, paradoxically, for similar reasons. Social democracy is often attacked from the left on the grounds that it cleaves too rigidly to the narrow 'econ-omistic' concerns of the working class — never mind the fact that social-democratic governments have tended rather to err on the side of *betraying* those working-class interests. The assumption seems to be that 'economistic' concerns are not only incomplete or inadequate, but actually *antagonistic* to the socialist struggle. Such an assumption would seem also to underlie the characterization of trade-unionism as an *obstacle* to revolution, rather than a limited form of class-consciousness representing the very social forces and interests upon which a revolution can be built. The corollary of these assumptions is that an appropriate politics will not grow out of the economic struggles of workers but must be brought to them from outside.

It is worth adding that, when political parties historically grounded in the working class, like the Labour Party, have for-feited the loyalty of their constituents, it has not been because they have blindly pursued socialist objectives against the prevailing opinions of the electorate — which, the Tory press notwith-standing, the Labour Party has never done; nor has it been — as the NTS would have us believe — because they have served work-ing class interests at the expense of some notional common good or national interest. On the contrary, the most dramatic electoral disasters have occurred precisely when such parties have too con-sistently departed from, and even betrayed, the class interests of their natural constituency. The attempt to 'broaden the electoral base' by abandoning their natural constituencies has always been a dubious strategy for parties of this kind.

In this respect, the issue is not whether Labour lost because it was too 'radical' or not radical enough, or even whether it was too much or too little committed to old socialist programmes, but rather whether it has, as a party of government, remained suf-ficiently tied to its social roots, sufficiently true to the interests of its working-class base, to have a 'natural' constituency at all. The last two Labour governments, for example — 1964-70 and 1974-79 — have both been defeated after periods of government particularly notable for their attacks on trade union rights and working-class interests — punitive incomes policies, the infamous *In Place of Strife*, the introduction of monetarism — which have simply been carried forward and developed by the Thatcher regime. Under such circumstances, when the 'natural' party of the working class ceases to represent the interests of its constituents, it is arguable that — leaving aside the sense of betrayal which might be enough to drive voters away — other, normally secondary factors may come to the fore in determining electoral preferences. It is at moments like this, when a reliable political expression of class interests does not exist, that people may respond, temporarily and with superficial commitment, to 'discourses' dissociated from their own social interests.

The Marxist conception of the working class as 'collective agent' presupposes that the object of political struggle is not the seizure of power (let alone the attainment of office), whether by election or by putsch, but rather the abolition of class. The taking of power is no doubt a necessary step in the transformation of society, but it is an instrument, not itself the object, of class struggle. The issue, then, is not simply the relative merits of electoralism and extra-parliamentary struggle. Different conditions will require different methods of attaining power, including electoral strategies. In advanced capitalist democracies, no movement that completely rejects electoral politics is ever likely to become more than a small and marginal fragment. And it is absurd to neglect the fact that the state is the point of concentration of all power in society. But the conduct of electoral politics, even when its goals are limited, must always be guided by the objectives of socialism and the final abolition of class.

The failure of working-class political organizations like the Labour Party to act as agents of socialist transformation — irrespective of the genuinely socialist commitments that many of its members undoubtedly have — has derived in great part from their acceptance of an electoralist logic — like that of the NTS — according to which the object of political action and rhetoric is precisely to *produce* the 'non-correspondence' of politics and class. This same logic has effectively enforced a rigid separation of political and economic struggles, not only by subscribing to a sharp distinction between political issues and purely 'industrial' disputes, but also by accepting the even more restrictive separation of parliamentary and extra-parliamentary domains. What has more than anything else disabled the Labour Party, among others, as an instrument of working-class organization and mobilization is a deep-rooted acceptance not only of purely electoralist principles but of a narrowly defined conception of politics as parliamentary activity. This delimitation of politics and its detachment from the arenas of class conflict — in a sense the ultimate ratification of the non-correspondence principle — has been the bedrock of capitalist hegemony from the beginning. The assumption implicit in this conception of politics is that the state is above class conflict, that it can and should represent a 'national community' transcending the sectional interests of class — an assumption that has had a long and tenacious tradition in the British Labour Party since Ramsay MacDonald.

The miners' strike is again a dramatic case in point. Here is how one observer has summed up the role of the Labour Party throughout the 1984-5 dispute and the features it had in common with the Party's role in 1926:

> An analysis of the two party leaders' responses to the 1926 and 1984 disputes reveals a series of common features: reluctance to get involved in the issue, underpinned by a hope that conflict could be avoided; fundamental doubts about the miners' tactics; a persistent demand that the state could serve as a mediator; a failure for the most part to articulate grievances expressed within the mining communities and by some backbenchers about the activities of the police.
>
> The similarities demonstrate certain durable themes within Labour politics that cut across the significant distinctions between 1926 and 1984. On both occasions, leaders attempted to operate a sharp distinction between industrial and political action. This surfaced in MacDonald's dismissal of sympathetic action and in Kinnock's claim that: 'There is no possibility and no justification for bringing down a British government by any means other than the ballot box.' Such pronouncements ignored the political dimensions of the disputes and erected a simplistic dichotomy in which industrial action was either directed to the replacement of the government or was narrowly economic. The refusal to admit any position in between blocked the possibility of developing effective relationships between industrial struggle and political mobilization.
>
> This reluctance has been linked with a concern to play down the centrality of class as a basis for socialist growth. For MacDonald this was part of a wider view that class conflict and class-based organizations offered no route to a socialist community; in Kinnock's case, it was perhaps a more pragmatic claim that changing employment patterns offered diminishing

scope for conventional class-based politics. ...

... In both cases, Labour's leaders continued to see the state as an essentially neutral instrument capable of fulfilling a reconciling role. At one level the state was seen as an essential tool for the settlement of such conflicts; at another, a faith in the underlying liberalism of the British State, helped to ensure that Labour's leaders failed to come to terms with the reality of police actions in the coalfield. Such an approach to the state is not only to be found in Labour's responses to industrial disputes; it has dominated party thinking from the beginning. ...[5]

The Labour Party's view of politics has thus inhibited its representation of working-class interests even within the narrow limits of parliamentary debate. There has certainly been no question of playing a role in the organization of class struggle and the formation of class unity. For the Labour Party, at least at the official national level, politics are not about organizing people around common struggles, or at least not class struggles. It is apparently not the job of a socialist party to unify and organize the labour movement outside the parliamentary domain. It may even be the sacred duty of such a party to dissociate itself from extra-parliamentary class struggles, perhaps even to thwart political action outside the holy precincts of parliament.

In the new 'true' socialism, this rather old view of politics has found its ultimate theoretical expression. The NTS case against the miners' strike will illustrate the point. A typical attack has been launched by Gavin Kitching in a nasty little reply to Raphael Samuel's criticism of Michael Ignatieff.[6] If the miners have failed to achieve their immediate objectives, argues Kitching, the fault lies with the NUM leadership who have betrayed their followers above all by neglecting to ensure the support of the trade union movement — or significant sectors of it — before embarking on this action. They seem to have assumed, he maintains — echoing Jimmy Reid — that 'once the miners' cavalry charge was in motion, the support troops would quickly rally'; and this false assumption could have been based on nothing 'except some gut-level essentialism about "the working class".' The support of other

---

[5] David Howell, 'Where's Ramsay MacKinnock? Labour Leadership and the Miners', in *Digging Deeper*, pp. 194-6.

[6] *New Statesman*, 11 January 1985; *New Statesman*, 25 January 1985.

workers could not be delivered — 'or at least not in any other than a fragmentary way' — because 'these people could not be convinced — as people — of the justice of the miners' case.' Interpreting and endorsing Ignatieff's view, Kitching maintains 'that unless they [power workers, dockers, railwaymen, and lorry drivers] were convinced — as individuals — they would not act, i.e. they had no prior identity as "workers" among whom appeals for "solidarity" would find "automatic", "essential" assent.' And if these people could have been brought to support the miners, it would have been by convincing them — discursively? — as *citizens* (needless to say, not by organizing them politically around their common interests as *workers*). Furthermore, in keeping with Ignatieff's conception of national fellowship, 'what would have convinced dockers as citizens, railwaymen as citizens, would have convinced many other citizens too.'

Kitching's analysis is revealing, and entirely consistent with the fundamental premises of the NTS. It may or may not be true that other workers — either 'as people' or as some other unnamed species — were unconvinced of the justice of the miners' case. It may be rather that people — as workers — were deterred by the risks inherent in the current economic situation. But one truly remarkable thing about Kitching's account is its silence on *politics*, and on the responsibilities of the — his — Labour Party. The demon Arthur Scargill and the leaders of the NUM failed in their 'duty of convincing these, some of their fellow citizens, of the *rightness* of the miners' claims and action', but Neil Kinnock and the Labour Party leadership apparently had no such duty — indeed were obliged to question the miners' 'rightness' and to assist the government in its efforts to divide the labour movement. They certainly had no obligation to participate in organizing the struggle.

Again, there is no conception here of class organization as a political task — a political task not because working-class interests must be artificially created, not even because class identities and interests may be subordinated to other identities and interests, but simply because the translation of *common interests* into *concerted action* requires organization and coordination. No doubt political organizations have an educative role to play in the development of class consciousness; but we should also acknowledge the extent to which the failure of 'objective' class situations to issue in concerted political action is not the result of a failure of consciousness — or, worse still, the non-existence of class and class interests — but simply a problem of *logistics*. Is it really plausible to imagine that workers separated by work-place, industry, and region, facing constant efforts by capital and the state to disorganize them, to manipulate the differences among them — of income, function in the labour process, gender, race — and transform *difference* into *division*, no matter how much they may share the experiences and interests of class, will spontaneously and automatically constitute an organized political force? And yet, this is what the NTS effectively demands to vindicate Marxism and its association of politics with class. Failing this simple correspondence, there is, in the NTS view, no 'essential' connection at all. If the working class does not spring full-grown from the head of capitalism as a unified, organized force for socialism, there is no essential connection between working-class interests and socialist politics; indeed, we are probably not entitled to speak of class interests at all. Again, we have the false alternatives: either the working class appears spontaneously and automatically as an organized revolutionary force (the phantom 'essentialist' view), or there is, in effect, no such thing as 'the working class', and no working-class interest. There are only people with contingent and discursively negotiable social identities.

IV

The principle that class struggle must be the guiding thread of socialist politics is not, then, merely a slogan, one of the pieties of 'orthodox' or 'vulgar' Marxism. It has very real practical implications which ought to affect our perceptions not only of political objectives but of even the most elementary mechanics of party politics. These different perceptions should also be acknowledged *theoretically*, in theories of class, ideology, and the state. The NTS is founded in theory and practice on a simple electoralism in which electoral victory is effectively an end in itself. The electoral purposes of party politics — consisting largely of cobbling together alliances capable of sustaining a parliamentary majority — are reflected in NTS theories of ideology and class. So current ideologies and political attitudes, however conjunctural and superficially grounded, are treated as if they were the primary and absolute determinants of class, or class determinations are altogether subordinated to ideological and political contingencies. This is very much in keeping with the logic of electoral alliances, which are constructed by taking people 'as they are', designing ideological 'common denominators' to paper over fundamental social antagonisms, and obscuring the distinctions between absolute class barriers and temporary, contingent divisions within classes.

If, however, political activity is guided by the objectives of socialism and shaped to the instrumentalities of class struggle required to achieve the abolition of class, then clearly this electoralist logic is not enough, even in the construction of electoral strategies. If a political party or movement is not only an electoral machine but also an instrument of mobilization, struggle, and ideological change in the service of socialist transformation, then it cannot be based on ephemeral social indentities and the superficial bonds of expediency. For its principles of cohesion, it must look to more fundamental and enduring social bonds; and for its motive force, it must appeal to interests much closer to the material foundations of social existence, interests that are commensurate with the objectives of socialism. If, in other words, a political party or movement is to engage in the struggle for power, electoral or otherwise, while acting as an instrument of mass mobilization and ideological transformation, if it is to pursue immediate objectives which at the same time advance the struggle for socialism, then that party or movement can only be above all a *class* party, guided by and organized around the interests of the working class.

This does not mean that there is no place for coalitions and alliances with other social movements. The nexus of politics and working-class interest can — and indeed should — be extended to social issues beyond the immediate material interests of class, to the politics of peace, gender, environment, and culture; and, as we have seen, it is in any case a mistake to treat these issues as if they take us 'beyond class politics'. But the vital interests of the collective labourer must remain the guiding thread for any political movement which has as its goal the construction of socialism. This may mean that, in some cases, alliances and coalitions will be explicitly limited and temporary, clearly directed at the attainment of limited specific objectives. Sometimes alliances will take the form of support by the working-class movement for the causes of others, without organizational unity. Sometimes, as in the miners' strike, the struggles of workers will engage other loyalties and interests and be strengthened by them, as the miners were strengthened by community ties and the solidarity of women. But just as in the miners' strike these other loyalties and interests were mobilized as a strong oppositional force by their articulation with the class interests of the workers, so other social movements can be forged into forces for socialism by their intersection with the interests of the working class.

There is no question that the socialist movement will have to find new forms of working-class organization and new ways of incorporating the emancipatory aspirations expressed by the 'new social movements'. The experience of the miners' strike has, again, pointed the way, revealing the possibilities of new solidarities, new forms of organization, and new points of contact between workers' struggles and other social movements. But the first principle of socialist organization must remain the essential correspondence between working-class interests and socialist politics. Unless class politics becomes the unifying force that binds together all emancipatory struggles, the 'new social movements' will remain on the margins of the existing social order, at best able to generate periodic and momentary displays of popular support but destined to leave the capitalist order intact, together with all its defences against human emancipation and the realization of 'universal human goods'.

While the power of the state is being used to fight the class war on behalf of capital, it cannot be the job of a socialist movement to encourage the divorce of politics from class, as the NTS project requires. On the contrary, the principal task is to encourage and to build upon the political impulses which grow out of working-class interests and struggles. That task is clearly not an easy one. Concerted action by widely scattered and disparate working-class formations, even when joined by common class interests, is not something that can happen spontaneously. A united working class in this sense is certainly not 'given' directly in the relations of production. But this is very far from saying that the building blocks of socialist politics are not to be found in the struggles, large and small, against capital which have constituted working-class history, or that a better foundation for socialism exists somewhere else. There are many obstacles to class organization; but to treat these obstacles as if they were absolute determinants, irrevocably overriding the common interests of class, is to accept the very mystifications that sustain the hegemony of capitalism.

There are many lessons to be learned from the thousands of working-class struggles that have taken place in Britain and elsewhere. Above all they have shown that, while the task is long and difficult, the material of socialism is there in the interests, solidarities, and strategic capacities of the working-class. In their victories and even in their defeats these struggles have shown us what might be accomplished if the labour movement had a political instrument ready to do its job, the tremendous goals that might be achieved if all the isolated and particular struggles for emancipation and 'universal goods' were unified not simply by the phantoms of 'discourse' or by the superficial bonds of electoral expediency but by the politics of *class*.

Index